P9-DTY-429

Building an Extranet

CONNECT YOUR INTRANET WITH VENDORS AND CUSTOMERS

JULIE BORT

BRADLEY FELIX

WILEY COMPUTER PUBLISHING

John Wiley & Sons, Inc.

New York ◆ Chichester ◆ Weinheim ◆ Brisbane ◆ Singapore ◆ Toronto

Riverside Community College
Library
MAY '98 4800 Magnolia Avenue
Riverside, California 92506

HD 30.37 .B67 1997

Bort, Julie, 1964-

Building an Extranet

Executive Publisher: Katherine Schowalter
Editor: Theresa Hudson
Associate Managing Editor: Angela Murphy
Text Design & Composition: North Market Street Graphics

Designations used by companies to distinguish their products are often claimed as trademarks. In all instances where John Wiley & Sons, Inc., is aware of a claim, the product names appear in initial capital or ALL CAPITAL LETTERS. Readers, however, should contact the appropriate companies for more complete information regarding trademarks and registration.

This text is printed on acid-free paper.

Copyright © 1997 by Julie Bort and Bradley Felix

Published by John Wiley & Sons, Inc.

All rights reserved. Published simultaneously in Canada.

This publication is designed to provide accurate and authoritative information in regard to the subject matter covered. It is sold with the understanding that the publisher is not engaged in rendering legal, accounting, or other professional service. If legal advice or other expert assistance is required, the services of a competent professional person should be sought.

Reproduction or translation of any part of this work beyond that permitted by section 107 or 108 of the 1976 United States Copyright Act without the permission of the copyright owner is unlawful. Requests for permission or further information should be addressed to the Permissions Department, John Wiley & Sons, Inc.

Library of Congress Cataloging-in-Publication Data:
Bort, Julie.
    Building an Extranet : connect your Intranet with vendors and
customers / Julie Bort, Bradley Felix.
       p.   cm.
    Includes index.
    ISBN 0-471-17910-8 (alk. paper)
    1. Business enterprises—Computer networks. 2. Intranets
(Computer networks) I. Felix, Bradley, 1973- . II. Title.
HD30.37.B67   1997
658'.0546—dc21   97-7641

Printed in the United States of America
10 9 8 7 6 5 4 3 2 1

contents

Chapter 2   Security   29

Chapter 3   Extranet Performance Issues   99

Chapter 8   Tools for Building an Extranet   239

preface

Who Should Read This Book?

The Internet and the technology that surrounds it are moving at lightning speeds—unlike any evolution ever seen by the software industry. Companies are buying in like mad, often without thinking through the business implications. At some point, they realize that having a Web page is well and fine, but it costs a lot to maintain and has a pretty low direct return-on-investment. On the other hand, by taking advantage of the Internet's best features—its platform independence and its wide area networking (WAN) nature—companies can really cash in. They can build secure connections with their business partners that allow them to work seamlessly together on *one* network while at the same time ensuring the privacy of their transactions.

As with the transition from separate PCs to local area networks (LANs), businesses will be able to share specified data and applications at astoundingly low costs. Businesses need information that will guide them in some of those practices, which they will be thirsty for within the next 6 to 12 months.

This book is therefore aimed at business managers, departmental managers, strategic planners, CFOs, and other executives looking for cost-effective ways to leverage their investment in Internet technology into a competitive advantage. It achieves this by explaining the business and competitive advantage of a business-to-business intranet. It also provides them with the information necessary to evaluate and develop a successful electronic commerce market.

At the same time, this book is also aimed at a wide range of information technology (IT) people. These include LAN managers, software developers, Webmasters, IT security managers, WAN managers, departmental IT managers, and chief information officers (CIOs). It includes sample code, concrete explanations of technologies, and sources where technical people can get assistance with their specific implementations.

In a nutshell, this book is of value to anyone who depends on a company's information technology to produce results.

We do make several assumptions about the reader. To begin with, we assume that, more than anything, you need help in understanding various technologies and the trade-offs associated with them. We also assume that, given this background, you are capable of deciding which technologies are appropriate for your particular needs and are then capable of acquiring the specific, in-depth technical knowledge required for a particular project. (We included lists of sources where your questions can be answered.) Walking readers through the implementation process of every specification that could apply to a project is simply beyond the scope of what we intended to do with this book, and, we believe, beyond what anyone can digest in a single reading.

Nevertheless, to get you started, we've included sample code of some of the more popular business-to-business implementations and have also filled these pages with many implementation tips and suggestions.

How This Book Is Organized

Because of the wide audience, *Building an Extranet* includes a range of information, from basic and background to highly technical, each marked accordingly. For business managers and other nontechnical executives, the book includes background and explanations of technology and the business implications in plain, easy-to-understand English.

From a technical standpoint, the book assumes the following things: (1) the reader is familiar with the Internet and the technologies that it is composed of, (2) the reader is currently managing Internet and intranet applications, and (3) the reader is looking for ways to increase the value of these technologies, while limiting the time, effort, and expense of managing new applications.

Most of the introduction is background, and can be skipped for those who are already familiar with the Internet, how it came into being, and what it offers. Chapters 1 through 4 offer primarily strategic information that explains technologies and how they apply to an extranet or other aspects of an intranet. These chapters are chock full of information to help any company create a rationale for expanding their intranet.

The most technical information will be contained in Chapters 5 and 6, including sample code as the basis of an order-entry system, a shopping cart application for electronic commerce, and a bidding system for suppliers. Chapter 7 will assist you in determining the costs and returns that such a project will bring to your company, while Chapter 8 will assist you in locating vendors with products that meet your needs. Chapter 9 outlines methods and places to go to get assistance with your project, from qualified system integrators to online venues for popping off questions. We close, in Chapter 10, with a look at what the future of these technologies will bring us.

What Is the Underlying Philosophy of This Book?

Ultimately, this book is about expanding a company's intranet to the next logical step—to include business partners or others who have need of intranet services remotely. It is for readers who are sold on the Internet and intranet as a business tool but are not so sure that simply posting static information is the best use of the technology.

Now, many people will tell you that such expansion is merely a matter of reconfiguring a firewall to allow access from the business partner's domain name (an Internet identification address—much like the name of a street). This is true to a point. While this is part of the solution, it isn't all a Webmaster needs to do. For instance, opening up an intranet from a particular domain name could allow access to anyone in that domain. This solution may not authenticate who the actual user is, nor does it protect information from being seen by hackers or otherwise exposed.

Also, an organization will want to control precisely what areas and which applications of the intranet a remote user can access. The company will also want management of applications, information, and so on. It will want to factor in the potential security risks of engaging in scripting or applets and know how to minimize these risks. The well-planned, well-implemented extranet does all of this and more. Within the pages of this book, you'll discover everything you need to get started on your extranet implementation: ideas for how to expand, security options, sample code of popular extranet applications, names of products specifically designed for or particularly useful to the extranet, and places where you can go to get your specific implementation questions answered.

Acknowledgments

Dozens of people offered time, knowledge, and assistance in the creation of this book and we are grateful to all of them for their contributions. However, several went above and beyond and for that we extend our warmest thanks. These include Matt Harrigan, CIO of MicroCosm Computer Resources, for his input on Internet security; Eric Rescorla, principal engineer of Terisa Systems and one of the creators of the S-HTTP protocol, for his insight into Web security issues; Bill Bilow, who provided extensive examples of JDBC applications; Jordan Redner, MIS director of Real Information Systems, for additional programming assistance; the SSL development team at Netscape Communications Corp., for their contributions on SSL; and several of Sun Microsystems' internal Web development specialists. Other companies that especially allowed us to pick the brains of some of their most knowledgeable people include Digital Equipment Corp. and Thawte Computing.

About the Authors

Julie Bort has been a technology journalist since 1987. She has written about virtually every aspect of the computing industry and her work has been published in a dozen countries. For the last three years she has specialized in the business and technical issues of enterprise computing. She is a regular contributor to *InfoWorld, VARBusiness, Client/Server Computing, Software* magazine and the *Denver Post,* among other publications.

    Bradley Felix is president and founder of Timberline Internet Services, Inc., (http://www.timberweb.com), a Web design, publishing, and application development firm. Felix is fluent in half a dozen computer languages, including the popular Internet choices of HTML, Java, PERL, and Visual Basic. He is also a knowledgeable system administrator in as many platforms, from DOS to VAX.

    The authors can be reached at extranet@timberweb.com.

An Indispensable Tool

In the summer of 1996, at a meeting with a group of executives at a large software vendor, an outside company was hired to assist the software vendor in producing some marketing publications. When the question of the editing process arose—each document was to pass through six people before it was approved—one of them frowned.

"It's too bad you're not on our intranet," one executive said to her new business partner.

The software company had an extensive intranet—its own internal World Wide Web—that allowed employees to communicate in a number of ways, including collaborating on documents. But alas, since the software vendor was now dealing with business partners, not actual employees with offices on one of the company's many campuses, half the team had no access to this tool, even though it would have made working on the project more efficient for everyone.

This story illustrates a growing situation among companies that have implemented an intranet intended for day-to-day business use. As employees adapt to the new work paradigm an intranet provides within the company, they find that easy access to static information isn't enough. They then move their intranets toward interactive technologies, document collaboration, telephone calls, workflow and database queries, and so forth. Yet, their business partners—vendors, contractors and customers, and others who often work together on the same projects—are excluded. While it would be possible to perform many of these applications over the Internet, one of the greatest benefits of the intranet would be lost—privacy.

Companies are beginning to address this situation with an adaptation of their intranet that we've coined an *extranet*. The extranet is a business-to-business intranet that allows limited, controlled, secure access between a company's intranet and designated, authenticated users from remote locations. This differs from the Internet conceptually, because it is discriminatory and not open to the public at large. The concept differs from an intranet in that it offers access to applications from remote locations and restricts the areas where the remote user may go.

But an extranet, with some planning and an extra measure of security, allows companies to selectively expand their intranets around their business partners. It spills into the space between "internal" and "public." It gives partners selective access to the online tools that a company has already paid for and implemented. It makes conducting business with those connected faster, better, easier, and cheaper. Moreover, by reusing the resources that a company already has online, the inherent return on investment in the intranet can exceed 1,000 percent, as studies have shown. Better yet, the same technologies can also be applied to road warriors and home office workers, making an extranet an infinitely practical affair.

Therein lies the purpose of this book. We will explain the concept of the extranet, offer information on all of the components you need to build one for your company, guide you through some of the most common uses (including sample code), and provide a reference of resources to get your specific questions answered.

Astounding Growth

Never in the entire history of information systems has any technology been embraced as quickly and as widely as the Internet is being grabbed at today. The growth statistics are astounding; as of 1995, usage of the Internet was doubling annually, with no signs of a slowdown at present. At that time, an estimated 35 million people used it regularly: some 10 million host computers were connected and some 70,000 networks. Moreover, roughly 96,000 new users across the world joined the ranks of the Internet *daily* in 1996. At this current rate of expansion, in 1997 we will see a rate of 192,000 new users per day, as shown in Figure I.1.

But the most shocking statistic is that, as of 1995, only an estimated 4 percent of the U.S. population was among the 35 million Internet users. Furthermore, only 7 percent of PC users were part of the growing cyberspace family. If the Internet will truly become an "information utility" rivaling that of television, clearly it's still in its infancy. Even if the present rate of expansion were to continue, doubling each year, it would be almost another five years before access became ubiquitous.

Nevertheless, these rapid growth statistics indicate that the Internet will become omnipresent in the industrial nations of the world, at least. Chances are, it has already impacted your workplace, and possibly your

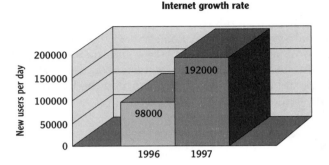

Figure I.1 Estimated Internet growth rate.

home, drawing you to our examination of where this technology will be tomorrow.

What is happening here? Well, media hype of the usefulness of the Internet as an *information superhighway* or *information utility* has contributed to the gold rush atmosphere. But hype aside, the various technologies that make up the Internet solve a real human need while simultaneously bypassing a traditional technology problem. The need is to communicate visually in a real-time but automated way, and with the end user in control. The need includes the ability to sift through vast amounts of information by concept. The Web and other technologies, such as e-mail, offer us the solution. Better yet, through platform independence, the Internet does this without having to know what type of PC it is talking to. Those presenting visual material need only post it once, the same for everybody, whether they use Macintoshes, Intel-based PCs, or RISC-based workstations. Peripheral Internet applications, such as File Transfer Protocol (FTP), Usenet, and Telnet also contribute to the informational power of the Internet. However, the Web has emerged as the ruler of the Internet universe, and is therefore the focus of most emerging technologies, including the extranet.

Before the Internet gained popularity with the average human being, communicating by the written word meant writing letters and waiting days for the U.S. mail to deliver, or asking someone to fax the needed material and hoping that it contained the information that was wanted, while being forced to wait for the other person (or a fax-on-demand machine) to comply. Information also had to be printed, which meant it was costly and time consuming to provide. Many times it was off-set printed in large volumes, adding to the expense and, additionally, making it difficult to change rapidly.

We don't believe that the U.S. Postal Service is in immediate danger of becoming obsolete; nor are we advising everyone to unplug their fax machines. But, just as the fax machine has taken the place of much of the world's postal needs, the Web has usurped the fax machine for many of today's immediate information needs.

Why Now?

This brings us to the question, *why now?* The Internet has actually been around since 1969. As long ago as 1986, the technologies it employed, such as the File Transfer Protocol, could have been used to meet this communication need. But the other pieces of the puzzle hadn't arrived yet. For one, the masses weren't particularly computer literate. Computers were far too costly to be sitting on every desktop. Worse, the world of computing was dominated by difficult, ugly, frustrating command-line interfaces. This meant that those who used the computer had to learn cryptic languages and memorize a lot of nonsensical commands, including precise punctuation, to get the surly computer to do what was wanted.

It wasn't until the advent, and then mass adoption, of graphical user interfaces (GUIs) for the PC that computers became a tool for the everyday worker. Today, icons, windows, colored text, pictures, and other images have changed how computers are manipulated, while advances in microchips, hard drives, and input/output technologies have improved how much the average computer can do at a cheaper cost. In a nutshell, PCs are faster, cheaper, and easier. Consequently, penetration of the PC into our lives has soared. In the world of business, penetration of the PC has reached nearly 100 percent. Likewise, roughly one-third of American homes have a PC. So, in this country, as in most industrialized nations, the average person is far more computer literate than was true even five years ago.

It was only a matter of time before the items that popularized the use of computers worked their way into the more established computing environments that continued to exist in this brave new world. For instance, while the Web was created in 1992, Mosaic, the GUI for it, didn't appear until 1994. Although it's hard to imagine a Web site without graphics, the Web was originally created as a means to link text documents to each other and was character based.

With the introduction of Mosaic the Internet was ready to be adopted by the average PC user. It also solved a hurdle never cleared by anyone else—platform independence. Prior to this, computers needed to speak the same operating system language in order to communicate. A Windows computer could talk only to another Windows computer, an Apple Macintosh only to another Macintosh, and Unix to Unix. Any attempt to communicate between operating systems required a lot of knowledge of how each operating system worked, and specialized tools that acted like translators, which left a lot to be desired. Yet, with today's versions of Mosaic—Web browsers such as Netscape Navigator, Spry Mosaic, and Microsoft Internet Explorer—communication between different operating systems is assured. This is because the Internet in all of its forms is built on standards—common ways of applying technology. While the browser itself must be built for the operating system of the machine it will be used on, the computer serving out information simply doesn't care if it's talking to Macintosh, Windows, or Unix machines. It speaks in a standardized way that all browsers understand.

With these legs in place, the creature stands today as a cheap answer to distributing visual information. The company need only publish one version, and store it electronically so that it is easily changed. Yet, this is only a fraction of what an intranet is capable of doing. Because an intranet is essentially a private Internet that uses a company's own network to send and transmit messages, it offers several advantages over the Internet, some of which can be compromised when creating an extranet.

1. An intranet can freely use larger graphics and fat files, as even the slowest network is 40 times faster than the fastest plain old telephone service (POTS) line (although some of that capacity may also be shared by applications other than the intranet, such as printing, file sharing, application serving, database querying, etc.).

2. An intranet offers a high level of security, because it requires that a machine be local in order to have access. Admittedly, some hackers can find ways around this local restriction, through compromising security holes such as open modems or conducting a "social engineering" attack, where hackers gain legitimate access to the network by conning employees. Still, inherently, an intranet is more secure, simply because it is private.

3. Because an intranet uses Internet standards it can therefore speak to any computer. Because an intranet is on a high bandwidth infrastructure, and is inherently more secure, the intranet is an ideal way to deploy interactive communications,

such as live, voice, or videoconference calls; download training videos or other movies; carrying on broadcast training sessions; and more.

Like potato chips, once people start using computers to perform these tasks, they want more and more.

Brief Explanation of the Technologies of the Internet

Having an intranet at all is a great way to extend the investment the company has in its PCs and network. Still, the vast majority of organizations that have invested in an intranet are still in the early stages of using it. It is relegated to being a passive tool, where information is posted and then browsed, much like the bulk of today's Web.

This book is about turning it into an interactive tool, in one specific way. Other books in this series from John Wiley & Sons can guide you through different ways to make an intranet interactive. These include

◆ Mellanie Hills, *Intranet Business Strategies*
◆ Mellanie Hills, *Intranet as Groupware*
◆ Mike Falkner, *Using Lotus Notes as an Intranet*
◆ Steve Guengerich, *Building the Corporate Intranet*
◆ Stephen Thomas, *Building Your Intranet with Windows NT 4.0*
◆ Richard Tanler, *The Intranet Data Warehouse*

But before any of that can be accomplished, a quick explanation of the technologies that comprise the Internet and its offspring technologies is in order. On the physical side, the Internet is what is known as a *client/server network*. Clients are machines that are requesting information and are being manipulated directly by the end users. The client is the PC that sits on the worker's desk or a notebook computer. Computers that dispense information are known as servers. These are usually faster and more powerful machines than what would typically be used as a client. A server may be a Windows PC dressed up with high-speed devices and lots of memory or storage; it could be a Unix workstation or even a mainframe.

Because the Internet is fundamentally based on Unix, its servers are often Unix workstations and, with increasing frequency, Microsoft Windows NT servers. Internet servers, in addition to storing Web pages, also control numerous other technologies, such as e-mail. They may also have databases for interactive applications or they may simply be networked to other servers that hold database information. Another set of Internet machines act as traffic cops, keeping a list of addresses and telling each electronic blip that makes up an Internet message where to go. Blips are known as *packets* and the machines that tell them where to go are *routers.* Hierarchies of routers determine where each packet of information needs to be sent. (See Figure I.2.)

Much like a street address, every connected computer has a unique number. This is its Internet Protocol (IP) address, and it is designated by a series of numerals separated by dots. However, since a series of dots and numbers is difficult for human beings to remember and use, the Internet uses what is called the *domain name system.* An organization is assigned an IP address (to ensure that no two Internet devices have the

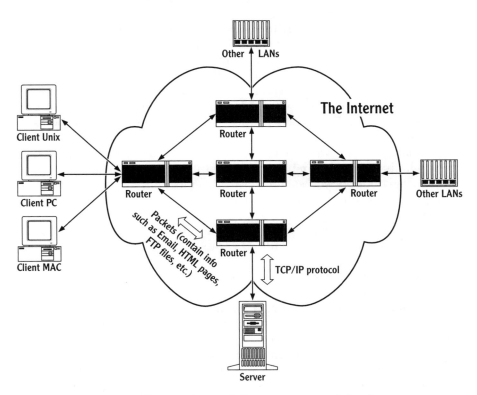

Figure I.2   A simplistic view of the structure of the Internet.

same address) by InterNIC (www.internic.net), an organization funded to oversee such administration of the Internet. On the other hand, that company can choose a domain name, provided that no one else is already using it and that the name follows the conventions established. For instance, the final three letters of a domain name give information on which type of network is connected, called a *domain.* The "com" extension indicates a commercial address, "gov" indicates government, "edu" indicates an educational facility, "org" indicates a noncommercial organization, "mil" indicates the military, and "net" means network, or an address that is concerned with the Internet. Outside the United States only two letters are used to identify domains, for instance, "uk" for the United Kingdom, "fr" for France, "au" for Australia, and "ca" for Canada. With its numeric address (which is actually composed of a series of addresses, so that a company can have more than one Internet computer as part of the Internet) and a domain name accepted by InterNIC, the company can "register" its domain name with a domain name server, usually maintained by the company's Internet Service Provider (ISP) as well as the InterNIC. The Uniform Resource Locator (URL) that a Web browser will use is actually a domain name that is mapped to a numeric address. In this way, human beings can more easily work with and remember addresses using names that make sense to them (words) while computers can work with addresses using names that make sense to them (numbers). Everybody's happy. More importantly, everybody's connected.

The last bit of hardware that makes up the Internet is the wiring. This is the telephone lines or network cabling that connects one machine to another, next door or across the world. The most important aspect of the wiring is the amount of data it can handle, known as *bandwidth.* It is designated in *bits per second.*

On the software side lie the applications. Today, the most accessed applications are the Web, e-mail, File Transfer Protocol, Telnet, and Usenet.

The *World Wide Web* is rapidly emerging as the most powerful application. It consists of a series of *hypertext files,* meaning that a user can jump from one file to another via *links* (addresses to other files embedded in the text of the original files). Since the graphical user interface face-lift (i.e., Mosaic), the Web can also include graphics such as drawings, photographs, or movies in its files. Users need a Mosaic-based browser to access the Web, in order to decode the text and images.

Web pages are constructed with HyperText Markup Language, commonly known as HTML. HTML is a subset of a larger standard named the Standard Generalized Markup Language (SGML). SGML is an international standard for electronic document exchange (a factoid that goes over big at trade-show cocktail parties). SGML was intended to overcome the limitations of ASCII—text devoid of any embellishments of appearance—but to do so in an open standard, rather than through proprietary technologies like Adobe Acrobat, which is still commonly used on the net and is usually designated by a .PDF extension. However, it has yet to take off significantly. Its major claim to fame is the birth of HTML.

The Web uses HyperText Transfer Protocol (HTTP), the file transfer and communication method used between browsers and Web servers for HTML documents. In fact, products that call themselves Web servers are actually HTTP servers.

E-mail is primarily used to send text in the form of memos, letters, or other written information from a single person to designated recipients, very much like a wired version of the U.S. postal service. E-mail is a *store-and-forward* technology, meaning that an e-mail message is sent to a server, which stores it and then forwards it to the user when that user logs in for it. It uses the Simple Mail Transfer Protocol (SMTP). This controls the connection of the sending and receiving machine.

The File Transfer Protocol (FTP) is the protocol used to copy files from one place on the Internet to another. For example, when a user *downloads* files, that person has copied the files from a server in the Internet to his or her local desktop PC. *Uploading* is the opposite—copying from local machine to a server. FTP can be embedded in a Web page which allows files to be easily downloaded from pretty HTML formatted text and graphics.

Usenet is a function of the Network News Transport Protocol (NNTP), which is similar to the SMTP protocol but is concerned with Usenet news articles, not individual e-mail messages. NNTP also includes some commands for updating newsgroup lists, article headings, and the postings of articles themselves. Newsgroups are e-mail discussion groups centered on specific topics. Users subscribe to them and can then read all of the messages sent to the group by all other subscribers.

Telnet is a network terminal protocol that allows a user to control a remote computer. Once a Telnet connection has been established, the remote computer treats the user as if it were accessing from a hard wire, rather than over the Internet. Telnet is used almost always as a text-based application, rather than a GUI-based one. Before the advent of Mosaic, Telnet was the common interface for such applications as FTP, e-mail, and even the Web (which was also text-based). Today these applications have migrated to GUI, but Telnet is still used often, especially by Unix Webmasters for server administration and also to exploit the powers of the Unix environment. It is also an especially favorite tool of hackers.

It's also important to note that all computers, in order to connect using Internet protocols, must be running Transmission Control Protocol/ Internet Protocol (TCP/IP) software. This can be embedded in the operating system. For instance, Windows 95 includes TCP/IP software, known as a *TCP/IP stack.* Or it can be purchased and used separately. There are many commercially available TCP/IP software stacks available. Whether embedded in the operating system or separate, TCP/IP is responsible for how various types of computers can all be part of the same computer network. Using this software, servers and clients can convert data into TCP/IP packets and back to the native language of the computer.

While most of us think of an intranet as being a mini–World Wide Web, the truth is that an intranet can make use of all of these Internet technologies. Moreover, most of today's Web browsers, particularly the latest, greatest 32-bit browsers such as Netscape 3.x and Internet Explorer 3.x, can support these functions as well, making the browser the central GUI for a variety of Internet applications.

What Differentiates the Intranet from the Internet?

In two words, it's *bandwidth* and *privacy.* With an Internet site, a company has several considerations.

◆ It needs to limit its graphics and large files in consideration of visitors with limited bandwidth, notably modems that operate, at best, at 28.8Kbps.

◆ The company wants to make sure that what is publicized on the Web is its consumer information.

◆ The company wants to be sure that the site is attractive and appealing, and offers content that brings people back.

With an intranet site, the company uses its own internal network exclusively, rather than the public network. So it eliminates those constraints. In most cases, the company is using, at a minimum, standard Ethernet, giving it 10Mbits of bandwidth to use, rather than the 28.8kilobits available to modems. In some cases, the company may also be using leased telephone lines at speeds of 56K for connections to remote offices. Also, the documents it wants to provide access to can be longer and more numerous, but they don't necessarily have to be pretty. Best of all, intranets are secure, if designed properly. Physically separated from the network, hackers cannot gain entrance through the traditional means that scare network managers—like sniffing the public networks to capture information. This does not mean that intranets are infallible, any more than the company's file/print and application sharing network is. They remain vulnerable to attack both from the inside and from the outside through unsecured modems, for instance. However, security has been vastly improved.

The lessened concern over security, coupled with the increase in bandwidth, makes intranets an ideal place to experiment with practical new technologies as they emerge.

Here's a typical history. Most intranets start their life as a multiplatform, multimedia repository of static information. End users may browse, even search, but what they find is an electronic form of a printed piece of paper (or video or audio file). It stays the same until someone changes it. This can be extremely useful and efficient. For instance, when the company insurance agent gives a seminar on the new policy human resources is offering, that seminar can be posted in a database, complete with slides or even videotape, and those who were unable to attend can then review it at a later date.

But, this intranet architecture only scratches the surface of what an intranet can do, and it doesn't necessarily do anything to help a company generate revenue or cut significant operating costs. The next step in most cases is to allow the intranet to process more data types. It may become a venue for video broadcasts from the CEO or for training videos. It may start to store images and computer-aided design (CAD) drawings. From there it may become interactive, supporting applications that allow employees to communicate in real-time collaboratively. This may be voice communications, "whiteboard" applications that allow two people to look at and annotate the same file at the same time, videoconferencing, "workflow," where documents are routed from one person to another automating certain tasks, and so forth. Any application that allows the Web to be a front end for a database backend can be created, giving rise to an endless array of possibilities.

At this point, as one IS manager put it, "It's a no-brainer to extend it to your strategic partners." In the next chapter, we'll explain why.

Summary

The Internet is growing at astounding rates, yet by many measures is still in its infancy. This combination of growth and newness is giving rise to an immediate future for information systems that only a few years ago would have been considered science fiction. The reason for the Internet's sudden appeal has to do with the convergence of social, economic, and technological factors. On the social side, industrial nations are more computer literate today than ever before. This has created a mass market for PCs, in particular, driving down costs, improving availability, and allowing computer literacy to rise that much higher. At the same time, computers have become both more powerful and easier to use, allowing even the lowest-end model to perform tasks only mainframes could do 15 years ago.

However, what specifically appeals to a growing number of organizations about the Internet is that it is standards based, meaning that the technology is owned democratically rather than by a single vendor and that it is constructed in such a way that any type of computer running any type of operating system can be part of the system.

Several Internet technologies are popular today, such as e-mail and Usenet, but the leader of them all is the World Wide Web. The Web allows users to jump from one document to another easily and also supports graphics very well.

The situation has lead to the mass adoption of intranets, or mini-Internets, that companies build for their own private use. However, as intranets embed themselves into the daily routines of employees, it quickly becomes apparent that the other side of the equation is missing, the business partner. Detailing the solution to this dilemma is the mission of this book.

## PART ONE

Overview

## chapter one

What Does Your Business Gain with an Extranet?

How Can You Expand Your Intranet to Make It More Productive?

By now, you already know what the intranet is and that it can be a great business tool. (If not, we recommend that you read the Introduction.) In fact, you probably already have one in place. Or, you are that commendable type of person that truly plans the direction of your company's technology future—a person who wants to know what the big-picture possibilities are before you invest. Either way, your nose is pointed in the right direction, in this book.

The truth is that the ways and means to expand your intranet are growing as fast as the adoption of the Internet itself. Thanks to a dozen new technologies, the intranet can be turned from a static Web server that allows employees to view data into one that runs a huge range of applications. For instance, end users can perform queries against a database or make entries to a database; they can conduct live chat sessions; they can share a file in real time; they can partake in videoconferencing; they can upload or download files; they can manage other servers across the network; they can perform standard print/file and application-sharing services. In short, the TCP/IP intranet can become a company's only LAN.

And it can do all this using standardized, inexpensive commodity technology that supports any front-end platform. Isn't this what the computing industry dreamed about in the late eighties when the term *open systems* was so widely adopted?

Database Queries

The single most significant development for interactive intranet applications is in allowing them to query an SQL DBMS, according to an Internet/intranet study of 300 developers, consultants, and specialists conducted by *VARBusiness* magazine. Two-thirds of respondents said that they are regularly working on projects which integrate a database backend to the Internet. Almost a quarter of them plan to specialize in database connectivity in 1997. Why? Because with a database backend, a Web page gains enormous flexibility. For instance, it can function as a kind of mini–data warehouse, allowing people to pull together ad hoc queries on sales figures or human resource data, for instance. It can process order requests, or be a source for a huge volume of files. In fact, all of the major SQL database vendors are developing tools that allow Web integration. The Java Database Connectivity API, (JDBC) is rapidly gaining in popularity to connect Java applets & applications to ODBC-Compliant Databases. And it can also be performed through the common gateway interface (CGI), a concept we discuss in Chapter 3.

Chat Sessions

Chat sessions allow employees to use their keyboards and an intranet to communicate in real time. There are a number of ways to allow chatting on the Internet. One of the most common ways is through the Internet Relay Chat (IRC). Again, like most of the technologies that make an intranet so appealing, IRC is a client/server application with client software available on a variety of platforms. So, users with PCs or Macintoshes or Unix clients can all partake of the same server. Essentially, users log into an IRC server and are served up with a list of topics on which to chat. When words are typed into the client, they are displayed on all of the end users' machines.

Videoconferencing

Again, a number of ways exist for performing videoconferencing over an intranet, but the most commonly used method in the

Internet world is an application called CUSeeMe, developed at Cornell University (hence the cute name). Because CUSeeMe was expressly developed to work with TCP/IP networks, it is particularly well suited for companies wanting to deploy desktop video-conferencing on their intranets. Like IRC, CUSeeMe requires users to log into a CUSeeMe server, called a *reflector*. The video data is actually sent across the network using a protocol called User Datagram Protocol (UDP), rather than TCP. UDP is more efficient for video, because, among other things, it doesn't request that dropped packets be resent. This could cause video to be rather jerky, but at least it doesn't further delay the already slow process of sending video over a network.

Whiteboards

Whiteboards is an application that allows several people to work on or annotate the same file. Using the Internet's IP multicast protocol, instead of the Internet's normal TCP, whiteboards can be set up that allow several people to work on the same file at the same time. IP multicast protocol allows a signal to be sent to several destinations simultaneously, rather than a single destination, as TCP specifies.

Real-Time Voice Conversations

A number of commercial products also exist that allow a TCP/IP network to be used for voice conversations. Some of these products require participants to log into a telephone server; others allow a call to be placed directly to someone's PC using the person's e-mail address as its telephone number. The latter method does, however, require that the receiving machine has a live, continuous connection to the Internet or intranet, not a dial-up connection or one that must be activated.

Things to Come

Many other technologies that add richness to an intranet are also available. Technologies such as virtual reality, broadcast video, and enhancements to the use of audio are being developed daily as we go to press. One that is especially promising for extranet applications is dubbed "Push Technology." These are clients that receive information automatically, rather than browsers which must seek out and request data. Although we cannot list them all here, any one of them might be the appropriate choice in a business-to-business intranet.

The Business Partner Extension

As wonderful as it is to improve internal communications, employees talking to one another is not the primary goal of most companies. A business needs customers, and it needs suppliers of items like raw materials, insurance policies, employee benefits plans, office equipment, and so on. It also frequently needs contractors and consultants. The better able a company is to improve communications with these people (whom we will refer to collectively as *partners*), the more money it will make or the more it will save.

Here's an example. Production engineers at a medical equipment manufacturer routinely publish the specifications of raw materials on their intranet, so it can be viewed by production managers and purchasing officials. The company uses a wide array of custom-dimension material, such as off-size bolts and screws. In the past, when the company's stock of its custom materials would decrease or the company had to change a custom part, the ordering process would involve having a production person contact a purchasing agent. That agent would then contact all of the potential suppliers and fax the specification. If the supplier had questions, the purchasing person would spend time tracking down engineers to get those questions answered. If the agent let any part of the process slip through the cracks, the material ordered would be late or wrong, delaying production and causing a backlog of customer orders.

About a year ago, the company, running low on a custom-dimension bolt, decided to open its intranet to its bolt manufacturing suppliers so they could view the specification on their own and submit a bid. Questions on the specification could be submitted directly to the appropriate engineer via an HTML form. By opening up the intranet, the company removed the burden from the purchasing agent and distributed it between the agent and the suppliers. (The agent still has to oversee the process.) The time spent by the purchasing agent faxing out information and relaying questions was gained while electronic communications directly between the supplier and the engineers made communicating more efficient.

The company saved time in reordering and in the bidding process, it saved money by eliminating wasted hours spent by purchasing personnel, and was better able to match orders with production.

Why Use an Extranet to Accomplish This?

Like the manufacturing company that already had the necessary documents online, the idea with an extranet is to leverage the existing investments in technology. So the effort of writing fabulous HTML documents, scanning in photos, and so on, does double duty, immensely increasing the return on the investment of creating them. (See Chapter 7 for more details on how to calculate the costs and ROI of an extranet.) Of course, not every extranet is built to use the same hardware, software, and data as is in use on a corporate intranet. For some companies, the most secure way to accomplish an extranet is to replicate the necessary data, place the data on its own server outside the firewall, and then heavily fortify that server with security measures to be sure that only authorized people use it, concepts which are discussed further in Chapter 2.

Still, even if the actual data and application used for a business-to-business connection is replicated—or even custom-developed—for the extranet (placed on a server purchased exclusively for this mission), because the Internet is based on standards, any number of other investments in technology could still be leveraged.

For instance, at the very least, the company's partners already have PCs and telephone service. In all probability they have Internet access, or are simply waiting for a good reason to get it (and this would be it). With that access they would have Web browsers and TCP/IP stacks. So developing an application based on Internet technologies means, at the very least, that the company need *not* supply its partners with a lot of special hardware or develop custom front ends. (Some hardware or software may need to be agreed upon, or supplied by the company, depending on the security scheme chosen. However, it is possible to choose a security scheme that is supported by the most popular hardware and browsers.)

By choosing to deploy an Internet-based application which is supported by the technology already in use by the partner, companies will avoid all hassles associated with custom clients, such as maintaining and supporting client hardware or software, or dealing with compatibility issues on the client side, or providing upgrades. Better yet, because the Internet is governed by standards, any extranet application developed to these standards will be virtually guaranteed to work with the browsers and TCP/IP stacks a business partner owns, reducing the time it takes to get an extranet application from idea to use.

Of course, exceptions abound, specifically when it comes to security, or when it comes to some of the more adventurous interactive applications that rely on newer or obscure protocols. That's why we advise companies who are beginning to create an extranet to do so sensibly. Start with what you have and what you know, and factor in what your business partners have and what they know.

Even though a videoconference link between your company and your biggest client may seem like a great idea, unless your company is already using the technology, this is going to represent a huge investment in hardware, software, training, and more. Done wrong, this will probably turn into a big ugly mess, with maybe some finger pointing. ("I did *not* suggest this project." "Did too." "Did *not.*" *"Did too!"* You get the point.)

However, an organization *can* develop a business-to-business application that it absolutely knows will operate as intended, not just on one partner's computers but on any of them. It need only restrict itself to the protocols that are in widespread use today: HTTP, FTP, SNMP, and Telnet, for example (not much of a restriction). At the same time, it should create a plan that allows it to migrate or add-on other protocols, like IPv6 Security (IPv6SEC), IP Mulitcast, and so on. If an extranet is created in this "conservative" fashion to start with, it can quickly pay for itself and for some of the fancy applications that might also be useful.

Here's an example. A large New York advertising agency created an intranet to allow its production department (on Macintosh PCs) to communicate better with its administration departments, accounting, human resources, and so forth (on Intel-based PCs). It then discovered that the HTTP protocol that handles graphics so well is an ideal way for customers to approve art. Drawings, photos, or other graphics can be stored in a database, called up through a CGI interface and viewed in minutes, even if the customer is halfway across the country. By making use of an HTML form, clients can respond to the art with their suggestions.

The system saves hundreds of dollars in hard costs almost immediately. It allows clients to give feedback early in the process, before a lot of time is spent on work that will be ultimately unsatisfactory. It eliminates money spent on overnight packages for approval, which could often be a back-and-forth process accruing major dollars over the course of a project, and it limits wasted color copies. The grand finale is that it creates tremendous goodwill between the agency and its clients.

In fact, the ROI on this extranet project was so alluring to the agency that it extended its customer-access extranet. The additional project was a database of newsprint ads. The database allows clients to log on, see an ad, obtain a listing of publications in which the ad appeared, and get feedback on the response to the ad, again, through a CGI interface, HTTP, and HTML documents.

As its next step, the company is considering a whiteboard application that would allow customers the same sort of early development input with ad copywriters.

What Differentiates an Extranet from an Internal-Only Intranet and the Public Internet?

Models of Extranet Applications

Extranets are built in all sorts of ways using all sorts of methods, but they do have a few elements in common. End users must be authenticated. This differs from a basic password-protected Web site on the Internet in that, with Web sites, few efforts are made to truly authenticate the identity of a person. One example of this is Silicon Investor, a Web site dedicated to investors of high technology companies (www.techstocks.com). Silicon Investor requires a password. The password is given through an HTML form and CGI script. This form asks for information about the applicant such as the person's name, occupation and e-mail address. Verification of the person's identity is through e-mail. After the form is submitted, a password is e-mailed to the address given in the form. If applicants are honest about their e-mail addresses, they will become authorized users. However, applicants need not be honest about the rest of their identity.

With an extranet, authenticated identity is important. Still, extranets can be classified into the following models.

◆ The secured Intranet access model
◆ The specialized application model
◆ The electronic commerce model (see Figures 1.1, 1.2, 1.3)

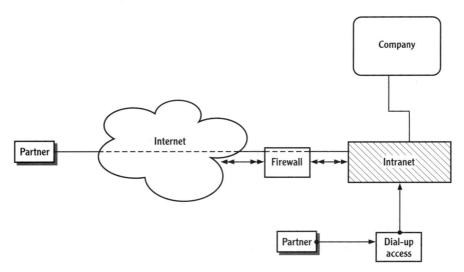

Figure 1.1   The secured intranet access model allows partners directly into the corporate intranet, either through the Internet or via a direct, dial-up connection.

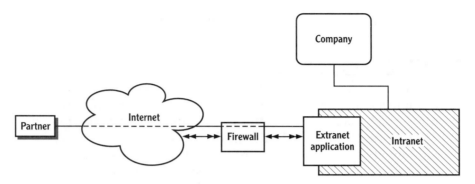

Figure 1.2 With the specialized application model, the extranet is an application developed specifically for partners that may also be part of the intranet.

The Secured Intranet Access Model

With the secured intranet access model of extranet application, the partner gains the ability to log directly onto a company's intranet to perform specified tasks. This requires the highest levels of security planning and also a lot of trust in the partners. An example of the secured intranet would be offering an extension of

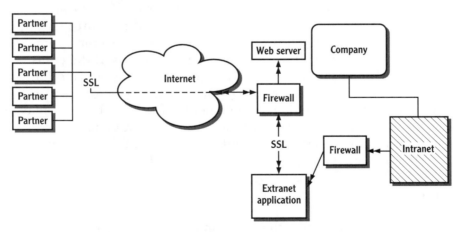

Figure 1.3 The electronic commerce model uses electronic commerce techniques to service a partner segment, including similar security architecture and transaction processing.

the collaborative software used on a corporate intranet to include access to a partner.

The Specialized Application Model

In this model, an application has been developed specifically for a particular partner, or for a category of partner in which only a few partners exist, such as raw material suppliers. Employees may be able to access the application from their intranet, but partners would have limited access to the intranet from this extranet site, if any. There is a moderate amount of trust of the partners because access is limited only to partners that the company knows well and may include processes that are mission critical. An example of a specialized application model would be an vendor bidding application in which the company's core vendors can bid on supplying raw materials for the company's manufacturing needs.

The Electronic Commerce Model

This method uses electronic commerce techniques to approach specific partner segments. It may be used when the partners segment contains hundreds of companies. It may involve commerce transactions, such as order entry, or it may not. However, it is typically capable of transactionlike operations, even if that transaction is not a sale. It implies limited trust toward the partners. An illustration of this model would be a database set up for a company's distribution channel or those partners that sell the company's products to consumers. This would contain information that would not be available to the public, such as wholesale pricing, incentive plans, and announcements of R&D projects. It may also allow resellers to place orders electronically, using a customer account number as payment information. In fact, we have outlined just such an application in Chapter 6.

Politically Speaking

The politics surrounding the creation of an extranet are vastly different from building an Internet presence on the Web. This is a bridge between a company and its most important business contacts, its partners. The extranet application had better work well, plain and simple.

The place to begin is with a thorough evaluation of the company's partners. Even though you may be reading this book because you have a specific partner in mind and a specific application, we strongly recommend that you step back and do an overall evaluation process.

One good method of evaluating partners is to stratify them by importance to the company. In this way, you can better evaluate the benefits and security risks of creating extranet applications for specific partners or entire partner segments. The following is a matrix that may work for you.

Strategic Partners

Strategic partners are so key that the company would be damaged if the relationship tumbled. For instance, a client that represents 25 percent or more of the company's revenue would definitely qualify. This would also include the amount of revenue that the customer influences. For instance, one customer may represent only 3 percent of the company's overall revenue but is a well-known firm that acts as a reference and has contributed to contracts worth 50 percent of the company's revenue.

A strategic partner may also be a company that is working on a joint development project. Or it could be the company's hired guns, such as the IT outsourcing firm, or those hired to do accounting, human resources, or investment management functions.

The supplier(s) of the custom-designed widget essential for your flagship product would most likely qualify to be part of this category as well. In some companies the coffee and candy bar vendor would be considered a strategic partner, because the productivity levels of the entire company depend on it. (Just kidding.)

Important Partners

Important partners are those that land on a somewhat lower tier than the strategic partners but are still significant. This may be the supplier of raw materials that can fulfill an order in 24 hours and at a lower cost than anyone else.

Or it is a customer that is eager to try the company's latest and greatest products and then work with the engineers to fine tune them. Or it is a longtime customer that once represented 50 percent of the company's revenue but today represents a consistent 10 percent (due to the growth of the company, of course).

It might also include professional partners such as lawyers, management consultants, or contract employees.

Practical Partners

Practical partners (*in other words, the rest*) are those other customers, vendors, suppliers, and consultants whose combined presence affects the success of the business, but who do not individually carry a lot of weight. These might be office supply vendors, repeat customers of small-ticket items, the insurance broker, and so on.

Implications for Extranet Applications   The implications of building an extranet with your strategic partners are tremendous. In fact, of the dozens of companies interviewed for this book who were in the process of building an extranet, nearly all of them were targeting this group first.

Why? Improving communications between a company and its most important partners could dramatically affect the bottom line. In fact, the return on investment for such communications can be 1,000 or more percent, according to a recent study on ROI of extended intranets conducted by International Data Corporation, a research company in Framingham, Massachusetts. Likewise, a frustrating experience could damage the bottom line.

Applications should therefore be simple and work reliably. Security is imperative. Should a security breach occur with these partners, the ramifications could be far greater than whatever data was lost. Trust will be compromised. The applications deployed for these partners will probably touch on some of the most sensitive data the company owns.

And yet, the potential paybacks are worth the extra efforts to secure the application. An application that makes it easier for a company's biggest customers to work with the company increases sales and further cements a relationship. An application that allows important vendors to do their jobs more efficiently and at less cost means savings can be passed on.

So, as extranets begin to be deployed, the importance of knowing the members of various partner groups is essential. A project that would cost $100,000 aimed at a strategic partner may be a reasonable expense. A project that would cost $20,000 for the benefit of a single practical partner may need to be rethought. Any project to include this group on a business-to-business intranet should have top-level executive buy-in.

Here's an illustration of how serious it can be to provide an extranet extension to a partner. At Sun Microsystems Computer Corporation, several extranet applications are accessible to different levels of partners through the Internet. Each application is targeted to a particular group and carries with it different levels of security. It also has an intranet it calls the Sun Wide Area Network. On rare occasions a business partner has been deemed important enough to need access to its intranet, primarily for database-access applications. Because the company's network is so strategic to its operations, the process of allowing someone onto the intranet may take up to two years. Approvals for the project must be gained from top management; IT professionals and other departments are involved. The application must be perfected, and, most importantly, a security scheme must be developed that is proven to protect Sun's resources.

When it comes to reaching important partners, the trade-off of security to payback decreases dramatically but may still be significant enough to warrant an extranet application. This is especially the case if the application can be applied to a group of important partners—such as raw material suppliers—rather than individual ones.

For practical partners, economies of scale take on even bigger significance. Because the importance of these partners is their collective influence, the application should serve the bulk of them. The payback for a security risk is low for an individual partner in this category (although it may be fairly high for the collective group).

Applications built for practical partners tend to use an electronic commerce model, rather than the business-to-business model. This could include applications such as the one employed by Federal Express, in which anyone can log in, enter a package tracking number, and receive data about the package. Security is loose—authentication is a function of the tracking number. If the wrong one is entered, the person receives rather meaningless data about the whereabouts of another package. The length of tracking numbers makes them virtually impossible to guess. So the situation isn't one that requires much protection.

All of these approaches are different from the goals of building a Web site for the Internet. In some cases, they are dramatically different. When trying to gain a presence on the Web, the idea is to build a site that will be visited by as many people as possible. To do this, a Web site should be entertaining. It should deliver the company message succinctly. It may try to collect demographic data from the people who visit, but it doesn't want the collection of that data to be such a barrier that people won't come.

Similarly, the extranet differs from the intranet in the people it will reach. Employees need information, not entertainment. Also, as long as other mission-critical resources are protected, the intranet can be a great place to experiment. Better that a newly created chat application crashes on employees than on a company's biggest customer.

Technically Speaking

Because an extranet is unique, both in the people it targets and the mission it has, it presents different technical challenges. In one sense, the extranet straddles the boundaries of a Web site or an intranet, and winds up with the worse of both worlds.

Whereas the intranet is a Web site set free from the stifling bandwidth constrictions of a 28.8 connection, the extranet may again have those restrictions imposed. While the intranet can rely heavily on the security access mechanisms in place on the network, the extranet requires extreme measures of security. Finally, although the intranet is free to have pretty, bandwidth-hungry graphic images and other fancy Web techniques, it doesn't really need them. Employees accessing intranet information are highly motivated to read it, even if it's ugly. (We are not arguing against infographics. Graphics that offer information, rather than entertainment, are unquestionably appropriate.) But the extranet, as a bridge to a company's most important partners, has more inspiration to look friendly and professional.

In comparison to the Internet, an extranet shares similar bandwidth concerns, but its emphasis on who is accessing this information is paramount. Also, while the ROI on a Web page can be somewhat vague—as is common in mass-marketing advertising—with the extranet it can, and should be, carefully measured. Why spend time and expense creating and maintaining an application if it isn't successfully performing its mission? If that mission is directly related to revenue generation, reduction in overhead, or at least customer service for your biggest clients, it needs to be tracked.

These differences translate into unique technical challenges. For one, the system created must be robust even though development tools are immature. The technologies comprising the Internet are changing at lightning speed. Tools that use, support, or enhance these new technologies, such as Java, Javascript, ActiveX, and even CGI, are appearing on the market with alarming speed. It is difficult to know if a tool even exists to perform a specific development task. If it is around, it can be hard to figure out if it is worth the investment and learning curve. The world is trying to pirouette before it has learned to stand.

Also, companies entering into this realm need to understand that, although putting up a Web site is easy, creating an interactive, secure application is *not* exactly basket weaving. Such applications are akin to building a client/server application, rather than posting HTML pages. As such, the people engaged in the task will need Web development skills, client/server development know-how, plus a dose of network systems integration smarts. In contrast, a webmaster these days need not know much about programming or networking—not even much about HTML.

Some of the issues that need to be thought through on this level include:

- ◆ Will the application reside on the creator's server or will it be replicated?
- ◆ If it is replicated, how will upgrades and maintenance be done?
- ◆ If it will remain remote, how will end users safely access it?
- ◆ Which parts of the application will be relegated to the server for backend processing?

◆ Which parts will be sent to the client for processing?

◆ Which tools will be responsible for that client-side processing and how will they be engineered to protect the client's PC from harm?

Are these issues complex? You bet.

Perhaps the biggest technical challenge is the lack of standards to guide a developer. This is a unique situation at odds with the entire 25-year history of the Internet. Internet standards are created in a democratic manner guided by those who elect to be part of the Internet Engineering Task Force (IETF). Workgroups within this task force gather opinions on how to standardize the execution of a particular technology. The process is long and involved and centers around documents called Request For Comments (RFC). The workgroup will submit an RFC that describes how a certain task should be performed. Other interested parties will submit comments in response; the workgroup will review them and then alter the standard-in-progress accordingly.

The technical problem for today's builders of extranets is that many of the technologies that are best suited for this highly secure project are commercial technologies owned by a particular company. The IETF is loath to endorse a specific company's technology by making it the basis of a standard. In fact, Internet culture demands that freeware and shareware solutions be readily available.

So important parts of standards get ignored, left out, or take eons of deliberation before they are addressed in a definitive way by the IETF. For example, in Chapter 2 we will discuss a technology called *virtual private networks* (VPNs). A core technology at the heart of VPNs is *encryption.* The IETF is working on a new IP standard, IP version 6, which will include a number of security features, among them VPNs. However, the IETF can't agree on certain key elements needed for VPNs to be a functional standard—one that creates interoperable VPNs. This hasn't stopped vendors, though, from attempting to support VPNs as they are somewhat outlined in the emerging specification.

This puts people creating extranets and intranets in a bind. If you believe what you read on the box of a shrinkwrapped product, the product supports a particular Internet standard. Internet standards, in the past, have been pretty reliable—not a lot of room for interpretation. One TCP/IP stack will pretty much provide an Internet connection as well as another, even if one is freeware and the other shrinkwrapped.

But with this new slate of products the Internet has been dragged kicking and screaming into some of the same thorny problems as the commercial client/server industry. A thin line exists between standards-compliant and proprietary. A vendor claiming to be one might also have the attributes of the other. All of these pitfalls can be safely avoided, however, with a bit of planning and a lot of knowledge.

What Does the Technology Buy You?

We believe that an extranet is the natural progression of most intranets. When planned well, the extranet can have a return on investment of over *1,000 percent* (see Chapter 7 for more information on this). While there is no limit to the type of collaborative applications that the extranet can be charged to do, a few ways seem to be better entry points than others. According to our research, here are the primary ways extranets are being used today.

The Extranet Content Provider (Suppliers on Your Intranet)

One of the easiest ways to nudge your organization into an extranet is to allow strategic partner-suppliers to provide content for your intranet. Several advantages exist for doing this. First of all, these partners can create Web content that specifically reflects its relationship to you. If they offer you special prices or packages, or if you've got a service contract, this information can be reflected in a supplier's page.

Customers can upload their quarterly reports, clips from the press, new products, management changeovers, phone lists, and so on—information that they already have in HTML format that would enable you to better serve them.

In all honesty, a strategic vendor will jump at the chance of being on your extranet faster than a strategic customer would. Of course, customers can be made to participate if doing this makes it easier and more cost-effective for you to service them. The key here is to make this option available only to those partners who fall into the strategic category; otherwise the company is either letting itself in for a big maintenance headache or a big security risk.

For example, Columbia Healthcare Corporation of Nashville, Tennessee is a syndicate of doctors and hospitals. It has an extensive intranet for its medical professional members. Recently, the company has identified ten strategic vendor partners that it is allowing to post information on its intranet.

One of the trade-offs in this type of extranet project, like many of them, is ease of administration versus security. The easiest way to administer extranet content providers is to let them be responsible for Web page development and the uploading of new Web pages. When developing pages for a company's intranet, they would be mandated to follow corporate Web page policies, such as using the corporate image map with links to the home page and other sites.

But uploading gets a little trickier. In order to allow them to upload they would have to have access to the Web server and the authority to write to their directory on that server. This may be more access and authority than a company is comfortable in granting. In that case, the project could revert to good 'ole sneaker net. This is the choice of Columbia Healthcare. Vendors who have been invited to participate in this extranet project mail disks to a Webmaster, who uploads them to the Web server. When all ten vendors come online as content providers, the task of making sure the latest Web pages were received and uploaded might be a pain. Furthermore, if the vendors don't have access to view their pages, they will have no way of playing watchdog over their content.

For Columbia, these maintenance problems are worth the headaches because they feel absolutely confident that the extranet can't be a vehicle for security breaches, especially when patient confidentiality is at stake via online records. However, it seems that there should be an easier way to do this while still maintaining the security of the rest of Columbia's systems. If vendors were restricted to a certain area of a Web server, which could authenticate them and monitor their activities, they could upload their own pages. That area might even be restricted from access to everyone but the Webmaster, who could then move the pages to the appropriate sections of the intranet, much like a moderated mailing list, or perhaps keep the entire extranet on a separate machine. These methods and a host of others can be done with confidence, security, and safety, by following some of the methods described in Chapters 2, 3, and 4.

The Extranet as a Customer Service Vehicle (Disseminating Messages to Your Customers)

Conversely, a company could engage an extranet application to provide content for its customers. It could allow these customers to come onto sections of its internal network to, say, view the HTML catalog available on the intranet.

Or it could establish separate servers that allow authorized access to specific customers. For instance, an extranet is a great vehicle for fulfilling service contracts, when those service contracts require the distribution of information. This is a particularly popular choice of software manufacturers who can use an extranet to upload bug patches, new versions of software, data sheets on related products, and so forth.

But even for a company that manufactures power boats, an extranet could be a valuable tool. It could post information on when individual customers should have their outboard motors serviced and lists of authorized service dealers. It could even allow users to book an appointment with a local dealer on the extranet application, over an Internet connection.

Using Internet broadcasting products, or Java-created applications, an extranet can also be a way to disseminate information about your company or your client over the extranet in a push-through way. For instance, if your company uses a "clipping" service that scans the media for mentions and articles on your company or its competitors, those clippings are often posted to the extranet. However, rather than sending them around in a mailing list, the headlines of articles could be broadcasted and scroll across the screens of those with an active browser. Or they can scroll at the bottom of the client's intranet home page. A good example of this is the C/Net home page (www.cnet.com). C/Net is a Web-based news service that uses this Java applet to offer peeks to its other Web pages.

The Extranet as Revenue Generator (New Products/Services)

A company can also choose to be an extranet content provider for fun and profit. Here's an example of an entire business that was created for exactly this reason. A startup called 401k Forum, Inc. of San Francisco provides a Web-based application that offers guidance to employees of Fortune 1,000 companies on how to manage their 401k funds (www.401kforum.com). This guidance is customized to both the specific pension plan that the Fortune 1,000 company offers and the idiosyncrasies of end user accessing (such as age, retirement goals, risk tolerance, etc.). Because 401k Forum's bread and butter is this custom Web application, the company won't replicate it and place individual systems on its customer's intranet. It needs to keep this code close to its chest, according to one of the system's developers, Michael Robertson, vice president of product development.

Additionally, replicating the application would pose some technical challenges, since the proprietary application is a complex one that relies on outside sources, such as financial data, analysis research on the 401k plans, and so on. So, the application remains on and runs on a server at 401k's headquarters. Its customers therefore connect over a secured Internet connection to access the application and get personalized advice on how to manage their 401k pension funds (Figure 1.4).

Another example of a company making a business out of being an extranet content provider is Trade Compass, Inc., of Washington, D.C. Trade Compass bills itself as a business-to-business Internet site (www.tradecompass.com). This company employs nearly every state-of-the art Internet technology available in its quest to be the foremost online source of international trade information. Its Internet Web site is a for-profit operation, in which subscription levels are sold which allow subscribers to access a certain number of reports. It also allows users to book freight forwarding space

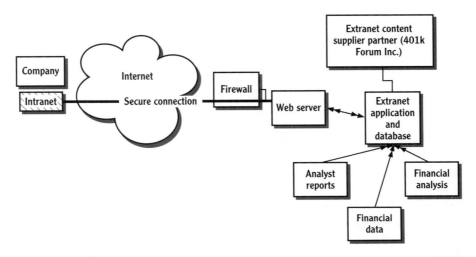

Figure 1.4 Some extranets are in the form of content suppliers such as 401k Forum Inc., which provides 401k investment information to a company's intranet. With 401k Forum, the extranet application actually resides at the 401k's site and is accessed via a secure connection over the Internet.

directly over the Internet for their international shipping needs. Qualified surfers can also search for sales leads, upload company contacts in a directory of business cards, and more.

Not surprisingly, then, Trade Compass operates as an extranet content provider of international trade information. It gleans its information from sources like the U.S. Inbound Manifest records. The manifest lists in mind-boggling detail every item that has been shipped into the United States along with the data on who shipped it, from which country, and so on. With an Oracle Express Server functioning as analysis tools, this manifest, along with other shipping data sources, can be used to find the answers to the most intricate details. For example, a textile company can keep track of how much cotton was shipped into the country to help it gage expected raw material costs.

Or an environmental organization can drill down to be informed on the incoming shipments of a particular pesticide. The system can also be used to analyze all shipments sent from France. Unlike 401k, however, the server, analysis tools, and database is a replicated system placed on the customer's intranet. A daily telecommunications feed, through the Internet or stand-alone, updates the data daily. This update could also be done through offline methods, such as the old standby magnetic storage.

The Potential of the Extranet

In Chapter 10 we'll play psychic and do our best to predict the direction of the extranet and its sister networks, the Internet and intranet. However, we wanted to take a few minutes here just to whet your imagination on the potential of this tool. The following are some ways that more advanced extranets can be used, but we don't recommend these applications as starting points (unless the company has the skill sets in-house and can demonstrate a business need that will produce an acceptable ROI).

Personalized Magazines

Many of today's search engines and Webzines allow end users to customize the information that they see. This can also be a good idea for businesses. But new tools are taking that one step further by allowing the search engine to learn from the end user's choices to create customized Web sites automatically.

The concept here is to take search engine agent technology, marry it with neural network technology (or another means to allow a computer to learn), and deliver a search engine that can be tailored to the preferences of a user. This has terrific implications for extranets. Take, for instance, the company that establishes an extranet to provide product, service, and worldwide location data as part of a service contract. By engaging a filtering search engine, every time a service contract customer logs on, that person will be presented with only the data that is most relevant, rather than being forced to surf through many pages to get to the stuff wanted. Companies that are working on personalized, agent-based searching technology include Empirical Media (of Pittsburgh) and a product called Wise Wire (http://login.wisewire.com).

Shareholder Communications

Another area that holds great promise as an extranet application is in the conducting of formal shareholder communications. Currently, many companies post shareholder information on their Web site as a matter of course. This includes quarterly earnings reports, letters to shareholders, and management changes. However, a whole set of shareholder communications seems destined to become a routine extranet application: regulated shareholder actions such as proxy votes. In this instance, shareholders would log onto a secured extranet server and, using a digital signature, cast their votes on shareholder referendums, such as electing officers.

Virtual Reality

Virtual reality and HTTP were seemingly made for each other. Virtual reality allows graphics to be manipulated in real time. Given the bandwidth needed for graphic files, HTTP handles graphics magnificently. Virtual reality is already showing up on home Web pages in the form of animated images via a modification of HTML called VRML. Imagine, however, an architectural firm that keeps images of its work in an extranet database for its clients to peruse. Using virtual reality, clients, at their leisure, can take a walk through their building-to-be and offer feedback at the design phase.

Strategic and Competitive Advantages

Buck Rogers applications aside, an extranet can become as essential a bridge between a company and its most important partners as the telephone has become. The goodwill created this way can be tremendous. Think of this: if a company's top customer knows that he has immediate $7 \times 24 \times 365$ access to resources that have been tailored specifically to meet his needs, what competitor could top that service? Best of all, no one need be awakened in the middle of the night to service this high-priority person.

Equally important are the reverse implications. Should a company fail to make use of Internet technologies, it will certainly loose customers to competitors who do. The intranet software market is expected to reach $10 billion by the year 2000, according to Forrester Research. The commercial world has seen the value of a standardized means of connecting computers at low per-seat costs. Companies that choose to ignore this phenomenon will surely be left behind.

The Inherent Disadvantages of Using an Extranet

Although we've spent the bulk of this chapter praising the potential of extranets and how they are being used today, the adoption of the technology does pose some risks.

Obviously, one of the bigger pitfalls is the potential for data network security loopholes where none existed before. However, other more subtle pitfalls exist: Complex client/server applications have always struggled with performance issues and extranet applications are no different. Where do you place the processing for each element of the program to be executed? How will scaleability be ensured so the server doesn't freeze when hundreds of people access it? How do you make sure that your modem users get the same reasonable performance as your ISDN or leased-line users? Put together any of these issues wrong and you'll have end users (your most important business partners) frustrated with your application and your company. Fortunately for you, we'll tell you how to avoid many common problems in Chapter 3.

While we have glowed about how an extranet can build invaluable goodwill, that goodwill could turn to venom if a company forgets the human factor. Try this experiment. Call the Internal Revenue Service's 800 number for taxpayers between January 1 and April 15. Want to bet you'll get a busy signal? How does it make you feel? That's the feeling you want to safeguard your business partners from having while they are using systems you've created to serve them.

An extranet system can be developed with the idea of offloading certain client or vendor communications completely. However, unless an avenue exists where live human beings can talk to each other, the extranet may wind up being your nemesis, much the way voice messaging got the nickname "mail jail" in the late 1980s when many companies fired the receptionist after installing it. Trapping a person into communicating with a machine is bad news. Machines can't cope with situations that are beyond their specific instructions. We'll talk about ways to avoid this in Chapter 4.

Another potential liability is the "sponge" project. A sponge project is one that absorbs all of the expertise and resources thrown at it and still doesn't achieve its mission. With all the new technologies emerging daily here, each trying to grab the mind share and pocket books of the commercial world, it's easy to get soaked. In Chapter 7 we'll walk you through the elements needed to perform an accurate ROI. From there, you should be able to budget time, money, and people to create an extranet and keep it up. You'll also have an idea of how to gage its effectiveness.

Furthermore, in Chapter 8 we will present you with a summary of some of the many products available to help you build and run your extranet applications along with some tips for how to evaluate them.

Finally, we'll guide you through finding help with an extranet project from experienced pros. We've even included a list of folks who claim to be Internet/intranet experts.

The risks are high with an extranet application, because of its target audience and the newness of many of the tools. But the benefits can be tremendous. Still, putting together an effective, productive extranet is entirely possible today in a way that didn't exist two years ago. The ubiquitous adoption of GUIs for both the client and the server, lowered costs of hardware and software, better performance, cheaper high-bandwidth options, and new security techniques developed for TCP/IP networks all are owed thanks. To find out how Internet technology has transformed itself from an open meadow into Fort Knox, read on.

Summary

By turning an intranet from a method of posting static information into an interactive development platform, those who invest in intranets will see a tremendous return on their investment. One of the primary methods of doing this is by creating an extranet application for a company's strategic partners. Extranet applications run the gamut of being Web content pages that vendors include on a company's intranet to being full-fledged collaborative computing environments. The advantage of using an extranet over a custom-developed client/server application is that most business partners already own, maintain, and manage the equipment necessary to use an extranet application.

However, an extranet does carry with it some stiff politics. Because this is a bridge with a company's most important business resources, such as big customers and major suppliers, such a project had better work well. Otherwise, the reputation of the company could be skewered. Certain technical challenges will have to be faced in order to ensure the application works properly. These challenges include working with immature tools and a lack of standards for security protocols. Other risks are performance problems, administrative headaches, and high costs of overblown, overoptimistic projects.

## chapter two

Security

The Internet was built without a thought about security. Intranets, which are private implementations of the Internet standards, can easily fall prey to that same lack of standards. This might be all right for intranets that limit themselves to electronic bulletin boards that do not span across the corporation's boundaries. In such a case, they easily fall under the domain of the general network security practices. For instance, a user name and password might be required to log on to the network and access the intranet. In that way, the intranet need not have any of its own security built in.

However, when building a business-to-business extranet, security must be intrinsic to the system because a company will no longer be controlling access of all parties concerned. If not, the extranet can become a gateway into the enterprise that lets the bad guys through.

In this chapter, we will outline the most popular options available for securing a Web site, and give you some information on the trade-offs of each. Undoubtedly, options exist or are being created that would secure extranet applications that haven't been mentioned here. Web security is an area that is under massive construction by a multitude of brilliant minds. The methods in this chapter are among the most popular (and most matured) options for securing your Web site.

Security Choices and Trade-offs

Before we can delve into the intricacies of Internet security technologies, we must gain a common understanding of security in general. A couple of truisms exist.

1. The more secure the system, the higher the cost to implement and administer.
2. The more security implemented, the more unavailable data is to end users and the slower the performance of the application.

With both truisms, the relationship between security and its effect is connected. The trick to thoughtful implementation of security measures is to strike a balance between securing the system and making it easy and useful for end users. Complicated login structures and password schemes make a system more secure but also more frustrating for the users it was intended to serve.

Six Goals of Computer Security

1. *Confidentiality:* verifying that information is private and therefore seen and accessed only by intended recipients
2. *Authentication:* identifying an individual or computer to ensure that the party attempting to access a given area is a member of the appropriate group, or is listed on an access list
3. *Nonrepudiation:* ensuring that people cannot deny their electronic actions
4. *Integrity:* verifying that information received is the information that was put there by the originator
5. *Access control:* verifying that the resources are under the exclusive control of the authorized parties and ensuring that the person attempting to access has the authority to do so
6. *Availability:* ensuring that data and server resources are up and running when needed, and that any downtime was not caused by a security-related incident. If goals

one through five have been achieved, availability will be a natural result.

How Security Issues Differ with an Extranet versus a Public Internet Connection or an Intranet

Security for a public Web site and for a private intranet have some major differences from an extranet site. The Web site is, for the most part, concerned only with security goals 2, 4, and 5, that is, authentication, integrity, and access control (to a lesser extent), respectively. The major exception to this, of course, is electronic commerce sites, in which all six goals are important. But even an electronic commerce site differs from an extranet site in that it is aimed at the mass consumer market. Its goal is to increase the number of users of the site, much like a retail shop wants to increase customer traffic and thereby increase the number of sales it makes.

A type of "electronic commerce hybrid" site has also been cropping up lately by the hundreds. These are sites that add minimal protections aimed at security goal 2, authentication. These are "members only" sites that have enacted basic authentication procedures on their Web servers. Examples of these include Silicon Investor (www.techstocks.com) and C/Net (www.cnet.com). However, in most of these cases the reason for authenticating end users is to accumulate general demographic data. As such, the users' true identity isn't really the point and the systems allow anyone who is willing to sign on to take part. For instance, the user may be asked to choose a login ID and password and then fill out a form giving demographic information. However, little or none of this demographic information is checked, except for an e-mail address. This type of basic authentication is easily thwarted by hackers and is not recommended for more serious attempts at authentication. (We will discuss this issue more thoroughly in the section on authentication later in this chapter.) On the flip side, surfers often get frustrated with these sites because they add to the ever-accumulating number of ID's and passwords users must remember.

An extranet differs from the electronic commerce and the advertising demographic models found on the Web in that it absolutely limits traffic from the start to specific individuals and/or sites. These people must be unequivocally identified and the information that is seen by them must be seen by no one else. While many of the security techniques used for electronic commerce Web sites can be applied to an extranet, additional security procedures must be enacted in order for the anonymous nature of the Web to be overcome, which is not desired by many Web users.

An extranet differs from intranet security concerns in that it may rely on the public network (the Internet) to connect its users. This opens up risks (and performance problems) that negate much of why an intranet is a great tool. If, indeed, the application will include access to the company's actual intranet, not simply an extranet application that resides on or near it, security steps must be taken that ensure that it is the *only* part of the network that extranet users can get into. Or an extranet can become its own system—a middlenet, as one end user described it—sitting outside of the core intranet and requiring the implementation of security protocols not used anywhere else in the enterprise. In order to do this, extranet developers need to adopt one or more of the new security protocols developed for bridging the gaps in Internet security, particularly over the Web.

The number-one problem developers face in doing so is that implementing protocols needed to achieve the ultimately secure site when creating a proprietary application requires a significant investment in development time. This is because tools have yet to appear that will allow developers to create a complete security solution. Even tools that claim to be "complete" are really only complete for one particular problem, and not for the whole enterprise. Commonly, such tools are aimed at electronic commerce using credit cards as a payment method.

No one solution provides the means to achieve all six security goals, as well as availability. However, several have been designed to be aware of and support all of the pieces. At the heart of almost all of them is the secret to securing data over a public network, a strange science known as cryptography. So before we dissect some of the protocols themselves, a quick look at this underlying technology is in order.

Some Cryptography Basics

First of all, let us say that cryptography is incredibly complex. It involves math that would make Albert Einstein scratch his head. So we are not launching into an "everything you need to know about cryptography" segment here. But, in order to understand what level of protection you are buying when you choose one protocol over another, a few key points about cryptography should be made clear.

Among the most important notions of cryptography is the method of key exchange. For the most part, two exist.

The simplest is *symmetric cryptography,* sometimes called "secret key" cryptography. Symmetric cryptography means that the same key is used for both encryption and decryption. (See Figure 2.1.) Examples of symmetric cryptography algorithms include DES and RC4. The important problem with symmetric cryptography is the process of key exchange. Here's an analogy: if you use a key to lock documents in a safe with a key, then ship the safe to the intended recipients, how do you get that key to them so they can unlock the safe and retrieve the documents? In the case of cryptography, do you mail a floppy with the key? send it in an e-mail? whisper it over the phone? Do you see the problem?

The answer to this is the public/private key exchange method, also known as *asymmetric cryptography.* RSA is probably the best known commercial example of such a public/private key exchange method because it is heavily marketed by encryption vendor RSA Data Security Inc. of Redwood City, Calif.; however, others exist, such as Diffie-Hellman. In the asymmetric model, two keys are used, each mathematically linked to the other. (See Figure 2.2.)

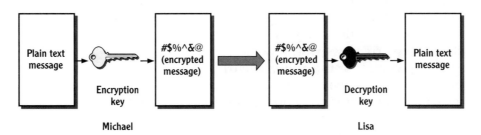

Figure 2.1   Symmetric encryption keeps prying eyes from viewing data, as long as a secure method exists for the key exchange.

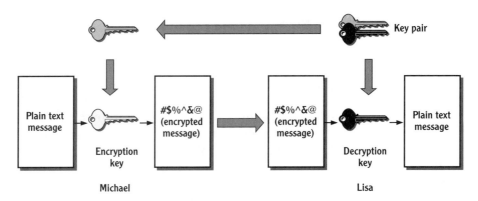

Figure 2.2 Asymmetric encryption uses mathematically linked key pairs: one public, one private.

The public key is used to encrypt data and it can be made openly available (although if it will be used for some ultrasensitive information, some security experts believe it should not be spread about with wild abandon, to avoid the possibilities of impersonation, for example). The private key is kept in the exclusive possession of the person, server, or application that will decrypt the data, and it is the only key that can be used for that purpose.

If, for example, Michael wants to send a message to Lisa, Michael obtains Lisa's public key, which is essentially publicly available. He then encrypts his message using this public key and sends it on its way. Lisa receives the message. Since it has been encrypted with *her* public key, the only way it can be decrypted it to use her private key. Obviously, the biggest requirement is that it must be virtually impossible to figure out the private key from the corresponding public key. Access to the public key must remain absolutely private as well.

The payment for the added security of public/private encryption is reduced speed. Symmetric systems are generally much faster when encoding/decoding. (Of course, hundreds of symmetric and asymmetric systems exist; each has its own speed attributes.) For this reason, many cryptography techniques actually mix symmetric and asymmetric methods. A random algorithm is generated and used to encrypt the data. That *algorithm* is then encrypted with the public key and sent to the recipient who decrypts the algorithm with the private key and can then decrypt the message itself. (See Figure 2.3.)

Where Is Cryptography Used?

Cryptography is a technology that is only part of a security solution. Encryption (and, of course, decryption) alone begins and ends with achieving security goal 1—confidentiality. It does nothing to ensure that the transmission of data wasn't intercepted, or that the originators are who they say they are, and so on. However, it can be part of a much bigger solution, depending on exactly what is being encrypted. For example, if encryption is used for the authentication process, it can make such a process much more secure. Some techniques used for encrypted authentication would be slogin, deslogin and ssh. Encryption is also essential for nonrepudiation techniques, represented by the digital signatures. A *digital signature* binds a document to the owner of a specific key and is intended to be the digital equivalent of paper signatures.

Key Size and Export Trouble

Another area of importance for encryption is key size. Obviously, the longer and more complex the key, the more difficult it is to break, but also the longer it takes to operate the encryption/decryption process.

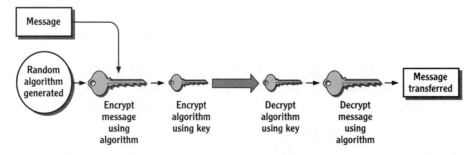

Figure 2.3 Asymmetric schemes offer extremely high levels of confidentiality in part because they use layers of encryption.

Currently, the largest key size that is generally used in most software security products is 1024 bits. Bigger keys exist as do smaller ones. In fact, recommended key sizes grow larger with time, as desktop technologies grow more powerful, allowing "crackers" to discover new ways to crack keys but also allowing users to be able to process longer keys without a performance degradation. Cryptography proponents are quick to point out that hardware improvements actually assist the user more than they do the hacker. Here's the argument: since it is easier to use keys than to crack them, the amount of brute force that must be thrown at these growing keys increases at a greater rate than the amount of processing power required to use larger keys.

But perhaps the biggest issue surrounding key size revolves around the export laws of the United States. The United States restricts the export of encryption software that will be used for confidentiality (although it is possible to export encryption software that will be used for digital signatures, as long as the exporter can prove that it cannot easily be converted for other uses).

Software that uses 40-bit keys are more easily approved for export with 512 bits being the upper limit of allowable export. For that reason, most international editions of software that use encryption for confidentiality use a 40-bit key size.

The rationale behind these restrictions goes something like this: If the government allowed encryption technology to be sent out into the world it could fall into the hands of terrorists or other *really bad people.* They could use it to encrypt messages about bombs and crop circles. The defense department would not be able to break into the messages to spy on the bad people. This is unacceptable. So, the U.S. government won't allow the more powerful encryption technology out of the country.

Of course, the rationale breaks down pretty quickly with even a tiny bit of scrutiny. No law exists that makes bad people buy encryption software products from U.S. companies. (And even if there were one, bad people don't follow laws.) Also, 1024-bit encryption technology is readily available from a number of companies based outside the United States. This also means that anyone developing an extranet application to be used outside of the

United States must succumb to 40- to 512-bit keys or purchase software from a non-U.S. source.

The government isn't completely blind to the flaws in its logic. Debate and congressional testimony over the value of the restriction has been going on for a half a dozen years. A lot of potential remedies are currently being chewed on and some action has been taken. For instance, discussion is now taking place on lifting all key-size restrictions, provided that manufacturers provide a viable means of key recovery for legitimate government access. Many encryption manufacturers already do have such processes developed and ready for use right now. The likelihood of rules being relaxed to that extent anytime soon isn't very high. However, as of January 1, 1997, new encryption rules do allow 56-bit keys to be exported if the exporting company provides a method of key recovery. Still, for companies that are unwilling or unable to adjust their technology to comply with the key recovery requirement, the limit for export will remain 40-bit algorithms. A slow trickle of companies have begun to receive permission to export the 56-bit algorithm including Digital Equipment Corporation, Trusted Information Systems, and Cylink Corporation Open Markets, known for its electronic commerce products, even received permission to export software that uses a 128-bit key.

One of the reasons for the government's change of heart is that encryption export has now come under the dominion of the United States Commerce Department, rather than the State Department. Also, at least three bills are pending in congress that would relax the key-size restrictions and other issues surrounding the export of encryption. Much of the Internet community, and the U.S. technology community in general, supports the lifting of key restrictions.

Meanwhile, a lot of debate rages as to the exact security risk of a 40-bit key. It is unquestionably less secure than a 1024-bit key, but does using a 40-bit key equal not using encryption at all? Some security experts claim that a hacker, armed with a $400 computer chip, can break a 40-bit key in a matter of hours, whereas cracking a 1024-bit key requires a supercomputer cranking on the problem for days. However, even so, significant effort is required to crack a

40-bit key. Unless a company has reason to believe that it would be a target for such persistence, a 40-bit key would probably be a viable compromise, particularly for companies who will be dealing with a lot of international traffic.

Reasons a company might be a target include hackers believing the payoff of such an effort would be tremendous (such as revealing bank account numbers), or if the company suspected it could be the victim of corporate espionage. For the average encrypted message trying to thwart the casual hacker, 40 bits would suffice. Still, companies that choose to use a 40-bit key should be aware that it is less safe than the typical confidentiality methods prevalently used within the United States. It is our opinion that companies should plan for the future and obtain a higher-bit-length key. Key lengths get longer over time because the power of the average desktop increases. This means that keys can be broken more easily by a Sunday hacker, and longer keys can be processed more quickly by an average user.

Still, it's important to point out that no encryption method is infallible anyway. It's simply a matter of degrees. Perhaps Edgar Allen Poe summed up the situation best when he wrote: "Human ingenuity cannot concoct a cipher which human ingenuity cannot resolve."

Speaking the Same Algorithm

Another area of concern when implementing cryptography is *interoperability*. Although two systems may both use, say, RSA, as their cryptographic system, implementation of it could vary from one product and/or platform to another. So, just because two business partners already use the same cryptographic system doesn't make it an automatic choice for an extranet implementation.

Work is being done to create a *platform-independent cryptography API* (PICA). In fact, an association that calls itself PICA formed in October 1996 to do just that. Its inaugural members were Apple, IBM, JavaSoft, Motorola, Netscape, Nortel, Novell, RSA, and Silicon Graphics. Its manifesto is to enable developers to add security features such as Secure Sockets Layer (SSL), DES, and "smartcards" to electronic commerce, banking, EDI, and other applications, regardless of the platform on which those applications reside. PICA also intends to work closely with standards bodies such as the Internet Engineering Task Force (IETF), which oversees the development of Internet standards, and the W3C, which is the working group whose specific focus is the Web. Of course, Microsoft is also championing its own cryptography API solution, the CryptoAPI.

Until that hallowed day when the mass adoption of a defacto API solves compatibility problems, we recommend that any extranet security systems stand on their own. Using a cryptographic system one has in-house is an excellent way to leverage an investment in training, but the cryptography should be implemented and tested specifically for the extranet application, not simply replicated from some other use.

Methods to Achieve Security Goal 1—Confidentiality

Obviously, confidentiality and authentication go hand in hand. You can't make sure that information stays only between intended parties if you don't know for certain who you are talking to. So most of the protocols we're about to discuss as means to achieve confidentiality also provide the means to authenticate to some extent. However, each actually combines different technologies to achieve these related, but separate, goals. It is also possible to augment these protocols with more ways to authenticate, so we will be taking a closer look at authentication as well.

The Secure Sockets Layer

Now that we've covered some cryptography basics, it's time to look at how cryptography is being applied to Web-specific security solutions to achieve confidentiality. This brings us directly to the Security Sockets Layer (SSL), a security protocol that, by most accounts, currently has the most momentum behind it for Web-based projects. SSL was developed by Netscape Communications Corporation (which explains its popularity) and is aimed at providing a private and reliable connection between two communicating applications. SSL is the protocol that is responsible for the key in the lower left-hand corner of Netscape's Navigator browser. If the key is broken, SSL has not been engaged. If the key is whole, however, an SSL session is occurring.

Essentially, the job of SSL is to be the basis of encrypted communications between a browser and an Internet server. Some people describe it as a security extension of TCP/IP, the protocol that handles communications for all Internet applications (e-mail, Usenet, the Web). However, it is actually a protocol that rides on top of a transport protocol, say the folks at Netscape. This means that it can work with a variety of transport protocols and isn't limited to TCP/IP.

TCP/IP uses a programming abstraction called a *socket* to implement the transport of packets between two parties on the Internet in a reliable manner. SSL is a security-enhanced abstraction of the socket. So, with SSL, it is the link between the browser and the server that is authenticated and secured, not the documents themselves. This accounts for one of the biggest assets of using SSL over other technologies aimed at securing Web sites: Its application-protocol-independent nature means it isn't limited to HTTP. SSL sessions can be used to create secure transactions over FTP, telnet, or other Internet protocols. Of course, this is easier said than done.

For example, in theory SSL provides security at the session level of the OSI model as shown in Figure 2.4, where a session consists of a series of connections. In theory, this means that it should not interact with the application level at all, just the presentation layer and the transport layer. However, in practice this simply isn't the case. Because SSL is, in effect, tied to the browser, the trouble comes in when people try to figure out how this level interacts with the application level. Many people mistakenly call it an application-level protocol.

The way people are dealing with the confusion currently is to assign different ports to different protocols. Ports indicate where the server is listening. If it is set to listen for a service at a specific port number, it will listen for requests for that service on only the specified port and no other. For example, with SSL one protocol is assigned to port x and its secure version is on port y. For HTTP, the unsecured port is by default 80 while the secured port is typically 443.

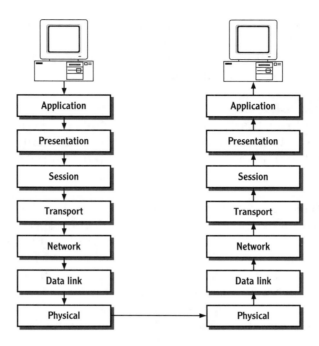

Figure 2.4   The OSI model.

TIP   *Some consultants that are frequent participants on Netscape's SSL newsgroup have suggested the following guide for assigning port numbers:*

https	*443/tcp*	*http protocol over SSL*
ssmtp	*465/tcp*	*smtp protocol over SSL*
snntp	*563/tcp*	*nntp protocol over SSL*
sldap	*636/tcp*	*Idap protocol over SSL*
spop3	*995/tcp*	*pop3 protocol over SSL*
ftps	*990/tcp*	*ftp protocol over SSL*

Still, some experts point out that the assigning of ports is functional but awkward. Ultimately, it would be better for the protocol being used to be extended so that it can trigger an SSL connection. But this would require everyone to agree on how such a situation would work. Because the IETF moves at the speed of worldwide democracy (slow!), such agreement will be a long time coming (if ever). Even then, it would also require implementation on all operating systems across the board.

How the Protocol Works

The protocol is actually composed of two layers, according to the March 1996 Internet draft version of the SSL Protocol version 3.0, written by the developers of the protocol (employees of Netscape).

NOTE   *An Internet draft is a work in progress. For that reason and others, we are not documenting specific technical details of the draft current as of the writing of this book (draft-freier-ssl-version3-01.txt). Still, because SSL itself is in its third version, and particularly now that it is a technology currently under review as a possible IETF standard, recent Internet drafts offer some of the best explanations of the technology available. To learn the current status of any Internet-Draft, please check the 1id-abstracts.txt listing contained in the Internet Drafts Shadow Directories on ds.internic.net (U.S. East Coast), nic.nordu.net (Europe), ftp.isi.edu (U.S. West Coast), or munnari.oz.au (Pacific Rim). Or look for the draft listed in the Internic's FTP directory /internet-drafts/ at ds.internic.net (ftp://ds.internic.net/internet-drafts/ as a browser URL).*

The lowest layer performs on top of a transport protocol such as TCP. (See Figure 2.5.) This is the SSL Record Protocol, whose primary goal is to encapsulate various higher-level protocols. For example, it will encapsulate the other SSL layer, the SSL Handshake Protocol. The SSL Handshake Protocol allows the server and client to authenticate each other and to negotiate which encryption algorithm and cryptographic key exchange method to use. This negotiation is done before the application protocol transmits or receives its first byte of data. Because of the encapsulation process, sniffers become ineffective tools against a SSL connection. *Sniffers* are devices that capture data as it traverses the network. Furthermore, even if a sniffer manages to capture the

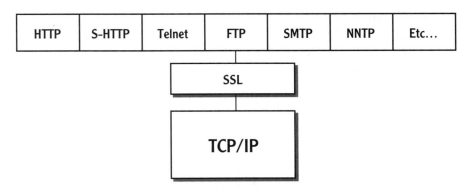

| HTTP | S-HTTP | Telnet | FTP | SMTP | NNTP | Etc... |

SSL

TCP/IP

Figure 2.5   SSL is a session-level protocol on the OSI Model. Therefore, it sits between TCP/IP and HTTP or other higher-level protocols.

transmitted key, that key is the browser's or server's public key and cannot be used to decrypt the succeeding packet stream.

Its authors say the SSL protocol has three basic properties:

◆ It establishes a private connection. After an initial handshake in which the secret encryption key is negotiated, encryption in enacted. Symmetric cryptography is used to secure the data itself (such as DES or RC4—two different types of symmetric cryptography). However, public/private key encryption is used to secure the transmission of the secret key. These keys are contained within the browser and server and the same key pair is usually used for every session a particular browser or server is engaged in. The key pair is generated by the browser when the software is loaded. However, it is possible to generate keys on-the-fly, which is an extremely secure way of dealing with key management, but also slows down the initial handshake process quite a bit.

◆ It allows the identity of both sides to be authenticated with digital signatures using asymmetric cryptography (such as RSA or the Digital Signature Standard, a NIST standard for digital signatures).

◆ It creates a reliable connection. Message transport includes a message integrity check (using a keyed *mes-*

sage authentication code [MAC] with secure hash functions, such as SHA, MD5 used for MAC computations). A MAC is a checksum derived by application of a particular authentication scheme, together with a secret key and applied to the message, and is used to ensure data has not been tampered with. A *hash* is a computation that takes variable-length input and returns fixed-length output. It is frequently used in cryptography.

The current version of SSL is 3.0. According to the authors, SSL 3.0 is a layered protocol. At each layer, messages may include fields for length, description, and content. SSL takes messages to be transmitted, fragments the data into manageable blocks, optionally compresses the data (which can help reduce the performance overhead associated with encryption), applies a MAC, encrypts, and transmits the result. Received data is decrypted, verified, decompressed, and reassembled, then delivered to higher-level clients.

Also, like so many of the technologies that turn the Web into something more than a place to read static multimedia documents, an SSL session is *stateful*. This means that it can track a series of events. A stateful session is unlike a typical HTTP connection, which views each event as separate, with no cause/effect (although the W3 consortium is currently reviewing ways to make the Web more inherently stateful).

An SSL session may include multiple secure connections. Or the two parties may have multiple simultaneous sessions. So, after a successful handshake and authentication, the user can access multiple secured pages, programs, or protocols. For example, with our shopping basket program featured in Chapter 6, if it was a used with an SSL connection and a customer was in the middle of an order but wanted to surf back to view other information at the site, the user could simply launch another browser and initiate another secure connection—without having to back out of the order page. Similarly, a user could be browsing with a secure connection to one site and launch another browser for a secure connection to another site. For example, that user could compare a bank statement from an electronic banking application with a mutual fund statement from an investment brokerage application.

S-HTTP

The major competition to SSL was supposed to be Secure HTTP (S-HTTP), which was developed by Enterprise Integration Technologies (http://www.eit.com), an Internet technologies developer and consultant. This specification, while still being promoted as a potential IETF standard, has by most accounts fallen flat on its face, although life still breaths in it and it could yet emerge as an important part of Internet security.

The problem has little to do with merit and much to do with popularity. Essentially, S-HTTP, while embedded in a few Web servers, has yet to become an official part of any major Web client. Although both Netscape and Microsoft have created implementations of it, they have still thrown their weight behind it. Between the two of them, they account for the browser market almost in its entirety.

NOTE *Reference implementations of Secure HTTP in the form of Secure NCSA Mosaic and Secure NCSA httpd are available from EIT and currently deployed to the CommerceNet consortium. Also, Terisa Systems, a developer of browser and Web server security toolkits, has developed and is shipping in beta a plug-in for Netscape Navigator that makes it S-HTTP capable, called "SecureWeb Documents." However, at the time this book is being written, it is too early to tell if this solution will garner much popularity.*

Still, because the specification is still on the dockets, and because a lot of discussion exists on how SHTTP and SSL may eventually merge or routinely be used together, we'll spend a little bit of ink on the spec in this chapter.

We should also note that it is entirely possible for extranet developers to build their own custom browser that supports S-HTTP. We generally advise against custom browsers because they give up much of the ROI advantages of using browsers already owned by business partners. Still, there are some scenarios where this makes sense. For instance, one of the security axioms often quoted by computer security experts is: "The more popular the technology, the more security loopholes are discovered in it. Then again, the more popular the technology, the more security loopholes are known." This goes hand in hand with the axiom: "Know thine enemy." The more hackers pound on a security technology, the more ways they will discover to get around it. However, as those ways are discovered and fixed, the technology eventually becomes more and more airtight—until the next major advance happens on one side or the other.

But, lesser-known technologies don't have the same opportunity to have their weaknesses exposed. So it's harder for hackers to gain knowledge about them. It's also less likely that they will spend their efforts trying. If 500 banks use technology A and one bank uses technology B, a hacker will garner a much bigger prize by learning about the holes in technology A. However, with a lesser-used technology, weaknesses could be sitting in the technology unexposed, all the while the users think they are protected. (This points back to the tightly woven, see-saw relationships of the security truisms stated at the beginning of this chapter.)

Therefore, it may be more secure to create an S-HTTP browser to use with an off-the-shelf S-HTTP server, provided the creator is a security expert and can make sure that S-HTTP is implemented correctly.

A Little Background

That said, we're going to delve off-track again, this time into the genealogy of S-HTTP and its major benefactors. The story illustrates one of the most astounding elements of the commercial side of the Internet—everyone's a relative.

EIT was founded in 1990, but was acquired five years later by VeriFone, Inc., one of the leaders in point-of-sale credit card authorization terminals. That's a natural fit, since S-HTTP's main thrust is to create an electronic commerce market in which credit card authorization would be a big deal. So, in addition to developing S-HTTP, EIT helped in the creation of CommerceNet, a large-scale market trial of Internet electronic commerce with members from banking, computer consulting, and other industry groups.

In addition, the company was a principal investor in Terisa Systems, a top vendor of toolkits for building secure Web servers and clients via S-HTTP and SSL. Terisa now lays claims to both Allan Schiffman, as Terisa's chief technical officer, and Eric Rescorla, as Teriesa's principal engineer. These two designed the Secure HTTP protocol when they were at EIT. Here's the interesting part. What other big names are investors in Terisa? America Online, CompuServe, IBM, RSA, and of course, Netscape Communications.

So, even though S-HTTP and SSL are, for all practical purposes, competing technologies, the situation is hardly Coke versus Pepsi (or even IBM versus Microsoft) because critical parties have investments in both.

The Spec Itself (Compared to SSL)

S-HTTP differs pretty dramatically from SSL in its approach. Its goal is to provide transaction security at the document level, rather than securing the connection as SSL does. It does this by allowing each document to be marked "private" (meaning it can be encrypted by the sender and, separately, also signed via a digital signature). For this reason, an S-HTTP operation is referred to as a "message" while an SSL operation is referred to as a "session" (borrowing terms that originated from each spec's authors). It can also be categorized as an application-level protocol on the OSI model.

Like SSL, S-HTTP has been submitted to the IETF to be considered as an Internet standard. Even a cursory examination of the Internet draft (draft-ietf-wts-shttp-03.txt) reveals why the specification is described as a substitution of HTTP. However, S-HTTP is in actuality a superset of the World Wide Web protocol and, its creators say, is intended to coexist with HTTP, rather than replace it. S-HTTP-aware clients can surf non-S-HTTP servers and S-HTTP servers can communicate fully with nonaware clients (although clients that don't support S-HTTP obviously could not partake of its security features).

However, unlike SSL, S-HTTP is application specific to HTTP. The advantage of having any application-level service, but particularly security, is that the service can be tailored to the specific application it will be used with. It can be so tailored because the service uses the same data unit as the application. This is the classic "end-to-end" argument in systems design.

In the case of HTTP, S-HTTP means that security services which are appropriate only to HTTP can be supported. For instance, S-HTTP easily accommodates different security properties for requests than for responses, whereas this is fairly difficult with SSLv3, some say (just as it would be with any transport layer security measure). Zeroing in on the application data model is also what accounts for S-HTTP's ability to digitally sign the messages themselves.

The disadvantage of S-HTTP is that it cannot be used over other Internet protocols. However, in theory, one could actually use SSL with S-HTTP. Many Internet security experts believe that this is likely to be the case in the future (or at least that the HTTP security standard finally adopted by the IETF will incorporate many of the good things about S-HTTP.)

With both protocols in use, a connection can be authenticated (via SSL) and the documents themselves can be signed (via S-HTTP). However, the merging of the two standards remains rhetorical until browser technology is developed that would be able to deal with both concurrently.

Microsoft's PCT

Perhaps a more important technology in the Web security wars is Microsoft's Private Communication Technology (PCT) specification, simply because any Microsoft baby has to be taken seriously. PCT, developed in conjunction with Visa International, is basically SSL that has been beefed up in a few ways. It is currently supported in Microsoft's products and, Microsoft claims, PCT is backward compatible with SSL. So PCT servers can talk to SSL clients, albeit without the PCT gizmos.

PCT authenticates the server and may optionally also authenticate the client. Its authors say it basically improves SSL's handshake phase, making it shorter while still allowing negotiation for more cryptographic details. For instance, negotiation for the choice of cryptographic algorithms and formats to use in a session has been extended with PCT. It covers a hash function type and a key exchange type in addition to a cipher type and server certificate type.

It also uses separate keys for authentication and encryption. (SSL uses the same key for both.) By doing this PCT allows applications to use authentication that is significantly stronger than the 40-bit key limit for encryption allowed by the U.S. government for export. Remember, longer keys can be used for authentication, as long as they aren't easily converted to keys to be used for privacy.

Also, with PCT, the client's response rests on the negotiated algorithm. This provides an added layer of security. If, on one session, the two negotiated a key that a hacker was able to sniff and crack, that key would not lead to the ability to decrypt other sessions.

PCT was originally developed to combat weaknesses in SSL 2.0, many of which have been corrected in SSL 3.0 (which is still being worked on by its developers and the IETF Transport Layer Security [TLS] Working Group and should emerge as an TLS standard). So, PCT may be less needed today then when it was announced to the world in 1995 in <draft-benaloh-pct-00.txt>. Ultimately, the TLS standard will probably include all of what Microsoft has fixed. However, according to Microsoft, PCT still exists today and is supported by Cylink Corporation, FTP Software, Inc., Internet Shopping Network, NetManage, Inc., Open-Market, Inc., Spyglass, Inc., and Starwave Corporation.

PCT is also one of the technologies delivered as part of the Microsoft Internet Security Framework (MISF). MISF is Microsoft's vision for performing data security goals, particularly exchanging information securely across public networks, controlling access from the public networks to the corporate network, and engaging in electronic commerce.

SET

Finally, we also advise you to keep your eye out for the Secure Electronic Transactions (SET) specification. SET details how bank card transactions on the Internet and other open networks will be secured using encryption technology. SET was developed by MasterCard International, Visa International, GTE, IBM, Microsoft,

Netscape Communications Corporation, SAIC, Terisa Systems, and VeriSign.

Like SSL and S-HTTP, SET was developed primarily to spur the use of credit card transactions over the Internet. In fact, the specification is almost entirely concerned with the three-party transaction required for credit card purchases. Those parties are the customers, the merchant, and the authorization parties (such as the issuing bank). It also details how organizations that assist in the process can be included, such as the payment card network—the people who handle the communications of an authorization, not the authorization itself (i.e., VeriFone).

In the summer of 1996, the SET folks swore that the specification would deal with bank card transactions and nothing else. Still, many security experts believe that it is capable of handling other types of communications and could be expanded if its progenitors saw a need.

When one examines the Internet draft and other SET documents, it doesn't take a huge leap of faith to see how easily this could be done. For instance, the goal of SET is to provide a means of confidential transmission, authenticate the parties involved, ensure the integrity of payment instructions for goods and services, and authenticate the identity of the cardholder and the merchant to each other. These are pretty much the same goals that SSL and S-HTTP have.

Like SSL, SET will use both symmetric and asymmetric cryptography—the first to encrypt the message, the latter to encrypt the symmetric key. (By the way, this method of encrypting an algorithm is often referred to as a *digital envelope.*) SET is also an application-level protocol.

However, a SET session is initiated at the point that an order is ready to be processed for payment. If the seller and buyer wish the order itself to be encrypted, another method of secure transaction must occur. SET relies heavily on digital signatures and certificates (explained later in this chapter) to allow security goal 3, nonrepudiation, to occur.

The application of a digital signature has a bit of a twist in it as well. Since the goal of SET is to provide protection for *all* parties in a credit card transaction, it is a three-way deal. The merchant, the buyer, and the issuing bank (which authorizes transactions) are involved in a SET session. Each one, then, must be authenticated and their electronic actions stamped so that nonrepudiation can occur.

As we were researching this book, end user products that support SET had yet to appear. However, given the heavyweight backing of its biggest proponents, both VISA and MasterCard, we feel confident that SET will become a popular method of dealing with electronic commerce. For extranet applications that mimic electronic commerce transactions and require credit card authorization, SET could be a valuable tool.

Recommendations

Of all the security protocols available for the Internet, SSL is quickly gaining the most support from the vendor community. Consequently, more users have adopted SSL as well. While the merits of this protocol can be debated, such discussions quickly boil down to the betamax vs. VHS debate—rather pointless now that VHS has clearly won the market. Therefore, for the most part, we believe that SSL is the right choice for extranet applications that require session-level security.

Still, the above security solutions aren't right for every extranet. For instance, they would be awkward for certain kinds of collaborative extranets—where the business partner is attempting to run existing applications over an extranet with some kind of client other than a browser. The same problems exist if numerous clients at a business partner's location will be attempting to gain access to a business's extranet, but from a single client, because of the issues surrounding authentication, which we will discuss next.

Virtual Private Networks

A better technology for these situations (and many others) is the *virtual private network* (VPN). This is a term that has been truly abused over the last two years. So, for the sake of clarity, we are defining a VPN as *a technology that simulates a private network.* A private network is defined as an infrastructure that is entirely owned or at least controlled (via leased lines) by the organization.

Tunneling

A VPN, then, simulates a private network at the link level of the OSI model (rather than at the application or session levels). Unlike the protocols we've talked about so far in this chapter, a VPN is a connection that occurs as part of the network infrastructure level. It is intended to secure all traffic as it traverses a public area, regardless of the application in which that traffic was generated. Of course, depending on the tools used to create it, a lot of refinements can be placed on a VPN so that it is confined to specific applications, IP nodes, and so on. But, simply speaking, this is not the case.

Here's how it works. At least two VPN devices are used. One uses the other's public key to encrypt packets as they cross. The other uses the private key to decrypt. In between is a public network. (See Figure 2.6.) Obviously, one of the primary public networks that can be used with a VPN is the Internet. (However, other networks can also be considered "public" such as a com-

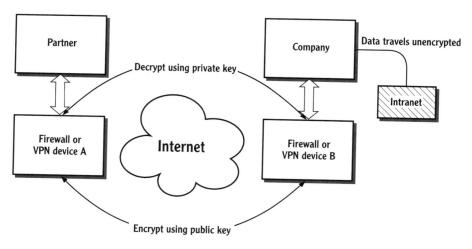

Figure 2.6 In most implementations of virtual private networks, the encryption/decryption process occurs at the network perimeter through a firewall or through a VPN-specific hardware device. All traffic between two (or more) sites is encrypted but travels in the clear once it passes through the perimeter.

pany's own intranet, if the data is not for general employee knowledge.) By using encryption at either end of the connection, a company is, in effect, creating a private "tunnel" on the Internet. This technique, not surprisingly, is called *tunneling.*

Tunneling can be a function of three types of products: the firewall, if it supports VPN, and most of the leading ones do; the router, if it supports encryption, and most of the leading vendors of IP tunnels do, such as Cisco (www.cisco.com) and Ascend Communications Inc. (www.ascend.com); or independent tunneling devices. To date, only a few independent VPN devices exist. Microsoft has one for NT Server, Digital Equipment Corporation offers one as an extension of the firewall, and Digital Signal Networks Technology offers one as a black box router add-on. (See Chapter 8 for more details on these products and companies.)

Tunnels can occur in two ways. The first is the *branch office* model, in which a pair of routers, firewalls, or tunnel devices encrypt all traffic as it passes between them. End users behind these devices remain oblivious to the fact and need not "activate" anything. A performance bottleneck can occur at the device performing the encryption and decryption, but that depends on the device. For example, the Eagle Firewall from Raptor Systems, Inc. has been known to saturate a T1 even while performing tunneling services.

The second means is a *PC-to-remote office* model. The tunnel occurs from a specific client to the firewall, router, or other device. The PC must have a VPN device driver, akin to a modem driver. The connection can then occur over any ISP, as the remote PC will encrypt the data and the remote office firewall, router, or independent device will decrypt. This method was created for the mobile user who needs to access intranet applications.

Network Translation

An adjunct to tunneling is also available. It is often referred to as *network translation.* Devices such as Cisco's IPxchange, and Private Internet Exchange from Network Translation, Inc. (of Palo Alto, CA), use a single IP address and can map or translate that into other IP addresses. This allows virtual networks to be created in which devices use IP addresses that are *not* registered with

InterNIC, the agency that dispenses IP addresses for use with the Internet. The security advantage to address translation is that it allows an entire network to hide behind the firewall's IP address. Also, companies that had been using TCP/IP as a network architecture long before the Internet became such a big deal often used unregistered addresses. Translation allows them to preserve these addresses and still have Internet connectivity.

Advantages of Tunneling

The biggest advantage of tunneling is that it is not a function of the application. So, if you had need to treat a business partner like a full-fledged remote office, tunneling would allow them to get to all of the network resources at headquarters securely. Tunnels at the firewall or specialized tunneling devices can also be configured to forward traffic to a specific server or director in a server. So a tunnel isn't necessarily an unrestricted key to the network.

Tunneling also doesn't require an on-the-fly key exchange. Both parties will already have one another's public keys, so there is no lengthy negotiation process at either end. Furthermore, tunneling will become an integral part of the next generation of IP. (See the sidebar, "Internet Protocols and Addresses.") In fact, because tunneling operates at a different level of the OSI model, it could be used with SSL and/or S-HTTP as well, for the ultraparanoid who will spare no expense for security. (Discussions are already taking place on standards or other methods that would integrate the three.)

Drawbacks of Tunneling

The biggest drawback of tunneling is that standards are sorely lacking. Despite whatever claims a vendor might make, the same two devices need to be on either end in order for tunneling to be effective with today's slew of products. (See Figure 2.7.) This goes against the grain of a system that has been established entirely on democratically agreed-upon standards.

Of course, standards are being created, but it may take a while before anything concrete is here for an average extranet developer to use. This is because the standards bodies are focusing on adding security to IP version 6, rather than IP version 4, which is what the Internet currently operates on.

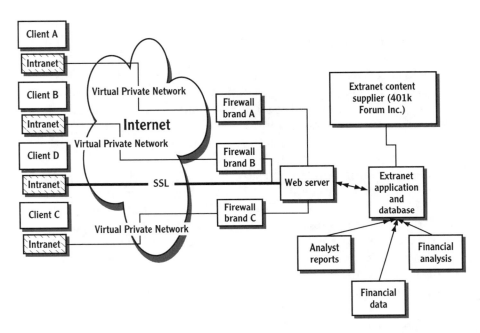

Figure 2.7 One disadvantage of VPNs is that they are typically proprietary, requiring the same product on both sides of the pipe. For companies such as 401k Forum Inc., an investment services company that provides extranet content over the Internet, this means being willing to implement several brands of firewalls to support their customers' implementations. It also means using SSL for clients that do not have VPN capabilities.

Another major drawback with tunneling is that, in its most basic form, it doesn't provide the level of granularity that security managers would like, especially when it comes to extranet applications. In theory, a tunnel provides a no-holds-barred connection. So a business partner would be entitled to roam the network at will just like a branch office or a local node.

Most firewall vendors that support the technology recognize that such a situation is unacceptable. The answer to this is to add some intelligence to the tunnel at the firewall level, if that is how the VPN was created. By allowing tunneling to be rule based, rather than simply on/off for a specific IP address, it can be con-

Internet Protocols and Addresses

The Internet currently operates on IP version 4. But because of the immense popularity of the Internet, and because it is being used in ways that it was never designed to be used (such as electronic commerce), we've outgrown the current system. Hence, the next generation of IP is being developed, IP version 6.

The Transmission Control Protocol (TCP) is responsible for turning data into packets and reassembling them at the destination, while the Internet Protocol (IP) handles getting packets to their proper destination. IP version 6 was mainly proposed to solve what's commonly referred to as an "address shortage" in IP version 4. In truth, the Internet is *not* out of addresses. But the most popular *class* of address is practically gone and the management of smaller classes which provide the same overall number of IP addresses can be a lot harder.

As a backgrounder, the IPv4 address scheme is a 32-bit hexadecimal notation broken into four octets (four bytes). The total address universe is, therefore, about 4 million. Class is determined by dividing the octets into fixed and assignable parts with the class of the address determined by its first part. With a Class A address, the first octet is fixed and indicates the network while the remaining three octets are assignable and therefore available for hosts. Class A blocks therefore allow 16 million addresses to be used for devices, such as routers or PCs.

With a Class B address, the first two octets are the fixed network address and the remaining two are left for hosts. This creates some 64,000 host addresses. With Class C, the first three octets are fixed and the final one is available for hosts, which gives birth to 245 assignable addresses. The IPv4 scheme also creates few Class A addresses and many Class Cs (See Table 2.1).

(Continued)

TABLE 2.1   Internet Addresses Are Available in Three Classes

Class	First Octet	Fixed versus Host Octets	Uses
A	1–126*	N.H.H.H.**	Only for the largest networks. Virtually impossible to get today.
B	128–191	N.N.H.H.	Reserved for large networks that can demonstrate a significant need. Difficult to get today.
C	192	N.N.N.H	More easily available. Often assigned in sets for those that would have qualified for Class A or B addresses previously.

 * Several numbers indicate special uses and are not used for regular IP addresses. These include 0 and 127.
 ** N = Network designation. H = Available to be assigned to hosts.

Because Class B provides enough addresses for all but the most massive networks, they remain the most sought after. However, as of the winter of 1995 roughly 65 percent of Class B addresses have already been assigned, leaving fewer than 7,000. In contrast, only 25 to 30 percent of the available Class C addresses are allocated, according to the Internet Network Information Center (InterNIC), the agency responsible for assigning address Classes. Consequently, InterNIC is holding Class B addresses pretty close to hand. In fact, they are even discouraging end users from trying to obtain their own Class C addresses, unless good reason can be shown why the company should *not* go through an ISP to "rent" addresses. As for Class B, only those organizations that can show an absolute need for a contiguous block of several thousand addresses has a hope of being issued one. Even for companies that can show this need, it's much more likely that InterNIC will assign multiple Class C addresses, rather than a Class B. This is because InterNIC no longer allows ease of address manage-

(Continued)

ment to be a factor when assigning the class. The main criteria in determining need of a Class B address is how many IP-addressable devices a company has, and whether its routers can deal with a multiple Class C environment.

So, the long-term solution is a whole new addressing scheme, which is in the works as IP version 6. (IP version 5 is an experimental protocol that never caught on.) Ipv6 provides a 128-bit address structure, versus today's 32-bit addresses in IPv4.

In addition to beefing up the hexadecimal notation, a slew of other enhancements are being proposed to the new IP. Among them are security features that allow the use of encryption. Encryption at the IP level is practically the definition of tunneling.

Some optimistic vendors have already begun to support IPv6's security features (known as IPsec), even though huge parts of it have yet to be decided (such as the key exchange method). Most rosy-vision experts expect that IPv6 Security, as it's called, will not be robust enough to become a true specification until 1998. Even if that's true, end users must be reminded that it's going to take a long time for the Internet

(Continued)

figured down to the detail of which users should activate the tunnel and for what IP addresses. However, because a VPN is intended to be a tunnel, not a thread, such security methods need to be thoroughly tested for holes before they are used. Well, so does the security system for SSL. But in the case of SSL, the company is risking the security of specific transactions. In the case of tunneling, the network is what's at risk.

A final drawback is that at some point, traffic could be traveling in the clear. In a typical installation, that point would be on the internal networks, if encryption/decryption occurs at the perimeter. If this is highly sensitive data that could be susceptible to insider attack, that may not be an acceptable option. Some devices to migrate from IPv4 to IPv6. Some say this transition will take as long as 10 years.

While an entire migration of the Internet won't be necessary just to use a tunnel (only two devices support IPv6), until it is relatively ubiquitous ad-hoc creation of tunnels will not be possible.

That hasn't stopped firewall vendors from building products to IPsec. In fact, a specification designed to facilitate interoperability between and among firewall and TCP/IP stack vendors has been created and interoperability tests performed. (That spec, known as S/WAN, is being championed by RSA Data Security, Inc.)

As of March 1996, eleven of RSA's partner companies and government organizations had been participating in the S/WAN interoperability tests, including Checkpoint, FTP Software, Gemini, IBM, Morning Star Technologies, NIST/NSA, Raptor, Secure Computing, TimeStep Corporation, Trusted Information Systems, and SOS. Updated results from ongoing interoperability tests which cover multiple aspects of IPsec and S/WAN are posted on RSA's Web site (http://www.rsa.com/rsa/SWAN/swan_test.htm).

such as NT's *Point-to-Point Tunneling* (PPT) can support, like its name says, point-to-point encryption and decryption—where the decryption happens at the server, rather than at the network perimeter (where the firewall resides). It is also possible to set up multiple firewalls and multiple tunnels within the organization. Encryption can happen at the source, the traffic can then continue through the perimeter firewall encrypted (if it is set up to allow it), and onto an *internal* firewall where it is decrypted.

Still, when it comes to collaboration, particularly between parties who can't be bothered with a lot of end-user or application-level security procedures, a tunnel can be a great solution. It also works well for extranet content providers who want to log in and make a dump of information to a server or a directory, or for numerous other instances when link-level security makes more sense.

Methods to Achieve Security Goals 2 and 3— Authentication and Nonrepudiation

Authentication is at least as important as confidentiality for any extranet application (and maybe more crucial). Authentication can be done at the user-, client-, and/or server-level. Some protocols innately perform authentication of one or all of the above. Others need additional technologies for authenticating all three.

Once authentication is absolute, it achieves security goal 3, nonrepudiation. Nonrepudiation in the electronic world differs from the legal concept of the term. In the electronic world, nonrepudiation is authentication taken to the *n*th degree. It means that an electronic action can be proven to have occurred by a specific individual. So, if an individual logs in to an order-entry extranet and makes an order, the security protections in place for nonrepudiation would mean that this person could not claim that someone else performed that act.

In the legal sense, however, nonrepudiation is intended to protect the act itself, not authenticate the source. This means that if someone enters into an agreement, that person does not have the right to back out. The issue that it was the actual party who entered into the agreement is beside the point (it was). What's at stake is whether that person could repudiate the deal.

Although authentication and nonrepudiation are siblings in the electronic world, different technologies actually provide one or the other. Authentication can occur in a number of ways such as password and login names at the server level, time-stamped passwords, and certificates. Nonrepudiation is a function of digital signatures.

Basic Authentication

Perhaps the easiest way to provide some level of authorization is by switching on the basic authentication features of the Web server. All major Web servers are capable of supporting basic authentication, which is essentially a password and a login name.

However, it is important for extranet developers to understand the kind of security this provides is so minimal as to be hardly a barrier at all. It will keep an innocent surfer from getting access to your server, but will hardly be a hiccup to a hacker. This is because basic authentication does not employ encryption. Every time a user logs in, that person sends the login ID and password in the clear. A sniffer program picks it up as it is typed and voila!— a hacker has valid authentication.

Even without a sniffer, basic authentication is flawed because it relies on passwords. Passwords are notoriously easy to guess. This is because many people use simple, common words as their passwords.

To give you an idea of how foolishly easy it is for a hacker to guess such passwords, here is a list of what a hacker will do in what's known as a *brute force attack* (guessing possible combinations until a match is found):

- Try the user's name, initials, account name, or other such personal information. (It's amazing how popular it is to use a pet's name as a password.)
- Try the words from dictionaries, using automated scripts.
- Try minor alterations of the personal information or dictionary words, such as capitalizing the first letter or replacing it with a control character.
- Try capitalizing other letters in the words or replacing them with control characters.

Studies have shown that such brute force attacks can have a 25 percent success rate in uncovering passwords. All a hacker may need is one password.

If this sounds like a lot of trouble for a hacker to go through, remember that dozens of password-cracking schemes have been created for hackers and are available on underground BBSs. In fact, some password-cracking programs are also available for security managers to use to test their own basic authentication security. One of the most popular is Crack, available at (ftp://sable.ox.ac.uk/pub/comp/security/software/crackers).

So, performing a brute attack with an automated cracking program is no more trouble than setting your VCR to record a program while you sleep.

Tips for Creating Guess-Resistant Passwords

Remember, the harder a password is to guess, the harder it might be to remember. Try to strike a balance here, or else expect to have one help desk employee dedicated to telling end users their forgotten passwords.

- Make passwords eight characters in length. This is short enough to be remembered but long enough to be tough to crack.
- All passwords must include at least one numeric digit and at least one symbolic character such as a punctuation mark or control character.
- All passwords should also vary CAPS/no caps.

Also extranet developers may want to consider employing a proactive password checker. This is a script that spells out the rules for password creation and then only accepts passwords that conform to them. Again, balance is everything. If too many password rules are in place, or they are so complex that the proactive checker rejects too many of them, users will complain (or simply not use the system). If rules are too few or too easy, the security basic authentication provides will be negligible.

Some applications have home-authored routines that generate a random password for the user. This is advantageous because you can guarantee that passwords will not be guessed. The disadvantage is that users tend to forget a personally meaningless password that has been assigned to them.

If possible, the extranet developer should create login IDs and passwords that can be placed directly into a password database. In this way, writes to the password database need never be allowed through the application, particularly if access to the application comes from an unsecured connection.

Session IDs

Another cheap and easy way to add a small measure of security is the session identification. When a user enters an authorized login

ID and password (or conforms to other authorization techniques) a session ID is issued and attached to the URL. The session ID will be unique to this session and will expire after a certain amount of time after disconnection, such as one hour. A session ID may be a time stamp with a few extra characters to make it unique, or it may be the access password with a time stamp and other unique characters, or it may be randomly generated numbers stored in a database. A URL with a session ID could look something like this: "http://www.yourcompany.com/cgibin/yourcgi.cgi?session_id=4838718569."

Of course, a session ID in and of itself is not a huge security solution. It won't prevent access by an unauthorized person who has managed to obtain an authorized login ID and password, but it will prevent someone from accessing an extranet site simply by knowing the URL. Session IDs are primarily used to provide audit trails or keep track of a user's activity on a site.

Smart Cards

Better than basic authentication are the numerous forms of one-time passwords. These passwords are generated on-the-fly from an external device that connects to the computer. Typically, they are created with the assistance of a small credit card–sized device generally known as a *smart card.*

The user of a smart card inserts it into the external device, which looks a lot like a credit card reader. The smart card generates a onetime, time-stamped password that is recognized by the server and access is obtained. Sniffing passwords becomes an exercise in irrelevance, because the same password is never used twice. Also, the user is free to travel among various clients as long as those clients support the smart card device.

Smart cards are available from a handful of vendors, but perhaps the best known is the SecureID from Security Dynamics (which is now the parent company of RSA Data Security, one of the leaders in public/private key encryption technology). (More are listed in Chapter 8.)

The catch to smart cards is that they must be supported on the server side and possibly by the firewall as well. Many firewall vendors have agreements with Security Dynamics. They also run the danger of being lost, damaged, or forgotten. Security experts also warn that smart cards are not entirely invincible against crackers' abilities, although they are considerably tougher to crack than simple password schemes.

However, an alternative has been developed by TriNet Services, Inc. of Raleigh, NC and Vasco Data Security, Inc. of Lombard, IL, called the Internet AccessKey. The patented Internet AccessKey is a Java program that creates a onetime password. Users equipped with an AccessKey (similar to the smart card credit card–sized device) log into a server that authenticates them by using the Internet AccessKey Java program. The program generates the password information which is displayed as a flashing bar code on the screen. The user holds the key over the screen and the response—the password—is revealed. The user enters the password, along with the correct ID, and access is obtained.

The beauty of the AccessKey is that it doesn't require a smart card reader on the client side—all of that function is now on the Web server.

Of course, not every token is physical. Onetime passwords can also be generated by an item called a *soft token.* This is software placed on the client that emulates a smart card. Each copy of a token-emulation software program is unique in that it uses its "secret seed," as the folks at Security Dynamics call it. This secret seed is different in each user's copy of the program, so it generates unique onetime passwords for user authentication.

Like smart cards, token-emulation software serves to authenticate without transmitting password information in the clear over a network.

Kerberos

Kerberos is also an authentication service that uses an encryption scheme for passwords. Kerberos uses secret-key ciphers for such encryption. It was developed specifically to authenticate requests for network sources, and as such is not a digital signature system.

Specifically, a Kerberos system employs a Kerberos server which handles the centralized key management and a few other functions for a Kerberos encryption system. This server contains a database with all the secret keys to all users who will be authenticated by the system.

Users log in to the Kerberos system, which decides to grant or deny access by decrypting the password and comparing it against the database. Of course, one of the risks of using the Kerberos system is that it's the proverbial Pandora's box. Should this server be compromised, hackers will be granted carte blanche. Not surprisingly, therefore, Kerberos often gets pounded on pretty heavily by hackers looking for holes; they have experienced some measure of success.

Kerberos can have a place in an extranet deployment, especially if the extranet is designed to grant somewhat broad access of network services to the business partner. However, virtually no electronic commerce implementations employ Kerberos as the primary authentication scheme. Should an extranet application be based on the electronic commerce model (such as an order entry system), we do *not* recommend Kerberos as the primary authentication scheme. We recommend *certificates* instead.

Certificates

Perhaps the method gaining the most support for authentication of Web-based systems is the X.509 certificate. In fact, these days, encryption and certificates go together like garlic and breath mints.

Trust Models and Certificate Authorities

Security in any form is about *trust,* or lack thereof. When it comes to electronic security, two trust models exist. One is a *direct relationship* trust model. Amy knows Barbara, so she trusts her. The other is the *trust hierarchy* model. This one gets convoluted quickly. If Amy trusts Barbara and Barbara trusts Chuck, does that mean Amy should also trust Chuck?

Enter the certificate. Certificates are the electronic world's version of a driver's license. They verify that a person or server is who it claims to be. If Amy trusts Barbara because Amy ran a full-scale private investigation on Barbara and if Amy trusts Chuck because she ran a similar investigation on Chuck, then Barbara can trust Chuck. If Amy issues a certificate of trust for all the people that she has investigated and now trusts, then these people can form the Amy Trust Club. Anyone wanting to get to know the secrets of the members of the club need only present their Amy Trust Club certificate and they will be told all.

Now, pretend Amy is really a server, not a person. She would be the definition of a *certificate authority* (CA). CAs use the trust hierarchy model and provide the service of being the "trusted big brother." (See Figure 2.8.) Obtaining certificates therefore usually requires a certain degree of investigation by the CA. The CA may request such things as proof of company name or articles of incorporation, depending on the level of certificate being obtained.

Although encryption protects the document from being seen by enemy forces, it does nothing to verify that the person holding the key is the authorized key holder. Certificates augment encryption by providing a means to achieve security goals 2, 3, and 4, authen-

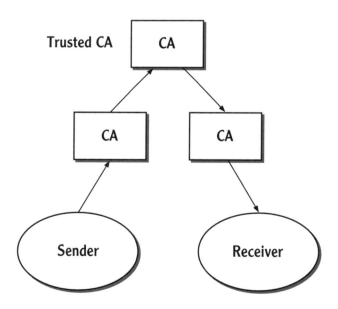

Figure 2.8 Certificates act like "trust brokers" vouching for the authenticity of certificate holders. Large certificate systems are frequently configured in hierarchies.

tication, nonrepudiation, and integrity. As such, they are becoming an increasingly important part of browser and Web server technology and the protocols that exist for performing secured transactions.

Furthermore, certificates are one of the primary security methods that thwart "man-in-the-middle" hacker attacks, where each party believes it is talking to the other but is really talking to the hacker.

Necessarily, the certificate must be issued by a recognized and trusted authority, the certificate authority mentioned above. Network users possess the CA's public key certificate (sometimes referred to as the "root key"), and can then use it to verify others' certificates. In this way, they know that the CA (whom they recognize and trust) vouches for the identity of the certificate holder.

The certificate is made available to the browser and can be offered automatically whenever a secure protocol, such as SSL, requests it. Most of the focus of Internet security and certificates is centered around certificates that meet ITU-T Recommendation X.509, which specifies the authentication service for X.500 directories and—what we are concerned with—the widely adopted X.509 certificate syntax. (ITU-T is the acronym for the International Telecommunications Union-Telecommunications standards body group formerly known as CCITT.)

An X.509 certificate provides several items of information on the certificate itself, such as the certificate authority, the validity period, the public key, and the name of the certificate holder, be it a person or a server. Most important, this type of certificate includes the digital signature of its possessor.

Certificates can be obtained through such third-party authorities as Verisign, and some lesser-known entities, such as Thawte (pronounced *thought*) Consulting, an international computer security consultant based in Raleigh, NC. Also, end users can be their own certificate authorities using products like NorTel's Entrust, Netscape's Certificate Server, and RSA's Bcert. In this way they can assign and manage their own certificates. Certificate issuing and management can also be outsourced to certificate authorities such as VeriSign, GTE, AT&T, BBN, or KeyWitness.

> **N**OTE   *It is important to know that browsers that support certificates will be looking for them from servers. The browser must be configured to accept the CA in order for a server's certificate to be considered valid. This can be more difficult with some browsers than with others. For instance, Microsoft Internet Explorer 3.0 does not provide a means to designate additional certificate authorities other than the ones it ships with from the browser. If a business partner uses IE 3.0 but the company wants to set up its own certificate-issuing infrastructure to issue its client certificates, it must write a script that will enable IE to accept the authority.*
>
> *The trusted root database of certificate authorities that IE ships with includes AT&T, internetMCI Mall, Keywitness Canada, Inc., and Verisign.*

Like government security clearances, certificates can come in several flavors, each representing greater research into the identity of the requester. For example, Verisign has three basic certificates. Class 1, in which Verisign checks for a unique name, verifies that the e-mail address is correct and that the requesting party is the one that has access to it. A Class 2 certificate means that Verisign has researched the requesting party's name, address, driver's license, social security number, and date of birth. A Class 3 certificate includes all of the items for a Class 2 plus a credit check.

CA Pros and Cons

Obviously, one of the drawbacks of using a third-party to issue a certificate is the time required for the private-eye work to be done. Other drawbacks include a lack of control over the criteria of a certificate issued and the rather "public" nature of obtaining one in this way. Certificate authorities, as you might imagine, can be the subject of attacks, all of which can be defended against, but nevertheless mean added level of risk. Organizations that do not want to display any security technique in the public wind generally do not choose to have a third party perform the certification. However, this could bring you into conflict with a partner's chosen browser, a solvable solution but one in which the obligation will be the company's to deal with. (See the Note above.)

On the other hand, the drawback to a company operating its own CA infrastructure is certificate management. Even with systems like Entrust that include management features, CA systems need to be baby-sat. For instance, most certificates are set to expire in a set amount of time, such as a year. Someone will have to see that expired certificates get reissued. Someone will also have to stay on top of issuing and revoking certificates, making sure new employees get theirs and ex-employees lose theirs. Other issues, such as where to store corporate versions of private keys, if a corporation wishes to keep these versions, also come into play.

However, a number of distinct advantages can be had for organizations that operate their own certificate-issuing infrastructure. If the issue is trust, no one can be more trustworthy than yourself. Better yet, certificates can more easily and quickly be customized and can use any criteria that a company believes is appropriate. Companies can also create certificate hierarchies if they control the infrastructure. This would allow someone with a basic corporate certificate access to all the SSL servers. However it would allow only people with a basic corporate certificate plus an extranet server certificate access to the extranet server from the inside.

Conversely, servers can be set up to allow access to a server or application from specific certificates. Business partners needing to access the extranet application can be issued a special certificate and only that certificate will qualify as authentication.

Digital Signatures

Digital signatures and certificates are sometimes referred to as one and the same (even the folks at VeriSign have at times been guilty of this). However, in actuality they are two separate technologies. Digital signatures, more than any other authentication technology discussed here, offer the most solid way to achieve security goal 3, nonrepudiation. Whereas the certificate offers information about the individual, the digital signature allows a document to be stamped in such a way that only the owner of the certificate can use it.

A number of technologies are used to create digital signatures.

PKCS #7, Message Digests

The *Public-Key Cryptography Standards* (PKCS) is a set of standards for public-key cryptography developed by RSA Laboratories, in conjunction with a consortium of other sources including Apple, Microsoft, DEC, Lotus, Sun, and MIT. Eleven of them currently exist. Each defines a general syntax for eleven uses of cryptography. PKCS #7 defines digital signatures and is a popular way that protocols provide for this technology. (The full standard can be found at ftp://ftp.rsa.com/pub/pkcs/ascii/pkcs-7.asc.)

PKCS # 7 uses message digests at the heart of creating a digital signature. In essence, a *message digest* is a unique value generated for a particular document or message. It is created by passing the message through a *oneway cryptographic function* (in other words, one that cannot be inverted), which then delivers a value (i.e., message digest). That unique value is encrypted using the sender's *private* key and is attached to the original message. The recipient uses the sender's public key to decrypt the message digest. Because the private key is used, the recipient of the message can be sure that the message truly came from the user. Because if even a single letter of the document is changed, it would alter the value of the message digest, so the receiver can also be sure that the message has arrived intact.

Different message digests exist that use different algorithms for creating the value and are appropriate for different uses. The most common ones are MD2, MD4, and MD5.

DSS

The *Digital Signal Standard* (DSS) is a National Institute of Standards & Technology (NIST) standard that applies the same sort of process as described above. Whereas PKCS # 7 is based on the RSA public/private cryptography, DSS is based on a different public/private key mathematics and one that competes w/RSA. The upshot is that the Digital Signature Algorithm makes it quicker to sign and document than to decrypt it. The RSA system is the reverse.

Many of the protocols that support digital signatures support both, since DSS is an open standard.

Digital Signature Schemes

In addition to these two standards, there are a number of digital signature schemes that control many aspects of how digital signatures can be applied. For instance, schemes cover issues such as whether the message can be signed by a recipient even if the recipient can't read it; whether each message must be signed individually (rather than a signature applied to a group of messages); whether anyone can authenticate a signature or only the recipient can, and numerous other situations. An excellent rundown of these schemes can be found on the FAQ composed by RSA (www.rsa.com/rsalabs).

Methods to Achieve Security Goal 4—Integrity

Just as security goal 3, nonrepudiation, is an extension of authentication, integrity is an extension of nonrepudiation. Nonrepudiation concerns itself mostly with messages sent specifically from one person to another. Various schemes outline how a message can be signed and delivered, and who can access it.

But what if you wanted to sidestep most of those issues and post something to your extranet and you wanted to allow anyone with authorized access to be able to retrieve it? What if that something was software? What if it was a static document? The answer lies in some of the other ways that exist to ensure integrity.

Digitally Signed Software

One of the biggest security concerns of interactive Web applications stems from the tools used to create the application. Three primary methods for creating such interactive applications include using CGI scripts (created in PERL or a variety of other languages) that perform rather rudimentary tasks, building Java applets, or building ActiveX objects. A lot of issues surround which one is best to use for what purpose, and we will discuss this more fully in Chapter 8. However, all share a similar security concern. How do you know that what the applet or object is about to do is safe? One way is to have the author of the document digitally sign it. In this way, any alterations to the code can be detected immediately.

Both Microsoft and Sun Microsystems are working on ways that allow Web developers to digitally sign their applets, the first adoption of which has already appeared on Microsoft's MSN Web page. Still, there seems to be a way to go before such a procedure is the norm, as the technology must be integrated into browsers and adopted en masse by developers. Until then, and even after, Web sites should offer certificates to verify that the site is who it claims to be.

MACs

Messages or other static documents can also be "signed" to prove integrity. One of the most common methods of doing this is the message authentication code (MAC). A MAC is a checksum tagged onto a document. Simply speaking, a *checksum* is a notation that verifies a document's length in a way that can't be easily replicated. MACs are checksums created by combining an authentication scheme, together with a secret key and appending the result to a message. MACs are computed and verified with the same key so they can be verified only by the intended receiver, unlike digital signatures, which could be used in such a way that they allow anyone to identify the sender. MACs are supported by SSL and S-HTTP, so could potentially be part of any application that includes a digital signature scheme.

Methods to Achieve Security Goal 5—Access Control (Server)

As important as it is to protect extranet documents from being seen by the wrong parties, it is equally important to protect the server itself against tampering. This means that only specific, designated individuals can upload information, delete information, change access privileges, and so on.

Security Concerns with Java and ActiveX

Java is essentially a development language, but because it has been created specifically for use with the Internet, it has some unique attributes not found in other development languages.

The types of programs Java creates are commonly referred to as *applets,* in part because Java has been designed to be processor independent and in part because these applets have been restricted in what they can do for security reasons.

Essentially, Java is a platform-independent bit of code, meaning that Java applets can perform on any PC, as long as that PC has a browser that supports the Java language. This is because applets are not compiled by the client's CPU. Instead they are interpreted by the browser, which takes care of making the applet understandable to whatever platform is accessing it. This extra layer of interpretation can drag down the speed of an application, but it also allows the applet to be more secure.

For instance, Java applets are prohibited from performing any function that might damage the client system, such as writing to a file on a local machine. Such restrictions stem from the fact that the applets are only allowed to perform within the interpreter. While this adds a level of security, the write-protected status of an applet means that Java programs might not be able to perform some useful tasks as well.

Competing with Java is Microsoft's ActiveX. ActiveX is also a means to create interactive applets. However, ActiveX is processor dependent. (At the time this book went to press, the only processor supported was, not surprisingly, Intel, although Microsoft has vowed to port it to other CPU platforms as well.)

The best description we've heard of ActiveX is that it is a "bunch of code" that is transferred from the server to the client's browser so that the applet can be performed. The code is compiled directly by the CPU.

(Continued)

This makes it extremely powerful, but also more risky. Since no interpretation is done by any application before the code is executed, ActiveX applets could, conceivably, reformat the surfer's hard disk or perform any other number of nasty tasks like shut down a machine.

Microsoft's main tack to combat security concerns is Authenticode, the ability to verify a program's source before you download it. Authenticode enables the surfer to identify who published the software before it is used and verify that no one tampered with it. Of course, this means that the Web site itself needs to be authenticated and that the digital signature has to be from someone who is authorized.

Most of these types of restrictions will be handled at the operating system levels and at the Web server level. A lot of this may seem obvious, and yet mistakes in configuring access control is one of the top items that hackers look for when they are trying to overtake a system. In the middle of 1996, the Department of Justice was embarrassed by just such an exploit. Hackers broke onto the department's Web site and replaced the original text and HTML code with text that was considerably unseemly. The incident made national headlines, much to the chagrin of the department's Webmasters, and also confused the unknowing surfers who visited the site before the attack was detected.

Here are a few tips for making sure that access control of your extranet server is top notch.

At the Operating-System Level with Unix Servers

◆ Turn off all services which are not essential to server operation; this especially includes the finger command and system mounting. The finger command is an especially favorite tool of hackers, as it is used to gain information about a system's users. Few applications need this finger command, so extranet developers should disable it immediately. System mounting, the sharing of storage space between remote computers, is also especially dangerous and rarely essential.

◆ Do not place or allow *any* .rhost files on the extranet server, whatsoever. A .rhost file is a file used for remote access purposes. It specifies what remote machines are allowed access on a particular account.

◆ Make sure you are using the most up-to-date version of sendmail, as sendmail is often compared to Swiss cheese when describing its security systems. The code itself is a jumbled mess, and security holes are constantly showing themselves. For instance, weaknesses in older versions of sendmail can allow a hacker to telnet into a port and then to use a variety of tricks to gain control of the machine, or have a password file e-mailed back. Either stay as up to date as possible or don't use it. Numerous other commercial mail packages exist that offer much tighter security.

◆ Consult security experts to be informed on some of the many other security loopholes hackers use on Unix systems. All of the above methods were easily discovered on the Internet, from books and magazines, and through the advice of consultants. Hundreds more exist that are only known to pros (both consultants and hackers).

◆ Join mailing lists for your operating system/platform. Yes, the amount of e-mail you will receive can become irritating, but there is a tremendous wealth of information in this source.

At the Web-Server Level

◆ Take advantage of the many access control mechanisms that allow access to various areas of the server. Set global access privileges, identify specific files to be accessed, and so on. Really scour this area of the documentation of the Web server to be used for the extranet and make sure every potential setting is configured to restrict access only to the appropriate people. If the documentation is unclear on a point, e-mail the vendor for answers, rather than making assumptions and declaring your extranet server secure.

◆ If possible, configure the extranet so that access can only be had from the machine that operates the Web server, not remotely. Many security-minded Web servers support this option.

◆ Remove any programming tools, compilers, linkers, and so on from the extranet server if at all possible. If not possible, be sure that these areas have restricted access set by the operating system and/or the Web server.

◆ Un-"suid" any programs that are not mission critical. Suid is "set user id" for an application. Suid has been responsible for some notorious security holes.

◆ Keep updated on current software. Even software one or two releases old poses a threat, because any security holes found in them will be well known by hackers. Current releases should include patches to any found holes. Remember, many holes are found and patched but not publicized. Just because you haven't heard of reports of holes doesn't mean they don't exist. (In fact, there are a whole bunch of people who hack programs for fun, just to send that information to the developer.)

Through the Firewall or Outside It?

Another important question should be answered when you design access control. Where should the server be placed in relation to the intranet and Internet?

The Case for Staying Outside the Firewall   One of the best solutions for where to place the extranet is to create a *middlenet.* A middlenet is an area that lies in between two security systems, often between two firewalls such as two Bastion hosts (which allow traffic to be application specific). Or, more commonly, the extranet is placed behind a screening router but in front of a corporate firewall. The public Web server may be placed along side it but the extranet server employs authentication and other techniques to protect its data. (See Figure 2.9.)

Those from inside the corporate firewall may have access to it and those who can meet specific security measures may also have access. But it is neither part of the public network nor of the intranet.

When using a middlenet it is best to place all databases, password files, and critical applications on the corporate side of the firewall, somewhere on the intranet. In this way, these important data sources and applications are doubly protected—once from the extranet security measures and a second time from the corporation's perimeter security measures. In this case, the Web server's main job is to make calls through a firewall to the protected information and then serve up the results of such queries, via CGI scripts, in pretty HTML format. Be sure to maintain as much

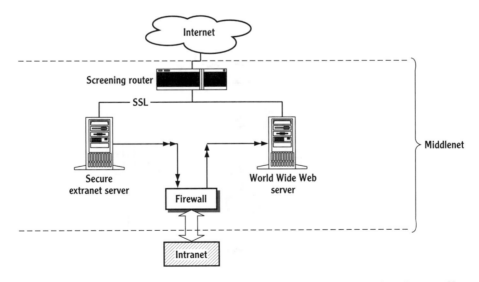

Figure 2.9 A middlenet places the extranet server (and usually the Webserver) in between two firewall-devices. These may be two Bastian Hosts firewalls, or like pictured here, between a screening router that performs packet filtering and the central firewall.

access security as possible on the database server inside the firewall as well. If a disgruntled employee has access to a database from within the corporation, all firewall and other security efforts are useless.

There may be cases where the extranet data will actually reside on the Web server. This is fine if the viewing of such data by unauthorized people will not harm the company. (See Figure 2.10.)

For instance, one software company uses a similar scheme for a password-protected database of information dedicated to maintenance contract customers. The information is in the form of static pages and a database. This data is somewhat sensitive, in that these people have paid for this (and other) services as part of the contract. However, because the only information that an unauthorized person could see would be documentation on products, the company does feel that the risk is worth the benefits of having less security to administer and of having the information closer to the user.

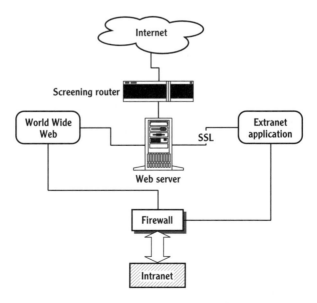

Figure 2.10 Sometimes an extranet may share the same server as a World Wide Web server.

Of course, such a middlenet approach has a few drawbacks, mainly that it isn't appropriate for every extranet. For instance, an extranet that allows partners to supply content to an intranet would not be a good choice for a middlenet configuration. In that case, the extranet content supplier would be forced to dump data to a middlenet extranet server; then that data would have to be replicated onto the intranet application. Although such a configuration is a plausible and secure way of using a partner as an intranet content supplier, it's also an expensive proposition, considering other methods to allow safe file transfers that wouldn't require the replication of hardware.

Another case where it wouldn't work is when the object of the extranet is to allow collaborate computing with existing internal applications. For instance, a business partner may be entering the network through the Internet in order to operate a custom engineering application via telnet. Replicating that custom application to an extranet server may be too expensive for the risk. A better method would be to create a VPN for the partner, and limit the tunnel's access to the specific directory where the custom application resides.

The Case for Going Through the Firewall   Of course, another option is to let selected outsiders right onto the intranet itself, through the firewall. This is the most efficient way to leverage the investment that's already been made in the intranet.

If the person trying to gain access is extremely trustworthy, or that person is actually an employee, then setting up access through the firewall is the right solution. For instance, if one of the primary goals of the extranet is to provide a safe means for mobile and remote employees to gain access to intranet applications, replicating these applications onto a middlenet server doesn't make a lot of sense from a cost standpoint.

Also, the best of today's firewalls offer a lot of granularity in the access control they provide. Many support onetime password schemes, can be configured to allow access of a specified IP address (that of the user's client), and can also allow traffic only to specific addresses. Also, once inside, access control to areas of the network or even to specific applications can be applied using standard network security measures.

Specifically, the best-of-breed firewalls support rules based on IP addresses and on IP address source/destination pairs. So a rule can be configured to allow traffic from a partner's firewall's IP address to the extranet server's IP address. Rules can also be set dependent on IP service protocol—Web and e-mail are allowed; telnet is not. Rules can be based on the direction of the traffic, from public to private, for example.

It should also be noted that certain types of firewalls are better suited for protection of access control from Internet connections than others. One of the largest threats that hackers employ is *IP spoofing*. This is a method of making packets appear as if they are coming from an authorized source, when in fact they are not. A common way to accomplish this is by using the IP address of internal clients, even though the connection is actually coming from the outside.

Screening routers that perform packet filtering are most susceptible to this ploy—especially if the router is not set to watch which port a packet comes from. If a packet comes from an outside port connected to the Internet, a router will know that the internal address on the packet cannot be correct and will reject the packets. Screening routers have their place in Internet security. They perform a first line of attack on packets, rejecting most of the packets that violate security policies. This keeps the software-based firewalls from becoming too much of a bottleneck. However, packet-filtering firewalls should *not* be relied on as the only firewall defense.

Domain and Type Enforcement A new method of access control is also being developed by Trusted Information Systems (TIS), a firewall vendor. It has been dubbed Domain and Type Enforcement (DTE). Research for DTE is being funded by DARPA. DTE is an operating system–level access control mechanism for Unix systems. It allows security policies to be attributed to every file, in addition to the Unix permissions already associated with a file. These policies would be based on organization-specific roles, rather than arbitrary attributes.

For instance, a company's controller would be allowed read and write access for any budget-related files while a company's engineer would be allowed only read access to certain financial files.

DTE files are typed as to the information they contain and to the sensitivity level. This augments the permissions Unix files already have today, namely that every file has an owner and is a member of a group. For example, an HTML document is owned by the user "S-HTTP" (the Web server) and is in the group "WWW." Permissions can be set on each of these, such as allowing S-HTTP read/write access, but WWW read-only access and everyone else read-only access as well.

In addition to working on the development of the operating system access controls, TIS is working to include DTE and cryptography into firewalls. TIS expects to have its TIS Firewall Tool-Kit modified to support DTE in 1997. As the work for this is being funded by the government, with the goal of modifying an industry-standard firewall, not simply TIS products, other firewall vendors can be expected to offer DTE-enabled products eventually as well. (Probably not before TIS gets them out—the company is already working on how DTE could be supported directly within its flagship product, the Gauntlet firewall.)

Methods for Ensuring Security Goal 6—Availability

When the connection is from your biggest customer wanting to place an order that would make payroll for a year, the last message that customer should see is an error message saying the server is not found or is not responding. Having other types of extranet servers go down from error or sabotage is no picnic either. In fact, a shaky physical connection can become an administrator's worst nightmare. On the other hand, when availability is secured, Webmasters are virtually assured sweet dreams. We said earlier in this chapter that availability is the result of a tight set of security methods. However, it can be planned for, rather than hoped for. Here we offer some tips on how to secure availability.

Physical Security

When it comes to securing for availability, it's important to remember that servers are part of the physical world, just as they are part of the electronic world. Make sure that the extranet server itself is locked up in an area that makes it safe from physical threat. All the firewalls in the world won't protect a server that winds up located in the employee lunchroom. If someone unplugs it, spills coffee on it, or steals it, the investment in the system is gone. This applies to all network components. If a server is locked in a safe room, but the network hub is in the secretary's office, damage can still be done. Or if the T1 runs across the ceiling of the mailroom . . . well, you get the idea.

Make sure that basic rules of network availability are used. Backups should be organized, complete, and done often, and backup tapes are to be kept somewhere safe. Authentication and access control should be airtight on the server physically. If someone logging onto the network can't get in, neither should an unauthorized person who waltzes up and starts typing at the keyboard.

That said, the other area of concern when securing availability is from *viruses* or *Trojan Horses,* executable files hidden in other authorized files, such as attachments to e-mail.

The Threat of Viruses

Viruses thrive in an internetworked domain. Because the Internet is the greatest of all internetworks, it is prime breeding ground. Be sure that antivirus software is running on the extranet machine, if it doesn't interfere with the operations of the application. Preferably such software should be running in the background, rather than activated for a once-a-day scan.

Even so, it might be wise to take even stronger antivirus steps.

Antivirus Checking at the Firewall

We predict that by the end of 1997 most of the major firewall vendors will be able to perform at least cursory antivirus scanning. The firewall, intended to be the front line against threats, is a logical place to perform such tasks, if it can be done without creating a performance backlog.

Setting Virus-Unfriendly Policies

Still, even as this capability becomes possible, it won't be all a security-minded Webmaster needs to do to be safe. Policies for and training of users will also help. For instance, e-mail attachments should be text, not word processor files. Word processor files that must be sent over public e-mail systems should be scanned by an antivirus system before being opening. Downloads of any executable file should be banned except by designated individuals trained in the company's security policies. If it's not possible to ban FTP transfers and still allow the extranet to perform its functions, all FTP files that are transferred into the intranet should be scanned by a current version of antivirus software before being used.

Type Enforcement

For a project, such as an extranet, where security is of extremely high concern, an organization might want to consider employing a firewall technology known as *type enforcement.* Security Computing offers a firewall called Sidewinder that uses a method of type enforcement that has been patented by Security Computing. Type enforcement, as it is being employed in Sidewinder, takes packet filtering into the next zone. It acts to separate Internet services, such as e-mail and/or FTP, so that one type of service cannon interact with another, unrelated one. In this way, it eliminates the "super user" (unlimited control) concept so that a single compromised service will not allow a hacker to gain control over the Sidewinder firewall.

But perhaps the Sidewinder's most interesting attribute is its ability to filter messages for content, at least for e-mail services. The current version of Sidewinder, 3.0 released September 1996, can filter messages based on size, binary, and key word search filters to screen incoming or outgoing mail messages. Sidewinder can filter mail using any combination of these filters, in any order. The size filter rejects the message if it contains a number of bytes greater than or equal to the threshold size. The binary filter looks at the pattern of the text to determine if it is normal, human-readable text. The key word filter provides a search for a specific set of characters, or key words, within an e-mail message. This can be used to help enforce antivirus policies, or any number of policies that dictate what outsiders gain access through the Internet and how they do it.

In fact, Security Computing has been issuing challenges to hackers to break the box. At the 1996 DEFCON, an annual hacker conference, the box beat the challenge.

The Case for Ditching the Internet Altogether

Until now, we've concentrated on talking about security methods for using an extranet application over the Internet. However, the Internet doesn't have to be the network of choice. Users have two other options. They could rent space for their extranet applications (or more) on a private TCP/IP network, a method akin to outsourcing an extranet/intranet. (See Figure 2.11.) Or they could use

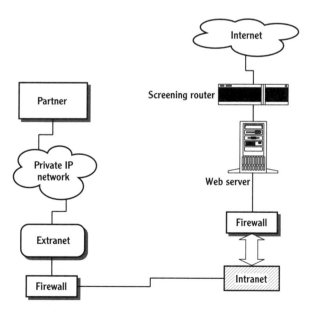

Figure 2.11 A private IP network offers an alternative to the Internet for extremely sensitive extranet applications.

the public telephone system with a remote access server placed as guardian. (Granted, the latter is a "retro-80s" concept . . . remember Tymnet? But it remains an effective option.) (See Figure 2.12.)

The Rented Tunnel

The "rented" tunnel refers to another method of creating a virtual private network. However, this has edged a lot closer to the concept of "private" than to the concept of "virtual." By this quip we mean that the network used to pass the signal from company to partner can be one of the commercial IP networks now reaching across the globe, rather than the Internet. Commercial IP network carriers include InfoNet as well as networks offered by the major ISPs such as UUNet, Netcom, and PSI, and the telecommunications and IP networks built by the telephone carriers such as Sprint, MCI, and AT&T.

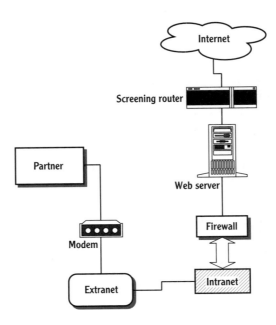

Figure 2.12 Extranet applications may also be accessed via a direct dial-up connection.

Optimally, in such a scene, the company would use the leased VPN as its intranet backbone and a business partner could be issued a connection on this VPN. Leasing makes particular sense for companies with many international locations. Between the company and its partners, a firewall would be used, in order to provide access control.

Rented VPNs have the following advantages over using the Internet. The numbers of renters using these systems can't compare with the sheer numbers of users on the Internet. Renters are segregated so that the companies see only themselves. This makes it much more difficult for an outsider to break into your system (but not impossible).

Performance is guaranteed because companies are paying a commercial provider for it. So, the network provider is accountable for performance degradation or security breaches that occur because of its negligence. This is simply not the case with performance or security problems that occur because data traverses the Internet. This doesn't mean that the Internet must be left entirely out of the loop. A VPN-to-Internet connection is possible, as most commercial TCP/IP network providers have routers in Internet network hubs that allow a connection to move from the private network to the public one.

The drawback, of course, is that it costs more to lease a VPN through a commercial IP network than it costs to use the Internet (even if the company is paying for ISP connections). Also, such a system means that the company that is renting the space must be responsible for the extranet extension. When both parties are using their own onramp to the Internet, each remains responsible for its own connection.

The Remote-Access Tunnel

The third option to protected, secure remote access is to employ the age-old *remote-access server*. In this case, the users dial into a remote-access server that supports TCP/IP using a remote-access PPP or SLIP client. The client deals with the connection and handshake and the extranet server can then be accessed with the Web browser.

Since information is not reaching across the Internet, the security threat from packet sniffers is eliminated. (But it is still possible for incredibly wily hackers to capture data streams by planting sniffers at a telecommunication switch, allowing sniffing of POTS.) Also, this allows access to an extranet for partners that do not have Internet service.

The drawback of this solution is the expense of the remote dial-up. Someone has to pay for long-distance telephone calls too, if partners are not in the same calling zone. For these reasons, we foresee the Internet as being the primary network that partners use to gain access to extranet services.

Risk Analysis

So, how do you know which one of these techniques, or which combination of them, is right for your extranet application? The answer lies in getting a handle on just what computer security is all about, setting policies. Securing a computer is like a visit to the doctor. Confidentiality is all important. Symptoms are assessed. A diagnosis is made and treatment is prescribed. If the treatment is not effective, another is attempted. If it is effective, the patient lives a normal life until a change in condition occurs and another diagnosis is in order.

When it comes to computers, the role of the doctor is the security professional. It is this person's job to keep the fragile little machines networked together into a single entity, healthy in today's hostile world of attackers and viruses. A diagnosis means evaluating the risk of the data on particular machines and across the network. That diagnosis also includes an analysis of the potential risk to other data on the network should this little computer be compromised. It is unwise to jump right in and apply specific security procedures to your extranet without a thorough risk analysis. Just as it is unwise for a doctor to prescribe treatment without a diagnosis.

Extranet applications need to be part of the big picture. For that reason, we're going to spend a little ink describing what's involved in this holistic approach.

Asset Management

Several factors contribute to a proper risk analysis. On an enterprise level, the place to start is with an inventory. Even better, that inventory should be automated by using one of the three dozen or so asset management products on the market. It is impossible to protect a network if the network's guards don't know what it is made of. That computer that the marketing department purchased on their own probably includes a modem. The modem may be connected directly and insecurely to a telephone line. This is a backdoor that would allow hackers to waltz completely around a firewall guarding the front.

If an extranet application is to be used to tunnel through the firewall into the intranet, such a modem could jeopardize it as well. So, be sure to fully understand what hardware your network consists of as well as the capabilities of each component.

Risk Assessment

Once you have an accurate inventory of all computers and communication devices on the network, its time to start answering some tough questions about them.

1. What are you trying to protect?
   - Mission-critical data, such as payroll information, accounts receivable, accounts payable, research and development, patient records?
   - Important data, such as product/pricing literature, personnel files, market research information, analysis of competitors?
   - Public data, such as press releases, contact information, quarterly reports, a prospectus?
2. *What are you trying to protect it from?*
   - Innocent blunders?
   - Internal threats such as disgruntled employees?
   - External threats such as hackers and corporate espionage?

3. *In what ways are you trying to protect it?*
   - From being seen by unauthorized users?
   - From being altered?
   - From being made unavailable?
   - From being able to be used to access other systems or to infect other systems?

4. *How damaging would it be to the company if the data was . . .*
   - Destroyed?
   - Viewed by the general public?
   - Viewed by competitors?
   - Altered to misinform?
   - Made unavailable to those seeking to use it?

By answering this series of questions for each piece of equipment and every byte of data, the company can proceed with a rational security plan.

For all mission-critical data, the highest standard the company will employ should exist. Does this mean that you must use retinal scanning devices as part of your authentication procedures for all accounting employees? Maybe; the answer to that is held in question 2. If the company has a real threat from sophisticated hired hackers conducting corporate espionage, then retinal scanners might be in order.

Once such a plan is in place, the company can evaluate where an extranet fits in. Is it as critical as the accounting database and should it warrant all the security measures and expense? Is it as unimportant as the public Web server and should it warrant mostly access control and availability measures? Probably it would be somewhere between the two.

For an extranet application, we also need to answer the following questions in our risk analysis:

1. How important is scaleability? Will this application be used only and forever by a handful of business partners or might it eventually be used by hundreds or thousands of people and sites?

2. Who will be responsible for purchasing and maintaining the client-side equipment and software—the organization or the business partner?

3. How will you create enforceable security procedures for end users who are not part of your organization, and then, how will you enforce them?

Only with formal security policies in place can a company make informed decisions about how to approach the security of an extranet application. For example, the Federal Deposit Insurance Corp. (FDIC) has a security policy that says absolutely no inbound traffic of any kind from the Internet is allowed. As a quasi-governmental organization entrusted with insuring the nation's bank deposits, its security managers recognize that it would be a tempting prize for a hacker to conquer. Still, no amount of convenience that could be derived from Internet-based applications is worth assuming that risk. At the same time, they rely on the Internet for e-mail and a Web presence. Therefore, any extranet application they create must remain separate from the central network, probably even by using good 'ole sneakernet when the machine must be updated or managed.

In the case of a company like Tyson Foods, which uses the Internet in a broad variety of ways and allows limited inbound traffic, a middlenet would suffice, using a commerce server that employs SSL.

For Roche Bioscience, where the object of the extranet is to allow scientists from different companies to collaborate on research, a VPN would be the right choice. In this way, people in diverse locations can access the same mainframe-based engineering applications and data with a minimal effort on the part of the users. The company, although assuming a security risk by allowing access to specific mainframe applications, gets the trade-off of lower data center costs by allowing partners to share existing data and applications.

The Layered Approach

Security, like warm clothing, is best layered. Every extranet application may not need to conform to all five security goals and some may need redundant methods to achieve a single goal. However,

Definitions of Attack

Brute force—an attack aimed at cracking passwords where every possibility is tried until a match is found

Data diddling—unauthorized altering of data

Denial of service—prevents the network or other services from functioning at all or at least normally

IP spoofing—an attack where the IP address is faked so that the data packets sent over the Internet appear to be generated by an authorized, inside network

Man-in-the-middle—an attack where each party believes it is interacting with the other, but is really interacting with an intruder who is snooping and then passing information along

Scanner—a program such as SATAN that probes a network for vulnerabilities in an automated way, or a program that dials telephone numbers to identify ones connected to modems

Sniffer—a program that monitors all traffic on a network to collect authorized passwords and data packets

Social engineering—an attack where hackers pose as employees in order to get authorized access to systems

Trojan Horse—an unauthorized program that gains entry to a system by attaching itself to authorized programs

Virus—a self-propagating program that damages the data on both the computer in which it is executed and others in some way

the more ways that an application is secured, the more barriers a hacker must break through in order to do harm. This has a twofold meaning: even a flawed implementation of security on one level will not automatically mean the hacker has free run. Also, the more barriers, the more time a company has to catch the thief, discover where the holes were, and seal them before any harm can be done.

Some firewalls support thief-trapping methods such as the well-known traceroute and nslookup commands that allow victims to gather information on their attackers.

What the Hackers Know that You Don't: Social Engineering

Computer security techniques for filtering packets, scanning documents, and generally prowling the electronic blips as they travel through the internetworked universe are only part of the picture. People who knowingly and, more often, unknowingly assist attackers are harder to control. And yet, no amount of electronic brick building will help a system if a hacker obtains authorized access through social engineering.

Social engineering is attacks based on the fallibility of human beings, rather than on networked computers. A hacker that is socially engineering an attack might get a job at the company or even pose as a worker to gain entrance into the building. The attacker may start calling employees on the phone, asking for information, pretending to be another employee. If it sounds impossible, think again. By gaining a little bit of information at a time, such as a valid name, phone extension, or employee ID number, a hacker could have enough knowledge to call a help desk and get a new password issued. Access is obtained and the firewall never even hiccuped.

To thwart social engineering, security policy designers have to:

1. Be aware that it exists.
2. Educate employees that it exists and as to what types of information are allowed or forbidden to be given out over the phone or to unknown people.
3. Have an alert process in place that allows employees to report suspicions of a social engineering attack. Employees should know who to contact, and for what reasons, and should be able to do so without fear of repercussions.

Auditing for Naughty Business

The final piece of security an extranet developer needs to consider is the plan for checking to see whether the systems in place are working, a process collectively known as "auditing." Auditing has two components: (1) looking for security loopholes and (2) compiling activity logs to determine whether wrongdoing is taking place. Both are necessary.

Unless an organization engages in thorough, effective, and ongoing auditing, it cannot possibly know if its security measure are working. One of the complaints we hear over and over again from security experts is that business managers seem to think that a security system is "set and go," but it's really a tug-of-war. A company implements security, checks it, and uses it. All is fine until the hackers develop a new program or algorithm, or manipulate a hardware device. Then security must be revamped to secure against this new threat.

Only if security is being constantly audited can those who implement and use it know how well it works, where a breach may have occurred, and what was compromised during that breach. Business managers must be educated to the concept that this is an ongoing battle. Security cannot simply be "set" and forgotten like cruise control on an Arizona highway.

Yet, studies show that a large percentage of companies fail to implement proper auditing procedures. A recent survey of 428 large organizations conducted by the Computer Security Institute, an association of IS managers responsible for security administration, found that over 20 percent of respondents had no idea if unauthorized use of computer systems had occurred within the last 12 months. (Even more scary, 42 percent said there had been unauthorized use, with only 37 percent believing there hadn't been.)

Most computer experts believe that the chances of attack are rising daily, especially for networks with Internet connections or remote access—meaning just about all of us. Experts say that the payoff for conducting a successful attack gets higher and higher as electronic commerce becomes commonplace.

In fact, one of the developers of SATAN, Wietse Venema, professor of Mathematics and Computing Science at Eindhoven University of Technology in The Netherlands, has written extensively on the lack of auditing. One area that he likes to point to as representative of the risk is a tiger team attack on U.S. government systems that was done in 1995. A *tiger team* is a group of paid penetration experts hired to find holes in a networked security system. (We've listed a few in Chapter 9, if you are interested in seeing how your own systems fare.)

In the attack Venema likes to point to, 8,932 systems were attacked, 7,860 systems were penetrated, 390 break-ins were detected, 19 break-ins were reported. Most people never even noticed they were compromised.

As we've mentioned, two types of auditing exist. One is *penetration testing.* This should be done when systems are set up and every time they are modified. It should also be done when new penetration testing tools are developed, as new security holes are discovered every day by ingenious hackers. Penetration testing can be done by hired tiger team officials, but that's overkill for most applications. Instead, extranet developers can employ some of the security auditing packages available on the market today. Some popular packages are listed in the box below. Still, packaged penetration testing will not get the results that professionals would, as they are likely to find far more complex ways that a system can be compromised.

The second aspect of auditing is reaping information from security logs. Perhaps the least glamorous part of computer security is these 'ole logs. However boring it might be to track security events and then pore over the logs looking for problems, it still must be done.

Audit trails have gotten a bad rap from many network managers because, improperly configured, they become disk-eating monsters that produce volumes of information where breaches are impossible to find (like a needle in a haystack).

Audit logs should be configured to look for items that indicate attack, not just failed logins. But on the other hand, it is rarely necessary to keep track of every opened file or every executable launched.

Items that should be looked at include:

Other Tips for Security Auditing

Create uniformity in auditing techniques. This makes any deviance easier to spot. For example, for Unix servers the following tools are available, many of them shareware or freeware:

SATAN (ftp://ciac.llnl.gov/pub/ciac/sectools/unix/satan) and COPS (ftp://ftp.cert.org/pub/tools/cops), both of which look for specific security loopholes that hackers commonly use. Tiger, a more recent version of COPS, can be found at (ftp://cert.org./pub/tools/tcp_wrappers).

ARPWatch, which detects bogus host systems pretending to be trusted hosts (ftp://coast.cs.purdue.edu/pub/tools/unix/arpwatch).

Crack, which tests for safe passwords (ftp://sable.ox.ac.uk/pub/comp/security/software/crackers).

Commercially, Internet Security Systems of Atlanta, GA offers the Internet Scanner (www.iss.net).

Qualix Group offers NetProbe (www.qualix.com).

For NT, a few commercial products exist (sorry you shareware fans, NT falls squarely in the for-profit world of Microsoft).

Intrusion Detection offers a version of Kane Security Analyst for Windows NT (www.intrusion.com).

Similarly, BindView Development Corporation offers BindView/NOSadmin for Windows NT (www.bindview.com).

Failed and successful logins
Failed user password attempts
Failed administrator password attempts
Successful changes to group access, additions, and deletions
Successful account policy changes including who, how, and what they changed
Guest accounts with excessive rights

Inactive accounts remaining active

Failed and successful attempts to use services not turned on

Failed and successful attempts to access root accounts

Failed and successful attempts to write into critical system areas (such as the directory where passwords are kept)

Failed and successful attempts to rename executable files or directories containing execution files

Repeated use of illegal commands

Users trying to run system programs

Fortunately, many of these tasks can be handled by scripts that have already been written. Poke around on the net to find them, then adjust them to your specific needs and use them, and finally, and most important, *heed* the results. All the monitoring in the world won't matter if the network administrator never gets around to reading the latest e-mail that says the modification data of the "adduser" script changed. (This indicates that someone, possibly a hacker, has replaced the "adduser" routine with another one that will, for example, store plain text passwords in some remote directory.)

Summary

With an extranet, security is everything. Computer security can be broken into six goals: confidentiality, authentication, nonrepudiation, integrity, access control, and availability. Each goal has its own set of tools and, in some cases, protocols, that will ensure it. Many protocols achieve two or more security goals.

Fortunately, the drive to secure the Web for electronic commerce has set some of the best Internet minds in the world onto security issues and the best security minds onto the Internet. Most of these solutions can be directly applied to an extranet application, even if it does not involve commerce.

The leading security protocol for Web-based applications is Netscape's SSL, for creating secure and reliable connections through encryption. Other protocols exist as well; these include S-HTTP and virtual private networks. Most experts believe that a variety of protocols will eventually emerge as methods of securing the Internet. The Internet itself is becoming more security oriented, and the next version of IP will include a number of security specifications, collectively known as IPsec. However, much work remains to be done on IPsec, and it could be a while before the next version of IP, IP version 6, is as ubiquitous as IP version 4 is today.

Security managers should also realize that an extranet should be part of an overall security plan which includes detailed policy making, a layered security approach for sensitive applications, and auditing in order to verify that security systems are working as intended.

## chapter three

Extranet Performance Issues

Performance of any Internet application is a big, wobbly subject. Problems can occur in the Internet connection (or the network, in the case of an intranet), the server, and the application. Each of these three levels can cause an extranet application to perform poorly. In this chapter, we will discuss some common problems of each, and offer some solutions. Some of our suggestions are forward-looking: they examine various vendors' R&D efforts. (We fully realize that such products may never materialize as intended, and yet they give a strong indication of what the market will soon offer.) Others are strategic, rather than tool oriented. Still others are tools that are available for the corporate developer now.

The Virtual WAN

With nearly ubiquitous access to the Internet now occurring in the commercial sector, the Internet has turned into a worldwide, public WAN. That's good news and bad news. It's good news because it is now possible to share data with almost anyone, as long as they are willing to adopt Internet standards and/or rent them via an Internet Service Provider (ISP).

The bad news is that we are now trusting important applications to a system that, for all practical purposes, is driving without a captain. It is a decentralized system where no single person or entity commands all of it. If a user experiences a slowdown in performance, if packets chronically never arrive at their final destinations, if a URL suddenly becomes inaccessible, it can be difficult to pinpoint the problem (and even more difficult to point fingers). Difficult, but not impossible.

Performance Problems of Internet Traffic

When it comes to the Internet itself, discussions of performance quickly get complex. We are dealing with an interconnected network wrapped around the world and composed of millions of computers and a dozen protocols. Moreover, the Internet is a system that was actually built with the underlying assumption that it may perform poorly under certain circumstances. (See the sidebar. We promise it's not the same old "ARPANET" story.)

What makes the matter of performance even more complicated is that the Internet is much more of a logical creature than a physical one, although it does, of course, have a physical component. That physical component pretty much can be described as millions of routers crazily spitting out packets to other routers, like a group of poker dealers gone mad. A packet is the Internet's standardized electronic blip. Routers can be connected to one another in a variety of ways: digital telephone lines, analog lines, satellite systems, and so on.

Obviously, if the whole physical make up of the Internet is dependent on the router, its actions are paramount. The router looks at a header contained on a packet, which contains the address of where the packet is going and where it came from. By following the guidelines of a specific protocol, and from that information, the router knows where to send its packets and what to do if it has a problem.

Because the Internet is a packet-switched network, a packet could conceivably pass through a dozen or more routers before it gets to its destination. Packet-switched networks are those in which there is no single, unbroken connection between sender and receiver.

A Brief History of the Physical Development of the Internet

Most of us are familiar with a simplified story of the Internet's development that goes something like this: In the 1960s a networking project was born and christened the Advanced Research Project Agency's ARPANET. ARPANET was used primarily for the military.

A decade later it added more U.S. government agencies and universities and another decade later added the nation's leading supercomputer centers and even more universities.

But the details of the story really point out how amazing the Internet is and how even more amazing it is for the commercial world to have found its value. After all, the commercial world's computing history is one of being dominated by some for-profit company or another, be it IBM and its mainframes in the 1970s or Microsoft and Intel and their PC platform in the 1990s.

But here we are, at the end of the millennium, discovering how to use the most open computing platform ever developed, which has been quietly working away for the select few for three decades.

How did we get here?

In the late 1960s, the country's major military focus was shifting toward the newly developed Cold War. The Rand Corporation, one of the foremost Cold War think tanks in the United States, began to ponder an odd problem. If a nuclear attack occurred, how would the nation's military powers continue to communicate? Centralized communication was sure to be one of the first military targets of any such attack. So, what system could be developed that would decentralize communications so that, even if it were attacked, it could still operate?

(Continued)

The result was the Rand Proposal, produced in 1964: develop a network that was designed from the beginning to be thought of as unreliable and to have in place systems that allowed it to continue to operate reliably, even though any given part of it might not be able to.

Each node would become equal. Hence the notion of packets was developed, so that a message would be the sum total of its packets. Packets would be free to choose the route in which they got to their final destination, with the route being rather unimportant, as long as they all finally made it and could be reassembled.

The idea was further refined by Rand, MIT, and UCLA with the first tests of a packet-switching network done by the National Physical Laboratory in Great Britain. In 1968, the project received funding from the Pentagon's Advanced Research Projects Agency to build a larger such network in the United States. In the fall of 1969, four nodes were installed at UCLA, and the system was baptized ARPANET. By 1971 ARPANET grew to fifteen nodes and a year later, 37 nodes. In fact, ARPANET continued to grow throughout the 1970s. In the mid-1970s, ARPANET's original protocol was enhanced into TCP/IP. TCP was an improved method of providing a source address, destination address, fragmentation (breaking data up into usable datagrams or packets), and routing for Internet traffic, while providing a reliable virtual circuit for IP. In other words, TCP handles the end-to-end reliability of this data.

By 1977, the open standard TCP/IP was discovered as a way that any other network could connect to ARPANET and was heavily pursued by universities and other research centers with a lot of big hardware. In fact, the two protocols were included in a popular release of the Berkeley Standard Unix, which was freely distributed to other universities.

In 1983, the military segment of ARPANET broke off into its own separate internetwork, leaving a vast network of

(Continued)

research facilities connected. So, in 1985 the National Science Foundation (NSF) funded a network anchored by several national supercomputer centers, including the National Center for Supercomputing Applications (NCSA) and Cornell University (who have remained strong centers of Internet application development ever since).

The NSF wanted to make these supercomputer centers available to any research center across the nation through 56K leased lines. The NSF funded the linking of the supercomputer centers together on a 56K line and the backbone was born. As most universities already had TCP/IP, any that hadn't already connected could readily do so.

A subculture began to develop, based on open and standardized computing. The TCP/IP standards were already in the public domain and anyone could join the link. Many diverse groups did. Such an expanse of the Internet was welcomed by the "free-love" Internet beatniks. But this type of free networking was also messy and uncontrolled.

Soon, protocols that allow the broadcasting of messages (Newsnet), e-mail, and file transfers became more widely known and used. Traffic grew in leaps. So, in 1987 the NSF awarded a contract to Merit Network, Inc. in partnership with IBM to upgrade the NSFNET backbone to T1-leased lines (1.544Mbps), which was completed in 1988.

This was the largest-scale networking project ever attempted to date. The backbone network included 13 sites, and its primary goal was to link the regional TCP/IP networks that had developed and wanted to interlink with other regional networks. MCI had joined the act, by this time, by helping to develop a network center in Ann Arbor Michigan, staffed 24 hours a day.

In 1990, Merit, IBM, and MCI spun off a nonprofit organization known as Advanced Network and Services, Inc. to manage the NSFNET backbone and to upgraded it to a 45Mbps T3 backbone. This was completed in 1991 and, at that time, con-

(Continued)

nected some 3,500 networks. The term "the Internet" now meant being connected to this NSFNET T3 backbone.

In 1993, the NSF wanted out of the backbone business. But how would they extricate themselves without the collapse of the ever-important Internet? The answer was the Network Access Points (NAPs). These were similar to a concept introduced a few years earlier by the commercial entities that were creating commercial TCP/IP backbones for use for networking with or without the Internet. In that earlier concept, commercial businesses such as MCI, Sprint, and others agreed to create physical locations where their backbones would intersect via NFSNET, so traffic could pass from one to another TCP/IP network.

However, the NAP proposal would eliminate NFSNET from the picture and instead allow traffic to intersect directly from one commercial network to another. Several physical locations would be created for network intersections.

In this way, anyone could develop a national or international backbone and sell connectivity to it, using the NAP as a juncture to gain access to other networks. A single backbone would not be burdened to carry all traffic.

In 1995, three NAPs were in place: one in San Francisco, operated by PacBell; one in Chicago, operated by Bellcore and Ameritech; and one in New York, operated by Sprint-Link, who was already overseeing international connections for the NSF. A fourth NAP was added in Washington D.C., operated by Metropolitan Fiber Systems, Inc. With the NAP system in place, NSFNET was laid to rest and officially shut down in April 1995.

Packet-switched networks are ideal for data because data can be broken into small sizes, sent whichever way the routers determine to be the quickest, and reassembled on the other end. This is exactly what TCP/IP does, where IP is the protocol that takes care

NOTE   *The converse of a packet-switched network is a circuit-switched network. This is where the connection seizes the entire channel from origination point to destination and must maintain that connection in order for communication to occur. An example of a circuit-switched network is a standard voice telephone call. A circuit-switched system can work with a packet-switched network, that is, the Internet, but it isn't as efficient as having a packet-switched connection from the start when it comes to data transmissions.*

of the decisions necessary to route the packet, without a care of what is contained in the packet (such as the sequencing number) and TCP handles breaking up the data into packets and reassembling them on the other end as well as verifying that the packets were transmitted properly and requesting that packets be resent if they were not.

Each packet can take a different route to get to its destination, even if the packets are part of the same message stream. If a packet gets dropped, or if its IP checksum or TCP checksum are not correct, TCP requests that the packet be resent.

NOTE   *Of course, IP's checksum only takes care of the IP portion of the packet—routing, and so on—but TCP's checksum takes care of verification of the content of a whole TCP/IP. This ensures that packets will all arrive at their destination, but doesn't mean that an application will perform well. However, an understanding of how the primary transportation protocol works is essential when planning for a high-performance application, and when diagnosing performance woes.*

How these routers know what to do with each packet is the logical structure of the Internet. Furthermore, many times these routers are working away without a human being in sight; if performance problems occur it can take a while for them to be detected and solved. The situation adds up to one in which performance can ebb and flow, depending on which Internet Service Provider is being used, how much other traffic is being sent over the Internet and over the particular routers your packets are using in a given moment, equipment problems, and myriad other factors.

Understanding NAPs

One of the biggest of the "other" factors that can affect performance is that packets may need to travel to a geographically distant spot, just to return a mile from its origination. For example, someone in Boise, Idaho logging onto an extranet server in Denver, Colorado may actually be sending packets to Chicago or San Francisco before they get to or return from Denver. This is due to the Internet's backbone structure. With an understanding of that structure, the extranet developer will be in a better position to evaluate performance issues and solutions. Because of its unique backbone system, some of the solutions that may be obvious for standard network performance problems simply won't work for the Internet. Here's why.

As we mentioned, physically, the Internet is a bunch of packet routers dutifully trying to deliver packets that are sent to them. In between these routers is a backbone, or in actuality, a handful of backbones, each one belonging to a different owner, including the U.S. federal government, some of the telecommunication providers such as MCI and Sprint, and some of the bigger, international ISPs such as UUNet, BBN Planet, and PSINet.

All in all, about a dozen backbones exist, if a backbone is defined as a T3 telecommunications "pipe" interconnecting with all of the other major backbones (a concept that we will explain more fully in the next few paragraphs). More backbone providers are coming on board each month, it seems. For instance, @home, cable giant TeleCommunications Inc.'s Internet service, is now also connected to other backbone providers.

Backbones are, for the most part, used to carry the traffic of other, smaller tributaries, rather than being an onramp to the Internet itself. The large commercial providers that own these backbones—T3 lines operating at speeds of at least 155Mbps—sell space on the backbone to smaller providers, who sell space to smaller providers, and so on. In fact, in the Gold Rush atmosphere that the Internet has created in the mid-1990s, a mind-boggling 7,200+ ISPs have sprung up to offer access. Yet, obviously, each does not have its own backbone. This makes the vast majority of ISPs middlemen (and, of course, suppliers of myriad other services such as Web site development or hosting).

In four spots in the world, these T3 backbones have major intersections called Network Access Points (NAPs). Physically, a NAP is a room with a bunch of heavy-duty routers connecting to a powerful switch, or series of switches, that allows traffic to move from one backbone to another. Technically, it is the switch itself that is the NAP. The exchanging of Internet traffic in this manner is generally referred to as "3peering."

These NAPs are located in San Francisco, Chicago, Washington D.C., and near New York in Pennsauken, NJ. Each NAP is run by a different entity. The San Francisco NAP is run by PacBell; Chicago by Ameritech and Bellcore; D.C. by Metropolitan Fiber Systems, Inc. (MFS); and the Pennsauken NAP by Sprint.

These four "official" NAPs are not the only place 3peering takes place. They are supplemented by some strategically located "unofficial" NAPs, owned and run either by the U.S. federal government or by MFS.

In fact, MFS's D.C. NAP was absorbed as a fourth official NAP after its use as an official NAP became increasingly widespread. MFS was already in the business of setting up commercial, citywide fiber-optic data networks long before it became a NAP operator. The idea of its networks was to create public regional WANs that allowed organizations to connect to branch offices (or others) less expensively than running their own leased lines within the city.

MFS still offers such services today, known as the Metropolitan Area Ethernet (MAE). Several MAE locations double as unofficial NAPs in which two or more ISPs have agreements with NFS to switch data from one backbone to another; others are primed and ready to service ISPs with an interest. The MAE site in San José is probably among the busiest MAE-turned-NAP. In fact, MFS refers to the D.C.-area NAP as MAE East and the San José site as MAE West (even though PacBell's official NFS-sponsored NAP lives just up the freeway in San Francisco). Still, MAE West is largely considered the unofficial fifth NAP.

Beyond these five points, 3peering occurs in some six other places. Some of them are other MFS MAEs and others are run by the federal government and deal most with military or NASA research traffic. These government sites are known as Federal Internet Exchange (FIX) points. FIX-EAST is located at the University of Maryland in College Park, MD, and FIX-WEST is located at the NASA Ames Research Center at Moffet Field in Mountain View, CA. However, FIX sites do not have the congregation of ISP direct connections as the official and unofficial NAPs do. MFS also operates MAEs in Dallas, Los Angeles, Houston, and other cities.

Each NAP basically performs the same task, switching, meaning they providing temporary connections between one backbone and another so that packets can be delivered. Incidentally, switching is *not* routing. The routing function is performed by routers which are owned, operated, and configured by the ISPs. ISPs must actually have *peer agreements* with every other backbone operator in order to set up shop at a NAP and commence 3peering. They must work out how the routers from one network with operate with the routers from another, and so on. ISPs also pay a substantial fee to be interconnected at a NAP, which is one reason why a backbone may never be a mom-and-pop ISP venture.

Another important concept about the NAPs to understand when thinking about Internet performance issues is that each is run by a different organization that uses a different methodology to perform the switching function. Not surprisingly, each employs its own "pet" methods. For instance, two of them employ their own implementation of Asynchronous Transfer Mode (ATM) switches: PacBell at the San Francisco NAP, and Ameritech at the Chicago NAP. ATM allows NAP customers (the ISPs) to pass TCP/IP traffic across the NAP backbone at broadband speeds between 45Mbps (for DS3 access) and 155Mbps (for OC3c access). The NSF requires that backbone and NAP traffic operate at speeds of at least 155Mbps.

NAP operators are continually working to improve the speed and performance of their site. For instance, PacBell is working on faster ATM switches and technologies and scouring the offerings from other vendors. It plans on offering Switched Virtual Connections (SVCs) in 1997, rather than its Permanent Virtual Circuits (PVCs) between ISPs. PVCs are preset point-to-point or point-to-mulitpoint switches, whereas SVCs are dynamic links between ISPs. These speeds are always being increased as faster-performing equipment becomes available. The PacBell NAP has recently acquired equipment from Cisco that will allow them to switch OC12 lines at an astounding 62Mbps.

In fact, all of the NAPs are doing their part to ensure that they are *not* the bottleneck. Operators aim for their NAPs to be up and running more than 99 percent of the time and, although much of the management is done remotely, they do have staff and systems in place for the execution of this lofty goal, including computer security methods.

However, think of the jackpot at stake for the hacker who penetrates a NAP and then installs a sniffer! Although the NAP operators would never admit that such an event could occur, some TCP/IP backbone providers have told us that many an undetected sniffer exists in these spots.

The Great Performance Cloud

If the extranet is using the Internet as its transport method—as most are—then extranet performance is at the mercy of the same performance issues as any other packet speeding its way along an Internet backbone. These performance issues are affected by how traffic is handled by backbones and what it must do to cross a NAP "bridge" onto another backbone. Because of the many paths a packet can take and the many other factors that can affect a data stream's success, pinpointing the exact cause of Internet performance problems is a cloudy affair.

Let's describe this in more detail. We all know that the backbone and its NAPs are not what most of us use as an onramp to the Internet. Instead an ISP will have one or more—dozens to hundreds for the larger ISPs—of 1.544Mbps T1s extended from the backbone. These become available as dedicated connections to companies or as a means to connect a group of smaller 56Kbps lines and *plain old telephone service* (POTS) modem banks. Envision the human cardiovascular system with three to five hearts and you'll have the schematic of a typical backbone (with each NAP acting as a heart). The rooms where T1 POTS connections are linked onto the backbone is an ISP's *point of presence* (POP). Large ISPs have POP locations throughout the United States and sometimes throughout the world. Small ISPs have only a single POP location. In any case, POPs are how most of us connect to the Internet.

So most traffic starts at a POP location. If an extranet user has a POP account on a different backbone from where the extranet server resides, the chance for performance problems rises significantly. Depending on the geographic location of server and client, traffic may have to travel through several routers to get to the NAP and then through several routers to get to its destination. Each hand-off represents a chance for something to get messed up.

If all the packets do not arrive properly, TCP must ask that a particular packet be resent, which doesn't exactly enhance speed and performance, but may not degrade it much, unless the packets are traveling across crowded territory.

This brings us immediately to a second critical concept of Internet performance: a packet's route cannot be controlled and it may have to travel to an area where a lot of traffic exists. Such a situation is sometimes perceived as a "brownout" where Internet traffic is so heavy in an area that a performance degradation occurs.

We're very fond of analogies, so here's one to describe the brownout situation. Picture the streets surrounding a football stadium. A person will have to deal with traffic on the day of a big game, even if that person's destination is the restaurant across the street from the stadium and not the game itself.

If an extranet application is linked to a company's Web home page and the home page is incredibly popular one afternoon, extranet surfers could be affected.

The Wrong Solution

Oddly enough, one solution that may *not* cure the brownout problem, or even enhance performance as much as common sense dictates it should, is the dedicated T1 line. Don't get us wrong, a T1 line represents a huge performance gain over, say, 28.8Kbps POTS. It's the dedicated part that doesn't gain much of a performance advantage.

This gets back to the concept of the Internet being a decentralized packet-switching environment—not circuit switched. Many of us are used to thinking of bandwidth in terms of circuit-switching technologies. That is, if a company leases a T1 line, that 1.544Mbps of bandwidth better be available whether it's being used or not. However, the Internet does not create an end-to-end channel connection. It simply sends packets to the nearest router that will route them on their way until they finally land at their destination.

So, even if a company hoards an entire T1 to itself—which it may truly need for any given burst of packets—this does not create a clear "channel" to the "heart" of the Internet where bandwidth is guaranteed. There is *no* channel and *no* heart.

The misconception over this issue comes from the fact that with circuit-switching networks a connection is made until it is broken. With packet switching, traffic is bursty and therefore so is the "connection." This means that while a company honestly may need the whole 1.544Mbps to send its extranet's applications thick and numerous packets, it will only need that bandwidth for an instant. Then, the T1 line sits around waiting for another burst, which in no way equals a performance gain.

The next burst can come from another company or another server sharing the T1 without any performance degradation at all. ISPs commonly connect to the backbone with a single T1 and yet sell T1 connections to numerous customers.

In fact, some research says that a single T1 servicing a packet-switching network is equivalent to about 14 circuit-switched T1s. That is, up to 14 T1 connections can be sold from a single T1 connection with no performance degradation to any.

ISPs understand this. So, even if a company has a T1 connection from the POP to the company, chances are the T1 connection from POP to backbone is being shared by multiple parties. That's okay from a performance standpoint as long as the ISP is carefully tracking usage and not grossly overselling, which can be determined from a usage report. We will discuss this shortly.

What Can an Extranet Creator Do about the Cloud?

First, extranet creators need to understand that the cloud exists. Ultimately, the best Internet performance will occur if the server and the client are on the same backbone. This can happen if both parties have accounts with the same ISP or with different ISPs that rent space from the same backbone.

Second, extranet providers can choose ISPs carefully and also follow the ISP's performance closely. The key to this is the usage report.

Usage Reports

How does a company know if the connection to the Internet is being choked by too much traffic? The ISP should be able to share those statistics via bandwidth usage reports. These are statistics that show the peak times and overall usage of the ISPs Internet connection. Remember, however, that the smaller the ISP, the more likely it has one or *more* layers of middlemen between itself and the backbone. It must get usage reports from the backbone supplier and that report is only going to reflect the ISP's area, not the bigger backbone picture. However, if any kind of a consistent bottleneck occurs, this is the area where it is likely to be—simply because it is where all of its users' traffic consistently travels.

We need another analogy to explain the situation. Automobile accidents are twice as likely to occur within a mile of the driver's home than anywhere else. True, this could be attributed in part to a tendency to drive on autopilot on this most familiar stretch. But, statistically speaking, it has more to do with the fact that we are on those roads more than any other. So, the odds of an accident there increase over, say, the street with the expensive restaurant that a person visits once a year.

The same situation occurs with traffic to and from an extranet's home of sorts, the ISP.

Still, ISPs that own their own backbone should be able to give a company a bigger picture of usage both stemming from the POP and on the backbone, if that ISP is willing to share such data.

When requesting usage reports, companies should be sure that they cover a typical two-week period. Avoid periods where there was likely to be extremely heavy traffic (like during an election) or unusually low traffic (like the period between Dec. 25 and Jan. 2). A usage report may, however, cover only 24 hours. Again, try to get several "typical" 24-hour periods.

In either case, the important points of a usage report are its peak times, and information such as how much capacity is being used. For instance, a peak of 80 percent during the hours of 8 to 10 A.M. might be okay if usage during the rest of the day is, say, 54 percent. Average usage of 80 percent or more throughout the day is a warning the ISP has some capacity issues that should be resolved.

Usage reports should be reviewed on both the incoming lines used by the company and the outgoing lines from the ISP POP to backbone.

Outages and Other Internet Failures

Another reason we have gone to great lengths to describe the Internet networking infrastructure is to lay to rest the popular claims that the Internet is primed for collapse. It isn't, and it can't be because there isn't one backbone any longer.

However, that doesn't mean that Internet users don't experience outages, downtimes of their backbone suppliers. Outages occur on occasion just as they occur with the regional telephone companies. Undue amounts of traffic that eddy around a specific Internet address also tend to cause packets to be dropped. Packet losses from such "congestion" can be as high as 10 to 40 percent. TCP, which includes a mechanism for requesting that dropped packets be retransmitted, can make the congestion problem worse, especially if the application doesn't really need every packet in order to function, such as video. (We'll talk about an alternative to this shortly.)

The Internet Engineering Task Force (http://www.ietf.cnri .reston.va.us), the closest thing we have to a guardian of the Internet, has recently created an Operations and Management Area that will look at management issues, of which outages is a part. President Clinton also promised to throw money at research for building faster backbones.

But these are still some far-off solutions that won't help extranet developers who need a rock-solid solution today. Several do exist, however. One is simply not to use the Internet. Along with alleviating a lot of security concerns, direct dial-up connections to a Web server through a secured dial-up server will also shift the burden from the Internet to the regular phone lines.

However, recent reports (http://www.atis.org/atis/nrsc/whatsne2.htm) on Regional Bell Operating Company (RBOC) service have concluded that about 33 million customers over the past three years have lost access to the public switched network for an average of five hours due to outages. That's 30,000 customers a day in the United States. So, such a shift may not be the ultimate answer either.

Another option is to set up the extranet application on a private, commercial TCP/IP backbone supplier. There are several companies that have large TCP/IP backbones. Think of them like intranet outsourcers. The drawback of course is that it significantly increases the investment that one or more parties to the extranet must make in order to participate. These companies charge significantly more than ISPs do for connections to the Internet.

Another solution might be to take advantage of some of the performance guarantee services that large ISPs have begun to offer. ISPs such as Apex Global Information Services, Inc. (AGIS) allow end users to place redundant backup servers at key POP locations. The idea is to guarantee fault-tolerance and acceptable performance levels by routing to mirrored-image servers. If one server goes down, is overloaded, or is the victim of a brownout, the other can pick up the slack. Of course, double the servers costs a lot more money. AGIS bills this service as CooLocation, a premium service for those with the need and the money to spend. Expect more ISPs to offer such value-added service as the 7,200 out there today converge into a more reasonable number that the market can sustain.

Network Performance Problems

Of course, the Internet isn't the only network involved in many an extranet application. The company's own network may also play a part. As such it is important to make sure that the network doesn't suffer performance problems as a result of any extranet application, and that the network is in good shape.

Network Capacity Planning Basics

As with any kind of capacity planning, the three steps involved are: (1) Get empirical data on existing performance. (2) Model expected loads caused by the new application. (3) Test actual loads against the results expected from the model and, of course, make adjustments.

The first part is the easiest. Information on network performance should be obtained by network management tools. Similar to the usage reports from ISPs, network performance tools will chart out usage, peak times, heavy use segments, and other performance metrics. Data should be collected over a number of days, or even over a year, if seasonal traffic has a big effect on network usage.

If such data is showing the network at capacity or near capacity, it's time to invest in the infrastructure so the company can truly take advantage of new technologies, such as an extranet.

Several Solutions

Don't panic if this is the case. It doesn't necessarily mean yanking out all of the Ethernet wiring and cards and moving on completely. A lot of times a company can add significant performance to an existing LAN with a forklift upgrade.

Some solutions here include perhaps creating a Fiber Distributed Data Interface (FDDI) ring, strategic placement of switches, and installing "blocking" systems that help keep bandwidth-intensive applications such as Internet phones from taking more than their share.

An FDDI ring for the servers (sometimes called a server farm) is a good idea for medium to large-size companies. Some consultants quip that 80 percent of the traffic is created by 20 percent of the devices. That 20 percent is mostly servers. Servers should be equipped with 100Mbps Ethernet network interface cards. They can also be placed on their own high-speed fiber ring backbone.

Like the Internet backbone architecture discussed above, this allows traffic to trickle down from where it is heaviest to where it is lightest, with the heaviest sections having the most bandwidth. Such a solution is a far better use of resources than to have everyone on the same network segment.

Switches, then, can be strategically placed in front of the server farm, which will boost the performance of your network segmentation scheme if the bottleneck was occurring at the servers. Switching creates temporary connections between one network segment and another and is one of the fastest ways to send packets on their way. Other high-traffic segments may also need their own switch.

Blocking systems can be accomplished by placing bandwidth-heavy extranet applications on their own segments, rather than distributing them throughout. For instance, an intranet phone can be on its own segment, although physically these phones are placed strategically throughout the company and/or on a segment open to a partner.

One other solution that is beginning to be developed by vendors such as Cisco is a technology Cisco calls *tag switching.* Because packets can be dropped if a router becomes overloaded and its cache fills, routing vendors are looking at ways to ease a router's load. One way is tag switching, in which IP routing marries Asynchronous Transfer Mode switching. Remember, ATM is currently being used in two of the nation's four NAPs, so it has proven itself to be a competent solution to Internet network woes. The idea goes something like this: ATM switches are integrated under the hood of Internet routers (i.e., IP routers). Perimeter routers at the intranet or at the ISP examine the header to determine where each IP packet is headed and then assigns it a tag corresponding to a predetermined multihop route from its adjacent router switch to another router switch.

Then the router switch uses the tag as an index to the router's tag table. This table tells the switch which outbound port to queue the packet. It also gives the packet the new tag needed for the next switch. The process thereby eliminates the need for each router along the way to examine the packet for the destination address and to then look up that address in its burgeoning routing table. Tags can be used to switch packets with traditional switches, if

ATM is not available. But if it is available, router switches can move even more quickly through the process.

Cisco isn't the only one working on a way to switch IP rather than exclusively route it. Ipsilon Networks, Inc. is researching IP switching. Bay Networks, Inc. is also developing integrated IP router switches specifically aimed at intranets.

The payoffs could be tremendous, as such a system would boost bandwidth performance much like a traditional switch boosts it today. This could mean that standard Ethernet networks would be much more capable of multicast (any-to-any) connections, even when using bandwidth-hungry audio or video applications.

For the dial-up extranet, the bottleneck would still be the modem. Even though modem vendors are currently working on ways to press modems to be 50+Kbps—nearly double today's speeds and approaching 56K leased lines—they are still a far cry from 10Mbits. Cable modems might be another solution for companies and partners located in the major metropolitan areas where cable operators have upgraded their broadcasting heads. It will be half a decade or more, however, before such upgrades reach rural areas ubiquitously (just as few RBOCs offer voice mail in such areas).

This discussion is, of course, a simplification of the process of network design. It is intended to make extranet developers think of how their work might affect the rest of the IS infrastructure, and offer some suggestions on how to overcome such problems.

Model Before Rollout

The second step of capacity planning requires some way to get feedback on the effect of an application before it's actually out there being used. Modeling tools for networks are extremely helpful for this, particularly those that allow what-if analysis. These allow you to play with variables rather than being limited to some kind of live feed.

For instance, the Marriott Corporation relies heavily on modeling in its application development process, a lesson learned from its mainframe days, although the company now uses a lot of client/server technologies. The key for Marriott is to carefully choose which bits of performance data will be used for the baseline data. That data should reflect both typical usage of network services and peak times, at least.

Once a baseline model is obtained, the effects of new applications such as those used with an extranet can be ascertained. However, the process is tricky. How do you model the impact of an application so it can be designed for minimal impact when the application doesn't exist yet? Modeling experts say start with an educated guess.

The truth is, the starting point *is* an educated guess. Make some assumptions about the application and, based on the empirical data gathered from the network management tool, conjure up the initial numbers.

For instance, if the extranet will replicate data to a middlenet server so that partners can be privy to certain Web sites, it is safe to assume that the only time network performance will be an issue is at the time the replication is done. That can probably be done at off-peak times, such as the middle of the night.

If the idea is to allow several partners, maybe those involved in a research project, complete access to the intranet, then one segment might be affected.

Once the model helps developers determine how to construct an application so that it minimally affects network performance, it is time to test. Testing should be done at the prototype phase, of course, but also at the production phase and from then onward.

Typically, applications that match modeled predictions on rollout won't start to cause a problem for at least a few weeks. After that, the power users will have mastered the new service and will be finding ways to use it more. They will also be performing unofficial training of other users. Within three to six months, the application will see a truer measure of its effect. So, it's important to test, test, test to thwart problems before they crash the network.

This may seem like a lot more work than anyone in the company has ever done for a Web-based application before. That could be true. Whereas Web sites can be built by someone who has never programmed anything before (and never will again), Interactive Web sites are really client/server development projects. Fail to treat them as such and they will almost certainly fail. That's not good for the company or its partners.

Feedback Tricks

On the other hand, a few tricks exist that will give a developer some feedback on network performance without installing a bunch of gadgets. Ping could be used as a gauge, for example. Any Unix system (as well as most NT systems) has a Ping command that verifies if other machines are "listening" and gives some statistics on how long they take to respond. Two identical machines on two different network segments that have significantly different Ping rates might indicate a congestion problem, for a test performed in the middle of the day. (A test performed in the middle of the night, when presumably no one is using the network, might indicate configuration problems, such as an old network card.)

Others advocate the old FTP gage. Using just about any FTP utility that shows file transfer speed, someone could FTP files around and then examine the FTP file transfer utility rates. However, some intranet performance experts advise against this trick—as the methods that various FTP utilities use to calculate rates cannot be relied upon.

Easy on the Graphics

A lot of folks think that the inherent speed of even basic Ethernet—10Mbits—is all that it takes to make sure intranet applications behave well. That's true for the company that uses its network for nothing else. How many companies do you suppose do that? Not many. Put simply, large graphics files can affect network performance. So, it is extremely important for extranet applications to go light on the graphics. Use only enough to make the page look professional. We'll cover some specific techniques for this in Chapter 4.

Sibling Protocols: TCP and UDP

Before we can delve into performance issues surrounding extranet applications based on HTTP, which comprise the vast majority of them, we need to talk about some performance issues that can arise from the use of applications that use other protocols.

Most of the traffic traveling across the Internet is using the TCP protocol, which is the protocol responsible for breaking a message into packets, and placing a header on the packet that includes the source, destination, and sequence number of the packet. This includes application-level protocols such as HTTP. However, if the goal of the extranet is to provide live video for conferencing or broadcasts, chances are that the HTTP over TCP combination won't be used. This is because with video each individual packet arriving intact is less important than a steady stream of packets arriving. Live video from an HTTP application, in fact, will probably use a technique called "streaming." Streaming uses the older User Datagram Protocol (UDP), which does not ask that dropped packets be resent and, consequently, does not keep checking to inventory arriving packets. Streaming video can be viewed as it is sent, rather than the extranet user having to wait until the entire video file is downloaded in order to be seen.

Any time UDP is used instead of TCP, it is important to note that missing packets will be presumed dead. So, if the collection of all packets is important, such as for e-mail, UDP should not be chosen.

On the other hand, if performance of a steadier stream of packets is more important than making absolutely sure all packets arrive, UDP might be a better choice. This does not necessarily mean the elimination of Web security, either. S-HTTP can support UDP just as it can be used with HTTP, for instance. However, SSL requires that a reliable transport method be in place—for which UDP does *not* qualify.

Web Server Performance Problems and How to Minimize Them

We've looked at the Internet and the network for performance problems. Since our research shows that most extranet applications are based on HTTP, the next step is to examine some performance issues of Web servers.

Hardware Performance Considerations

On the hardware side, servers need to be well-sized for the task that they are to perform. If the extranet will only serve a select few business partners who need access to specific Web pages or applications, just about any PC server will do, with a 486 or better processor and a good 16M of RAM.

On the other hand, should an extranet application be one that serves hundreds or thousands of clients and fields millions of hits per week, it faces a completely different set of performance problems. An example of an extranet application that falls into this category is an application that will perform Web-based service agreement support. Ideally, the salespeople will sell increasing numbers of service agreements and customers will grow to increasingly depend on the Web as a form of support. This could lead to those "millions of hits."

In between these two extremes lie most of the extranet applications being employed today. The key to knowing how much hardware a given application will need is in matching the capabilities of the server with those of the client and also with usage. A company should not use an old 386 server if its partners rely primarily on Pentium desktops. This will create a bottleneck at the server. On the other hand, graphics, text, and design that perform great on a screaming Alpha RISC box should not be used if the partner's clients are a bunch of 486SX machines. However, it is also important to plan for the future. If a partner's clients are likely to be upgraded sometime in the future, it makes more sense to start with enough hardware on the serve side to handle that upgrade from the start.

The trick is knowing how usage of the application will create performance demands. The secret once again lies in modeling.

We mentioned modeling in the section "Model Before Roll-Out" but want to go into it in more depth here. Modeling can involve complicated mathematical manipulations, much like encryption does. Bernie Domanski, president of Domanski Sciences, Inc., a consultant in Englishtown, New Jersey, and a renowned authority on modeling, once quipped to us that modeling was more than a little like rocket science.

Modeling comes in two forms: *monitoring* and *projecting.* Monitoring is gathering performance data and presenting it in graphical form. Projecting is taking that data and adding what-if scenarios to project how planned variables will affect performance.

A growing number of tools are coming out on the market to perform monitoring. These include Insight from Accrue Software, Inc. (http://www.accrue.com/), Analysis Pro 2.0 from netGenisis Corporation (http://www.netgenesis.com/), Internet Monitor from Optimal Networks, Inc. (http://www.optimal.com/) (a company that offers a variety of modeling tools for various parts of a system including the LAN, WAN, and server), and Patrol from BMC Software, Inc. (http://www.bmc.com/).

Of course, many of today's bona fide network management suites also provide performance metrics such as Spectrum from Cabletron Systems, Inc. (http://www.cabletron.com/) and the Tivoli Management Environment from Tivoli Systems (http://www.tivoli.com/). The latter includes a module called net.Commander for monitoring Web servers.

We could go on, but we'll leave the rest of the product roundup to Chapter 8. However, monitoring is only half the battle when it comes to modeling for performance.

The other is what-if scenarios. Ideally, the application is designed to perform well from the start, rather than built with fingers crossed and problems solved later at the monitoring stage. The surest way to make that happen is by using a modeling tool that lets a person add data to see the effect.

For example, if an application is to allow suppliers to bid on new contracts and it will reside on an existing intranet server, the modeling tool would take a baseline of existing performance metrics. Application developers would then do a rough prototype, enough to give them some idea of how much CPU power and memory various aspects of the application require. They would then plug those numbers into the modeling tool to get a feel for what would happen to the server, application, and other cohabitating applications if 10, 20, 100 people used the application at once. Programmers can then go back and tune areas of the application that hog too many resources, if such areas exist. Or it may be that to effectively support the application, developers will need to upgrade resources.

How Do You Know if You Even Need Modeling Tools?

We'd like to preach that *every* development project should engage in some form of modeling for performance. Statistics show that 80 percent of client/server projects fail, not because they don't offer the features needed, but because they perform unacceptably poorly. Modeling is one of those up-front costs that keep the whole project afloat happily. But these tools, which can be quite complex, also range in price from about $500 to over $100,000. A good rule of thumb is that a modeling tool should cost about 10 percent of the entire project's budget. However, a modeling tool may be worth more money if it can be categorized as an infrastructure expense, rather than as a part of this project. It can gain that stamp of approval if it will be used for other development projects and if the company has come to perform an increasing amount of application development rather than purchasing straight shrinkwrapped code or hiring out for such projects.

If this is a truly tiny project, then we realize it may make more sense to skip the projection modeling phase and use experienced guestimates based on the monitoring performance phase. This means good 'ole trial and error. Get the monitoring statistics, create a prototype, use it to gather more monitoring statistics, and so on. In its simplest form, modeling could be done through the analysis of the Web server log file. Many Web servers offer an *extended log file* ("elf") log format, which eats more disk space but logs much more information. Software packages, ranging from freeware to full-blown commercial packages, are then available to analyze this data. These include "wwwstat" (available at http://www.ics.uci.edu/pub/websoft/wwwstat/), and "WebReporter" from Open Market Inc., Cambridge, MA, (www.openmarket.com).

The trial-and-error approach is not efficient—as it could send programmers back to the drawing board to fix performance problems later—but it's cheap in terms of up-front capital expenditures and training time on tools.

Which Operating System?

Another area that's critical when planning for hardware performance is scaleability. A debate is raging right now over what types of scaling options are best, but most experts believe that some form of clustering is optimal. Clustering is a method of distributing the computational load among various servers. The idea is that each computer operates in a sort of CPU commune, where CPU cycles can be lent out to any processes requiring extra power. It is distributed computing at its essence and is a very powerful way of scaling hardware.

However, when it comes to Web servers, the debate on clustering immediately becomes a debate of operating systems. From a performance standpoint, the two primary candidates for most Web servers are Windows NT and some form of Unix. Surprisingly, a lot of Windows 95 machines are also being asked to be Web servers. But unless the Web server will be dishing out static information to a limited number of clients, we strongly advise against Windows 95 as a Web server operating system. This recommendation is made for several reasons. First and foremost, Windows 95 isn't a true multitasking machine. It assigns importance to each process, with foreground processes taking on less importance than background ones.

This greatly reduces any chance of high performance, as multiple users performing multiple operations on a Web server will wind up queued instead of served.

Also, Windows 95 was not intended to be a server, even though it includes some peer-to-peer networking components. Application development tools and sophisticated Web servers don't exist for this platform as they do for the others. And Windows 95 flat out isn't as stable as NT or Unix, which doesn't bode well for a server that is expected to be up 7×24. (Seven days a week, 24 hours a day.)

Still, for the extranet application that will rely on the occasional connection, or for an extranet extension onto a peer-to-peer intranet built with the TCP/IP tools that ship with Windows 95, it's important to note that the desktop OS can be an alternative.

However, for the more heavyweight extranet endeavor, the question remains, should the OS be Unix or Windows NT? The answer today depends on just how much you anticipate your application will need to scale and what kind of security and management trade-offs you are willing to make.

In terms of clustering, engaging a Unix server can be almost a sure bet. Clustering for various forms of Unix has been around for many years from the biggest names in computer manufacturing such as IBM, Digital, and HP. Unix clustering architectures have been used, pounded on, and proven.

A lot of performance data is available for any Unix server that supports clustering. Also, more free and shareware tools are available for every Unix platform than there are for commercially conceived NT.

On the other hand, Unix was designed as an open system. Although many Unix vendors have added considerable security features to their operating systems, Unix remains a hacker's favorite, for good reason. These open, complex, multithreading systems are far easier to crack than NT.

In fact, NT was actually designed to conform to the government's toughest computer security standards—the C2 rating. A C2 rating designates that a product conforms to the publication *Trusted Computer System Evaluation Criteria,* also known as the "Orange Book," produced by the U.S. Department of Defense's National Computer Security Center (NCSC).

The C2 rating is considered a sort of baseline testimonial to a product's security attributes. It covers implementation of access control, authentication, and auditing.

On the other hand, as far as clustering and NT goes, this technology is only now becoming available, with less than a handful of vendors shipping servers today that will support NT clustering. However, one of these vendors is Tandem Corporation, a company that has built its reputation on fault-tolerant clustering systems.

Microsoft is also currently working on an initiative to embed native clustering in its next version of NT—Cairo. The initiative, code-named "WolfPack," allows up to two 4-CPU servers to mirror and work redundantly. It's not the only initiative to turn typical Intel-based desktop into clustered workstations. In fact, Intel's intelligent 120 bus architecture has received the most nods to date. The 120 is a processor-independent technology that allows workstations to be clustered, even if they are running multiple operating systems, applications, and disk arrays. Such a cluster can be viewed and managed as a single system with a network management system that supports the bus architecture.

The upshot is that if you need immense scaleability immediately, we recommend going with a proven Unix system and servers that support clustering technology. Unix vendors routinely build clusters that span 100 different processors, through multiprocessor servers. NT can cluster, but at a lower level, more in the range of eight to ten processors.

Of course, Microsoft contends that NT can be scaled to lengths equal to Unix and that may very well prove to be true. However, few installations have yet tried it and, after all, NT is still a relatively young product. Unless your organization is an NT shop that will benefit from determining where its scaleability threshold is, it might be best to go with a proven system, if such power is needed.

However, if less than a full-scale attack is needed, NT offers a security advantage and earns our hearty recommendation.

Web Server Software Considerations

The choice of operating systems is going to dictate in a large part the choice of Web servers a company will make. Like any other product, performance differs among HTTP implementations of Web server products as well. The computer trade press runs ongoing "Web Server Shootouts." We urge you to examine such tests as they can offer a lot of objective performance data in an easily digestible and comparable manner. Of course, corporate users may want to augment these results with more real-world performance tests themselves. Fortunately, Web server vendors typically adhere in part to the "free computing" Internet culture of days gone past. That is, free evaluation copies will be available on the vendor's Web sites for such performance testing.

No matter how a company tests, the two areas that testers should watch closely are "average connections per second" and "average response time." The first will reveal how many connections a server can handle before it is saturated. This is important because monitoring software may not give the whole picture. Most monitoring software offers statistics on what a user did once connected, but will give no feedback on how many users were turned away.

But how many potential business partners will be denied access can be an important performance problem and one that a company may not even be aware of if it isn't a metric being watched. Generally, Unix systems running on RISC or SPARC CPUs will outperform any Intel-based clients here. In fact, such Unix boxes can handle up to six times as many clients in a test situation as Intel-based machines, with an Intel-based machine becoming overloaded at 20 or fewer clients if each is pounding out the page requests.

Another number to analyze when evaluating a Web server's performance is the average response time. This is the time it takes a server to dish out a page. Although most tests performed by testing centers and vendors will measure static Web pages, it is still an indication of how speedy the server is.

Many Web server home pages contain information about the performance of the product. Of course, each will be offering only such information, or analysis of it, that promotes their wares, but that doesn't mean such data is completely bogus. Shoppers should browse vendors' pages to discover what performance features each Web server offers and what kind of tests were performed to prove one Web server is "better" than another.

Extranet Application Problems and How to Minimize Them

Beyond the hardware, the application itself can be the performance dog. When discussing the application, the term "performance" now takes on two meanings:

1. The application performs the services that are needed and expected.
2. It also performs these tasks well—with high efficiency, few if any crashes, and no bugs.

We're going to walk you through a few strategies for ensuring that high performance in both its forms is part of your extranet application.

Managing Expectations

One of the hardest aspects for any technical person to master is the politics of a new implementation, and an extranet is loaded with politics. In fact, many a Web site is an extremely political creature. It is often under the domain of the marketing department, rather than the Information Systems department, for instance. This means that the most experienced Webmasters in a company may *not* know much about client/server application development. The intranet or extranet may be the first time that Webmasters and IS people collaborate. Therefore, intranets and extranets are often the first place that these two sides meet to battle it out over control of the territory.

Please prepare for these issues. To help you do so, we've compiled a list of helpful suggestions to get any extranet project off and running.

- *Place control of the project under the domain of IS people from the beginning.* One of the most expensive mistakes most companies make is to enlist Webmasters from departments other than IS. That's fine for page creation. However, once more advanced application development becomes involved, these Webmasters often have to suffer through woeful inexperience and discovery of the tried and true development practices already honed by IS. In contrast, the IS department already has the know-how to build high-performance applications, or at least has a stronger background to figure out how to solve such problems.

- *Reuse code wherever possible.* Along with centralized command comes the ability to leverage the work of all the players. If multiple departments are housing their own Web servers and their own Web applications, they should create a centralized database mechanism that is keyword searchable to keep track of who has developed what. This way code can be leveraged, time can be saved, and money can actually be made.

- *Include members of applicable departments on the prototype team.* If the company does have an official Webmaster from the marketing department, include that person in the development process, at least at the prototyping sessions. This is *not* just a nice touchy-feely suggestion to keep people's feelings from getting hurt, or to stop interdepartmental wars. It is actually the best way to create consistent-looking Web pages. Consistent Web pages are important, particularly when a Web strategy will cut across internal, external, and public lines.

◆ *Give people a visual prototype to work from as soon as possible.* This prototype should contain a proposed "look and feel" of the application but should not be a complete set of processes. For example, if an extranet application will be offered to service contract customers, create an initial page that represents the way the site will look, what items it will include, and so on. Allow the service contract department to review it, and if at all possible, let customers review the prototype too. (It doesn't do a lot of good to create a service for customers that doesn't offer them what they want and need.) Allow all parties to give feedback on the look and feel.

◆ *Define functions, not architecture.* This seems like a no-brainer, however, it is surprising how easily developers can get caught up in the how-tos before all of the what-to-dos are worked out or even discussed. Think of the functions as the program's directives. What is the experience that users will have with it?

  ◆ *Right:* The order status extranet application will offer a list of recent orders and allow customers to customize that list by date, PO numbers, and other variables.

  ◆ *Wrong:* The order status extranet application will make calls to the accounts receivable ODBC database, then use a CGI interface to create on-the-fly HTML pages.

  Why is this distinction important? Because developers should be free to come up with ways to accomplish the goals of the application. If they are restricted to carrying out a preconceived architecture, they will be precluded from developing better, higher-performing applications.

◆ *Define a scope of work.* By the end of the review process of the initial visual prototype, a complete list of functions should be in the hands of the application developers. Of course, even as we write the word "complete" we know that this list will be modified many times over before the project is done. However, sculpting out the scope of this project in the beginning so that changes require *justification* is absolutely essential. If the door remains open for *major* changes and shifts in perspective throughout the whole developmental process, the project can become a sinkhole in terms of man hours that eats up the vast potential ROI and reduces the payback to a pittance.

◆ *Define the attributes and constraints.* Although we do not want to limit the developers from finding high performance solutions, we also need to give them framework in which to find these solutions. For instance, a great solution to slow performance could be to beef up the hardware to the fastest workstation around. However, that workstation may be beyond the budget of this project. Therefore, the developers should be sure that they understand what their limits are and what the attributes are of the tools they have at hand. If the company has agreed to migrate its infrastructure to NT, then the operating system for the extranet server must be NT, rather than Unix; that's an attribute that should be made clear. Likewise, if the extranet application must run on a hand-me-down 486/66, that's a constraint the developers should know.

◆ *Provide ongoing feedback.* Another good idea is to set up a system where ongoing preferences can be ascertained. If two solutions are possible, which one would the team prefer? Be careful here, as the company does not want to bog down every decision with groupthink—making the group reign over the process. However, developers who can count on ongoing feedback can be sure that their application will meet expectations.

◆ *Manage expectations.* This is a tough one. Key to this is an understanding of how this project was sold to the various people that bought into it. If sales is funding the project, and they were told that it will increase incremental sales of services without a lot of maintenance and overhead, then the developers must be aware that this is a primary goal of the project.

Developers can then further manage expectations by not imbuing the project with possibilities that haven't been thought through. For example, developers shouldn't casually announce that the next step is to tie the order-status site to the procurement system, so an entire order can be automated. Such an announcement must only come after the technical, political, and security problems have been examined. A lot of developers think the inverse is true. That the best course of action is to find out if people want a feature, then go about building it. However, this relates back to the scope of work. Developers must balance the scope of work they have now before making promises on phase two. Take the most likely course that will allow the application to be modified when a future scope of work is thoughtfully defined.

At the same time, be sure that users have realistic expectations about the performance of the features that have been agreed upon, feature by feature.

Developing a Fast, Scaleable Application

With the first definition of performance under control, it is time for extranet developers to tackle the second definition, speed and reliability of the application.

As the Web becomes the platform of choice for ever more development projects, a knowledge base of Web performance is growing. Here we're going to offer some of the better, universal suggestions for creating high-performance applications.

The CGI Performance Hit

Contrary to what common sense might tell us, dynamic page generation via CGI doesn't necessarily produce a significant overhead.

Pages can still be pulled together quickly even when generated on the fly via CGI and the level of customization dynamic pages offer makes the millisecond delay worthwhile. However, when these pages don't zip out to the client quickly, it typically indicates a problem with the program itself, not the gateway.

For example, Perl scripts have a higher overhead and cause more of a performance hit than a program that provides the same function as an executable binary. That's because Perl is an interpreted language. It requires that the software running it interpret it for the underlying hardware, rather than allowing the hardware to operate the code itself. With an interpreted language like Perl, the interpreter itself gets loaded into system memory every time someone executes the application. This definitely causes performance issues.

In contrast, binary code, such as that written in C or C++, is run directly by the CPU. With binary code, there should be no more overhead than if a user ran the program at the command line, and very little more overhead if thousands of users are hitting it from all over the world. This makes it faster than interpreted code. The obvious drawback to binary code is that it must be developed specifically for the particular platform—Intel, RISC, SPARC, and so on. (This is one of the primary differences between Java and ActiveX.)

However, Perl has become a popular way to create CGI code for a lot of reasons. For instance, since Perl does not require compilation, it significantly reduces development time and consequently it allows fast on-the-fly changes/fixes. Developers also love how easy it is to use. Although it will always take a small performance hit over compiled languages, in most cases interpretation at runtime is plenty fast. The hit in performance can be offset in some instances by Perl's basic architecture. Perl was written specifically for handling text, which is a common need in any Web application. Perl can actually be faster in performing text-handling tasks than other languages.

So, for those who love Perl and want to continue to use it to write CGI scripts, one idea is to configure the Perl interpreter so that it remains loaded in memory, rather than having to be launched every time a script is executed. Take care to allow it to be loaded in memory only on machines in which access control is absolute; potential hacker access to the Perl interpreter is unnecessarily dangerous. Also be aware that many platforms do not allow the Perl interpreter to actually be loaded into memory.

In any case, lengthy scripts—particularly those that will be restricted over a plain old telephone service line—need every ounce of performance possible and should therefore be written in a compiled language. The same holds true for scripts that will need to scale to an extraordinarily large number of users and for scripts that will be handling a lot of graphics.

Increasingly, a number of object-oriented development tools are emerging onto the market that allow traditional three-tier client/server architecture to be built expressly for extranets and intranets. These include Progress Software's WebSpeed, Prolifics' Prolifics, and NetDyamics Studio. Three-tier architecture refers to having the application with three components: the client (which creates queries), the server (which holds the business logic and passes the queries to and from the client and database) and the database (which stores the data). Web-specific development tools that have many traditional online transaction processing (OLTP) database characteristics and have been duly dubbed by some as Internet Transaction Processing (ITP) environments. The components have been molded to fit the Web, of course. For instance, the client is the browser, the server dishes out the results of the query in HTML or Java—and sometimes even uses Java as the language to contain the applications business logic—code that tells the application what it is to do.

The huge gains of these products occur from the development end, which we will talk about in Chapter 4. However, from a performance perspective, complex applications developed using such tools should perform better, because such tools have been optimized expressly for this ITP task and because they ease a developer's work, so the developer can fine-tune an application better. The best advice is to test before building the full-scale application. Build a small portion of the application both in C and in Perl and see which one performs better.

Graphics Smarts

We've harped over and over again about restricting graphics on the extranet system but we realize that a certain number of graphics needs to be present in order to create a professional page. We also realize that graphics are a wonderful edition to text. So, we are not advocating the elimination of graphics altogether. But from a performance standpoint, less is more. Our rule of thumb is that pages should load in no more than 30 seconds when clocked against a 14.4 modem and preferably in 15 seconds when clocked with a 28.8 or faster modem. If the developer knows that the site will always be used over a network or other high-speed connection, clock the page using a 56Kbps connection, such as a leased line. To help extranet developers accomplish this goal, here are some suggestions on handling graphics.

Specifically, *dynamic page generation* should be limited to text. Try to avoid dynamic graphics. Because they are dynamically generated, they don't carry a standardized file name, which means that they don't cache well. The browser, not having a standardized file name to use as a comparison, won't be able to compare that file name to its cache list. Even though the image may be only slightly different with each reload, there will be no cache. Therefore, if an extranet user jumps on the site six times a day, each time that user will have to wait for the dynamic graphic to be generated. Talk about annoying!

Also, a large number of small graphics causes a bigger performance hit than a small number of large graphics because each graphic file requires its own HTTP session. So, *don't litter a page with a bunch of spot graphics.* If several small graphics are necessary to creating a corporate look and feel on a Web site, bundle them together into one medium-sized graphic.

Along the same lines as cautious use of spot graphics, *use image maps instead of separate graphics* for navigating the page. Always tell the browser that an image map is coming, using the optional ISMAP qualifier to the image (<IMG>) tag: For example, <IMG

SRC="URL" ISMAP>, then use the mapfile, either client side or server side.

The Graphics Interchange Format (GIF) supports 256 different colors, but *don't use more than four*. In fact, two is better, if using two colors doesn't violate the corporate color code. Every additional color has a compound effect on the time it takes to load a page. So, be sure you understand how to shrink your image files as small as they can go without sacrificing quality. For example, if an image only has three colors, be sure it is saved as a .GIF with only three colors and not as an 8-bit .GIF. This can be the responsibility of the graphic designers at a corporate site.

◆ *Create a caching scheme.* Cache the most popular lengthy pages of an extranet application in the server's memory to speed their retrieval. This sounds simple but takes a bit of planning because these cached pages will be bumped when users access less popular pages. An algorithm needs to be in place that will help the system determine which pages to cache and which ones to replace if they are accessed. This algorithm should *not* simply cache the most popular pages. The idea is to speed up access to richer pages which take longer to load. Therefore each page should be weighted with a caching value, which is determined by how popular the page is multiplied by how long it takes to load. The highest-weighted pages will be the ones to be cached. Lower-weighted pages will be replaced by higher-weighted ones after they are accessed.

Weighted Pages

Home page: popularity 100 × time to load .6 seconds = 600
Catalog: popularity 50 × time to load 45 seconds = 2250
Order page: popularity 20 × time to load 10 seconds = 200

- *Segregate servers.* Do not combine general information Web pages on the same server that is hosting chat software or videoconferencing. This will slow the performance of what should be speedy pages because resources will be hogged by these high-powered Web applications. If possible, place such resource-intensive applications on their own high-performance server.

- *Use redundant and/or clustered servers.* This is backup the server way. Have at least one alternate sever that can pick up when the performance of another lags, a process called distributed server management. This server may be a complete mirror used only as a backup or, better yet, it may make use of load-balancing software so that the two act like a minicluster. Such software includes Interactive Network Dispatcher from IBM www.ics .raleigh.ibm.com/ics/issfact.htm and Resonate Dispatch from Resonate Inc. of Mountain View, California (www. resonateinc.com). More servers can add to the cluster as volume of hits demand.

- *International performance.* Remember that not all countries have the high-speed telecommunication infrastructure enjoyed by the United States. If your partners will include international sites, keep applications as skinny and as fast as possible. If the extranet application will be used for high-bandwidth activities such as telephone conversations or video broadcasts, investigate outsourcing an intranet to a private TCP/IP international backbone provider such as Sprint or InfoNet.

Products that Minimize Performance Problems

We have compiled an extensive list of vendors that offer performance-enhancing products in Chapter 8 under the subheading "Performance Evaluation Tools." But before we shunt you over there, we want to give you some shopping tips for performance equipment.

Tools for the Web are developing and shipping at such a rapid pace that keeping up from week to week is a nightmare. For this reason, we believe in being a little more flexible when shopping for Web products than when shopping in other areas. For instance, we believe that using 1.0 versions of performance products may be fine. There may be areas in which such first generation tools do not work optimally, but if they actually increase your performance in the meantime, you're still better off than you were before.

However, in order to see if these products really work, testing is strongly recommended. Every performance product that is being considered should be tested in the following manner:

1. Get a baseline of where performance stands today.
2. On a sample system, engage the product and compare performance with the baseline sample.
3. Test for latency of graphics, load on the CPU, and disk space used and other performance metrics that will give you an idea if the product is worthwhile.
4. Run real-world tests in which varying numbers of people try to access the extranet at the same time, to get a performance metric.
5. Run real-world tests in which varying numbers of people try to access the extranet at the same time with the performance product engaged, to get a performance metric.
6. Perform ROI analysis of the cost of the product versus the performance gained (this is explained more fully in Chapter 7).
7. Engage the product first only with partners who might be willing to play "beta" with it for you.
8. Deploy the product only after a significant amount of gain has been shown and an acceptable ROI is the result.

Summary

Performance of an extranet application literally spans the globe. Performance problems that occur at the internetwork level, if the

Internet is used, may be the toughest to solve. The best way to do so is to understand that the Internet is a packet-switched technology and to sign on with a good ISP. Having partners on the same backbone is also a big plus. At the network level, performance problems can occur if the network is overloaded or if an application is too resource hungry. The way to solve the former is to use various methods of increasing bandwidth ranging from simple design techniques and switches to an all-out upgrade. The way to solve the latter is by prototyping and modeling, rather than developing via trial and error.

Even with modeling, developers should follow a lot of tried-and-true tips for creating sure-hit and super-fast Web-based applications. Finally, developers should carefully evaluate the true gains of new products that claim to minimize performance problems.

## chapter four

Managing the Back End

Closely knit with extranet performance issues is back-end management. Where as "performance" is a look at how an application behaves from the end user's point of view (functionality, speed, reliability, etc.), back-end management is a look at performance issues from an administrator's point of view (technical choices, maintenance, integration with other applications, etc.). Here we take a look at some of the problems that will be common to most extranet applications: those based on HTTP.

The Web: Ruler of the Internet

The World Wide Web operates in much the same way that human beings think, jumping from link to link, using images, sounds, and words. This has made it a very practical platform for most of the energy that is being poured into the Internet and its spinoff implementations, intranets and extranets.

For these reasons, the vast majority of extranet applications will ground themselves firmly in a standard HTTP implementation using TCP, gaining all that the Web has to offer and suffering all of its drawbacks. The number-one pro and con for HTTP is its statelessness. Statelessness is when each request, or action on the Web, stands on its own. Servers don't need to remember what happened with previous requests in order to service a new one, nor do they need to. Requests are what the server sees when a user clicks on an underlined link. Statelessness is the "Web" part of the protocol. It's what allows end users to jump from one page to another seamlessly and fairly error free (just as a person's thoughts might ramble from one subject to another on a lazy Sunday afternoon).

Statelessness is wonderful when the only goal is to read static information. However, as soon as a Webmaster wants to create an interactive application, statelessness becomes a problem. According to the guardians of the Web, the World Wide Web Consortium, W3C, (www.w3.org), "Statelessness is a mixed blessing because many potential Web applications, particularly extranet applications, need to track a history in order to perform."

The shopping baskets application presented in Chapter 6 is an example of this. It simply can't be done without keeping track of the history of a user's actions. Keeping track means one of two options: creating an enormous file on the server that keeps statistical information on each visitor or embedding a tiny bit of data on the client that keeps such statistical data. The latter is an increasingly popular method, and one that has been available for widespread use on the Web since Netscape Navigator 2.0. It is known as "cookies."

Cookies: Sweet Statefulness

CGI's scripting capabilities are a solid step in the right direction toward giving the Web the capabilities of a stateful system. It can execute scripts that perform consecutive requests. However, a problem remains: how does a Web site remember these consecutive requests, so that a modicum of history can be incorporated into an application? "History" is a critical element of electronic systems. It is, for example, the "save" command. Without it, many of the traditional types of programs cannot be performed. One of the answers is *cookies*—bits of textual information about the requests a particular browser made on a particular Web site held in trust by the browser.

Cookies, whose name comes from unclear origins, simply track state information on Web requests by storing small pieces of information within a browser for later use. That information remains stored on the client's hard drive, useful only to the server of the Web site that put it there. The information allows the particular

Web server to track requests that assist it in an application. For an in-depth look at this, consult Chapter 6, in which we present a shopping cart application that uses cookies.

Beyond applications such as shopping carts and custom messages, cookies can allow Webmasters to track which areas of the site people jump to, rather than counting random hits impossible to distinguish as a new visitor or one that was scanning the entire site. This is a valid use of such technology. How can Webmasters determine whether what they do is well received without empirical feedback?

Other common uses of cookies include the customizable Web site, an application that may be well suited for an extranet. In fact, both Netscape and Microsoft offer good examples of this on their Web sites, usually available just after you install their respective browser software.

Security Worries about Cookies

A lot of misconceptions about cookies exist, most notably that they are a huge security risk and/or an invasion of privacy. These types of concerns stem from a basic misunderstanding about what cookies are and how they perform.

Cookies do *not* collect personal information about the user or rummage around a hard drive. If users send personal information like credit card numbers or e-mail addresses to a Web server, the Web server could place such data into a cookie, without the user being aware that it has done so. However, cookies should be designed so that that information becomes accessible only to that one site; no other site can access cookie information deposited from another site. Information is stored as a string of numerals in files in a cookie file. The only clear words that will appear are that of the Web site. End users could simply delete the entries of sites where they performed credit card transactions, if concern overtakes them.

Also, cookies are *not* programs that execute on the client side. In fact, the only entity that finds a cookie useful is the Web server application that placed it there. It is much like a server asking the browser to hold a list of words. Without the script that says in what ways those words work together to be useful, they are just random words.

For example, during a visit to one of the best cookie sites on the Web, Andy's Netscape HTTP Cookie Notes (http://www. illuminatus.com/cookie.fcgi), we took advantage of a script that lets a user see his or her own cookie file. It was the first visit the new browser on Julie's desktop had made to the site, so the cookie file was set to: "Count=1"—hardly dangerous information about this author. What did the cookie allow Andy's site to do? It greeted us with a newcomer's welcome message. On the next visit, the browser's file was changed to "Count=2." This let the site greet us with a "welcome back" message.

Another misconception is that cookies are akin to Big Brother, tracking all of the online doings of a user. While it's true that cookies can be used within a site to get feedback from browsers, cookies are designed to be site specific. If a surfer downloads software from one site, signs a guestbook at another, reads some data on an intranet, and accesses an extranet application from the same browser, no one is keeping tabs. The cookie only talks to the one that put it there. The following is a sample excerpt from a cookie file on a typical Netscape Navigator browser:

```
# Netscape HTTP Cookie File
# http://www.netscape.com/newsref/std/cookie_spec.html
# This is a generated file!  Do not edit.
.msn.com      TRUE  /      FALSE 937396800   MC1
.foodstuff.com     TRUE  /   FALSE 882397291   MSF113     1
.excite.com TRUE  /      FALSE 946641600   UID    38373AA632B972CE
.isn.com      TRUE  /      FALSE 946684799   session    21475691
.toyota.com TRUE  /      FALSE 946684799   LT_UID     OonmtG3q1iH1G
.foodstuff.com     TRUE  /   FALSE 883801067   MSF102     1
```

Another security concern stems from early implementations of Javascript and Java, in Netscape Navigator particularly, that could allow hackers to run unrestricted programs on the hard disk, such as spy on hard drive information or collect an e-mail address. These problems have been fixed in current releases of Navigator. The fear that cookies are some kind of loophole back to these holes remains unwarranted.

Some security administrators worry about information that is embedded in the browser, not connected to an authenticated user.

This means that anyone using a machine with that browser is now in possession of the cookie. So, if a machine was used to access an order-status extranet site of a vendor, an unauthorized user could potentially use that machine and gain information about orders. Several simple security mechanisms can be employed to overcome this problem at the customer site, such as good access control measures and strong physical security policies. However, this also means that you should *never* store authentication information in cookies. You can use basic authentication instead. The difference is that cookies last, regardless of whether you restart your browser. With basic authentication, each time you shut down your browser all authentication information is lost.

Also, cookies include expiration dates, which means that a database of knowledge is not being kept by the cookie. When using cookies in an extranet, developers should be sure to establish an expiration date scheme that makes sense and actually works. It may be seen as a drawback, but since cookies are stored on the client, their expiration date/time is based on the *client's* computer time, not the server's. However, the initial expiration date and time is set by the server.

For example, if your company and server are in California and your customers are in New York, and you have your cookies set to expire in two hours, customers in New York won't even be able to use your application because the cookies will never even get set in the browser, due to the three-hour time difference. Still, the key to using cookies, particularly in an interactive application, is to have the cookies expire as soon as possible without disabling users from being able to access the application. For international customers, this might get especially tricky. You may be forced to use expiration periods of one or more days. On the other hand, if the information you are dealing with doesn't require extreme levels of security, you may think about higher expiration dates that stretch to days or even months. Such would be the case for the custom-browser application.

However, if you think that your customers will be using the same computer to access the same cookie-based application on a fairly regular basis, then their browser may be storing old information that no one really wants. If this is the case, be sure to reset your cookie values when a user enters your application.

Another worry stems from the fact that cookies write information to the client's hard drive. However, such writes are extremely restricted. Cookies are limited to entries of no more than 255 characters into a cookie file kept by the browser. Therefore, it is best to keep cookie information succinct and keep track of expiration periods so as not to contribute to overflowing the cookie limit on a client browser (this will also help save you from irritating technical support problems).

The sum total of these concerns is that many companies have set a security policy that disallows the use of cookies on company browsers. So, although cookies represent a safe and easy way to solve the technical problem of a stateless protocol, extranet developers who use the process may have some political hurdles to clear first.

Extranet developers must understand that such concerns about cookies exist and, when using them, spend a bit of time educating targeted business partners about the lack of risk. This may be a simple pop-up screen that directs concerned extranet users to a cookie FAQ. Several good ones exist, including Andy's page at http://www.illuminatus.com/cookie.fcgi. Or they may create an FAQ of their own which outlines how the site uses cookies and lets partners view their own cookie information.

Extranet developers should also be considerate in their use of cookies. We would advise against placing e-mail addresses, credit card information, or other personal data collected from the user in the cookie, particularly if the application could perform properly without it. It is much better to assign an end user an ID than to use an e-mail address as the ID. It is much better to ask the customer to type in the credit card number each time it is needed than to store it in a cookie in an effort to be convenient. Such precautions will keep undue concerns over the safety of cookies at your site at a minimum.

For applications aimed at specific partners, it might be worthwhile to check their security policy on cookies before spending time developing an application that depends on them. If the answer is "no go" on cookies, extranet developers can then try to educate these managers on cookies and hope they lift their ban on them. Or they can develop an application that offers cookies only as an option. Or they forgo the easy solution that cookies offer for a process that will be more generally accepted.

For instance, it is entirely possible to develop a state-tracking application itself. Several examples of applications exist where user information is tracked in a simple file, or even a full database, on the server. This is done usually either because cookies were not accepted or cookies had not yet been developed. For example, Cisco Systems developed an application for providing seminars over the Web. It included a user identification based on a database of customers. Session tracking occurred via the URL. The URL was passed to the database, and the database then generated a unique key that allowed attributes to be assigned per user. It was able to keep a history on specific users of the site without the use of cookies. Searching the net will often reveal scripts in your language of choice, sometimes without cost.

Scripts that keep track of sessions can also be stored on the server and used only while the browser is connected. There are some advantages to this approach. One is that expiration dates can be completely controlled by the server, as that is the only time and date that is relevant. There are a number of obvious disadvantages to this solution, however. One is that return visitors could not be recognized as such. Another is that it taps into precious server CPU and disk space resources if the server must keep track of every visitor's requests.

NOTE   *Both Netscape Navigator 3.0 and Microsoft Internet Explorer 3.0 offer the option of alerting users when servers attempt to set a cookie on a client. It can be set in Navigator by the Options/Network Preferences menu in the Select Protocols/Alert Before window, with the check box labeled Accepting a Cookie. This will trigger a pop-up box that alerts a client that an attempt is being made to set a cookie, what the values of the cookie are, and when the cookie will expire. It can be set in Internet Explorer by clicking on View/Options and the Advanced tab, then checking the box labeled Warn before accepting cookies (see Figure 4.1).*

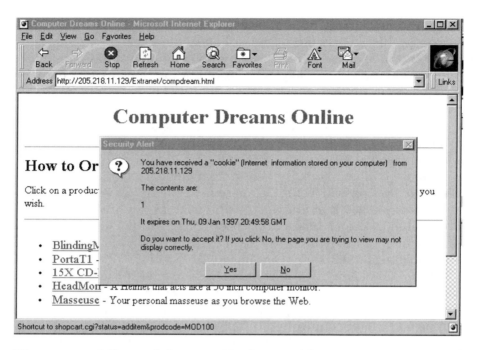

Figure 4.1 Microsoft Internet Explorer with option set to warn of attempts to set cookies.

Recommendations

We recommend the use of cookies in applications where state information is critical over other methods of providing state information today. However, we also advise extranet developers who use cookies to do so conscientiously. While cookies do not pose a serious security risk as they are being used today, the more constrained they are, and the less often they contain information a hacker could find useful, the more likely it is that they will stay safe. We believe extranet developers who use cookies should act as advocates of them, offering information on how their cookies are used and remaining sensitive to the fears that surround this solution.

ActiveX versus Java

Microsoft has a way of butting heads against the rest of the software development community, forcing developers to choose. When it comes to extranet development, this paradigm is replicated in the ActiveX versus Java debate. In truth, it is possible to have both of them work together, as Java is an interpreted language and ActiveX is binary code compiled for the Intel platform. But why would you want to? Either one can be used to create applets that will be usable by 90 percent of the owners of desktops (that's due to Microsoft's domination in the world of PCs). So, it essentially comes down to a choice between the two.

We've talked a bit about ActiveX versus Java elsewhere in this book; however, when it comes to making back-end choices for interactive applications, this one can be crucial. So we're going to delve into the subject a bit deeper now. Let's start with an examination of exactly what these two tools are.

Essentially, both represent a concept some call *component software.* This is reusable code that is downloaded and executed as needed by some sort of container. In the case of Web development, the container is a browser. The attraction here is that the component software allows the browser to do some very powerful and customized things, yet code is small and fairly easy to create, and it resides in a central place available to anyone with the right container (a browser) and a connection.

If the object of the executable is to perform a fairly simple script, the developer may want to embed executable scripts in HTML-defined Web pages. This is the function of JavaScript or Microsoft's Visual Basic Script. Some common uses for these simple scripting tools are pop-up alerts, form controls (such as requiring form fields to be filled in by a user), simple text animation, and so on. Again, as the development community begins to use these tools with more frequency, a greater store of free scripts and examples can be found on the Internet itself. We hope that you browse around for them.

However, if the executable is to be more complex, more powerful tools are in order. This brings us to ActiveX and Java.

ActiveX Primer

ActiveX, like Java, is actually a term that is used to refer to a set of technologies. These technologies include the ActiveX components themselves, which is what most of us think of when we talk about ActiveX applets, called ActiveX Controls. As a legacy of the technology's predecessor, Object Linking and Embedding (OLE), ActiveX Documents exist. These make non-HTML documents, such as Microsoft Excel or Word files, viewable through a Web browser. Active Scripting allows the developer to control several ActiveX controls at once, or even ActiveX controls and Java applets simultaneously from the browser. An example of a script is an ActiveX control that activates, calls, and executes a Java applet, then executes other ActiveX controls. A good source of information about ActiveX can be found at the Microsoft site (http://www.microsoft.com/activex/).

All of this rests on a development framework that manages the shared use of components. This framework is called the Distributed Component Object Model (DCOM) and it's important. It is gaining a growing acceptance as the component management framework of choice because it is from Microsoft, it specifically supports ActiveX controls, and it was available far and away before the next competitive framework, Java Beans. DCOM is a networked version of Microsoft's Component Object Model, a method for creating reusable code (known as objects a few years back; today, popularly called *components*).

Research suggests that Microsoft is more popular than Java with the folks who create Web applications for a living, such as Internet/intranet value-added resellers (VARs), the industry term for computer consultants. A recent study conducted by *VARBusiness* magazine showed that while about a third of the VARs surveyed use Java, and about 40 percent use ActiveX, few rely on Java as a primary component language. In fact, 21 percent of 112 respondents use ActiveX on a regular basis, as opposed to 9 percent who use Java. This is despite some serious security concerns about ActiveX components—namely, nothing exists to restrict them from being malicious and wiping out a surfer's hard drive or collecting personal information from another application, for exam-

Object Brokers and the Web

One of the more interesting wars being waged right now among Web application tool vendors is that of the development framework. Since the idea of components is to write them once then reuse them, issues of how to distribute, manage, and track objects become serious immediately. What do you do if two applications need the same object at the same time? How does an application find an object that might be stored on any number of servers? The answer is an Object Request Broker (ORB), a piece of middleware that takes charge of object management.

The ORB solution to managing distributed objects is not new. The Object Management Group (OMG) has been working on a means to handle the problem in client/server networks since it was formed in 1989. The standard it created for doing so is the Common Object Request Broker Architecture (CORBA). CORBA is currently in its second version and is at last gaining momentum, with dozens of products from as many vendors that implement it.

Microsoft's Distributed Component Object Model and its Component Object Model essentially compete with CORBA-based products. Not surprisingly then, Microsoft's Web rival, Netscape, has aligned itself with the OMG. Netscape announced that it would support the OMG's Internet Inter-ORB protocol as its object management development platform. (This announcement caused industry watchers to proclaim that the IIOP could become the basis for the future of HTTP, largely because of Netscape's support of it.)

A lot of finger pointing and bickering has ensued through the latter part of 1996 and early 1997 on this topic. Much of it was criticism of Microsoft for hoarding COM and DCOM as proprietary standards. In October 1996, Microsoft announced that it would turn these standards over to The Open Group standards body (www.rdg.opengroup.org), and hence give

(Continued)

COM/DCOM to the world. The Open Group is best known for its Distributed Computing Environment (DCE). DCE is a standard for all sorts of distributing computing issues such as access control, and name services. However, Microsoft has dragged its feet on actually doing so. Vendors in the OMG camp said that Microsoft's entire open systems gesture was laughable, and accused Microsoft (known for the occasional federal investigation into unfair trade practices) of withholding key parts of its technology, such as Win32 APIs.

Microsoft countered by saying that Webmasters will be protected, no matter how the process of opening the standard ensues, because products will begin to emerge that will bridge COM/DCOM and CORBA. In fact, the OMG is currently working on a Request for Papers (RFP) that does exactly that. RFPs are the mechanism by which the development community creates its technology standards. After an RFP is put out, the public is free to submit papers that document ideas of how to solve a particular technology problem, in this case, a bridge between COM/DCOM and CORBA.

Extranet developers who plan on investing heavily in objects for Web applications should watch these developments closely, as this war will determine how cross-platform objects can be handled. A good source for staying tuned is the OMG's Web site at www.omg.org.

ple. One of the more famous incidents that demonstrates the potential security threat of executable code such as ActiveX was demonstrated by a group of German hackers who call themselves the the Chaos Computer Club (http://berlin.ccc.de/WarmWelcome.html/). In February 1997, Chaos claimed to have built an ActiveX component that would conduct a phony money transfer on PCs running certain financial software. The club demonstrated the control in action on German TV, German media reported. Microsoft officials were quick to point out that no reports of the wayward ActiveX control were actually reported, but the potential power of the technology in the wrong hands remains obvious. Microsoft has attempted to combat this security concern, not by restricting the capabilities of the controls, but by instituting a method where control authors can sign their work and be held accountable. (See Chapter 2 for a broader discussion of this.)

One of the reasons for its popularity with this hard-core development crowd (despite security issues) is that over 1,000 ActiveX components are already available for reuse from itself and third-party developers, Microsoft touts. We give you a taste of these in Chapter 8, in the section on ActiveX. Also, the lack of restrictions on controls make them able to perform in some extremely powerful ways. The DCOM framework allows developers to better manage their controls, once they are created, so that they can be efficiently reused.

However, ActiveX has another major liability attached to it— platform dependence. As compiled binaries, ActiveX controls must be written for specific CPUs and operating systems. Until recently, the Intel/Windows platform was the only one supported. At the end of 1996, Microsoft announced support for Macintoshes. It has continually announced that it plans further support for Unix.

For extranet developers who know that their partners will be using Windows PCs or Macs, ActiveX remains a sweet option, considering how many components are already available (many are not free, though). But for extranet developers whose partners may be using other platforms, ActiveX is not a viable option for essential interactive elements. Also when making this important choice, developers should remember to keep the future in mind: will a company's partners *always* be using the same platform? Is there evidence that ActiveX will gain enough popularity that platform dependence will not be an issue?

Java Primer

ActiveX controls compete directly with Java applets, but the means by which Sun Microsystems' Java accomplishes its executable code differs considerably from Microsoft's ActiveX. From an end user's standpoint, Java applets are interpreted, not compiled. However, from a developer's standpoint, Java applets are compiled. They come in the form of FileName.class, which is the binary compiled code, and FileName.java is the source code that gets compiled by the developer. From there, the Java interpreter within the browser interprets the source code for the platform. In Chapter 3, we talked about the performance trade-offs of compiled executables versus interpreted executables in our section on CGI performance. The same holds true for Java versus ActiveX. Java applets will have a greater lag time than ActiveX because the interpreter must be loaded into memory and then creates an extra layer of processing between the PC's browser and its CPU.

Yet an interpreted language offers a distinct advantage over ActiveX—platform independence. This means that developers can write a Java applet once, and any platform that has a Java interpreter can use that same code—no more porting on the part of the developer.

Here's how it works. Every Java-enabled browser contains an interpreter, a Java Virtual Machine (VM). The VM knows what platform it lives on, be it Windows, Macintosh, or Unix, and it can listen to Java and interpret it to that platform. When a user activates a Java applet, the VM is loaded and executes the code, making it understandable to the platform it resides on.

Platform independence isn't Java's only benefit. Because a Java applet can only be executed in its own VM, it is a much more secure application. The VM is restricted from performing certain tasks, like writing to the hard drive. In addition, thousands of applets are also available for this platform (see www.gamelan.com for the premier database of sample Java applets and applications). Furthermore, Java is a full-fledged language. It has been said that Java combines the best of various languages such as C++ and others. It is a language that is rather different, not so much in syntax but in structure and terminology. So, C++ extranet developers will still need to spend some time climbing a learning curve when they initially work with Java.

Also, ActiveX and Java are not mutually exclusive for a Web application—just for an applet. In fact, developers can mix and match ActiveX components with Java components, allowing developers to shop from a greater pool of stock components. This is because Microsoft has created its own VM, used within its Internet Explorer browser. Microsoft officials contend that this implementation of a VM has become the de facto standard for a Windows Java interpreter, and it has been adopted by other companies who embed Windows Java Virtual Machines in their wares, such as Borland, Symantec, and the Powersoft division of Sybase. What makes this particular Windows VM so attractive is that with it, any ActiveX-supported browser can run Java applets from within an ActiveX framework. Therefore, ActiveX Scripting can be executed by the browser. Microsoft has also developed a server component, the ActiveX Server Framework. It includes a number of Web server–based functions such as the security schemes (like Authenticode), database access, and other tasks.

Sun Microsystems is none too pleased with adaptations of the VM. The creators of Java fear that such a tactic will lead to the same incompatibility problems that has splintered Unix and kept it from becoming the world's preferred operating system over Microsoft Windows. Of course, Microsoft denies that its implementation of the Java Virtual Machine specification is less compatible with Java applets than any other virtual machine. Still, we believe that a basis definitely exists for Sun's fears. While developing our own Java application for Chapter 5, we ran into some compatibility problems. Our Java application worked fine with all browsers except the commercially available Internet Explorer 3.0, which gave us a Java "language verify" error. Problems such as these nullify one of Java's biggest selling points—write the code once and have it available to any platform.

This situation immediately leads to another concern that building slightly different virtual machines will allow Microsoft to continue to dominate the desktop industry. That is, if a developer wants access to the tremendous installed base of Windows users, it must license the Windows VM from Microsoft (the same strategy that Microsoft used so successfully with Windows, and which landed it under the scrutiny of the Federal Trade Commission for alleged illegal and monopolistic practices). Such a situation is not in the best interests of the commercial community, who have finally been handed the reigns over computer technology with the mass adoption of the standards-based, democratic Internet, rather than vendor-based technologies.

Sun is combating any further adaptations of the VM by Microsoft (or others who may be tempted) with an initiative it calls "100 Percent Pure Java." The idea of 100 Percent Pure Java is to create a standard set of APIs which will assure Java developers that if they write a Java app, it will run on any VM. A suite of more than 50 tests in the Java Developers Kit is intended to ensure that entities that have licensed and embedded the Java Virtual Machine build compliant implementations. Independent testing, sponsored by Sun, as well as certification and branding are all part of the program. Over a hundred companies are in support of the initiative, including a slew of traditional Microsoft adversaries such as Apple Computer, Inc., IBM, Oracle Corporation, and Netscape Communications Corporation. More information on the initiative can be obtained on Sun's Java Web site at http://java.sun.com.

Extranet developers should be aware of this contention among major market players over VM implementations and that it could mean that Java applications developed today may not work with all Java-enabled browsers.

Recommendations

We are going to cop out on you here; developers may not really have much of a choice, based on the restrictions that each tool has. If the application must be accessible to a wide variety of platforms, the security benefits of using an interpreter are desirable, and a performance degradation is acceptable, Java is the choice.

If the application will be used only by Windows or Macintosh users (although a Unix version will be forthcoming), every ounce of performance is mandatory, and the application can be used by other types of containers than just Web browsers, ActiveX is the right choice.

If none of these items poses a restriction for your company, the choice might come down to a matter of style. We recommend experimenting with both Java and ActiveX and seeing which one fits the developer's preferences. C and C++ programmers may prefer working with a true language, Java; however, we must warn you that its unique structure may make for a steeper learning curve. We include a Java application in Chapter 5 that illustrates its usage. Visual Basic lovers will probably prefer ActiveX.

Building Human-Friendly Extranet Web Sites

Perhaps one of the biggest issues when it comes to Web sites, in our view, is making them human friendly. Cookies and cool applets won't excuse a basic visual design that frustrates, confuses, or overwhelms the user. Although an extranet may be mostly text, its great lure is that it is essentially a visual tool. It relies on a graphical user interface (GUI). Like any visual tool, it should be created to work according to the way human beings process and relate to images. At the same time, the Web, as an electronic beast, has its own unique graphic design issues such as hyperlinking (a person can't hyperlink between one page of a magazine and another, as a comparison). As the Web gains in popularity, a growing reservoir of knowledge is emerging from which graphic design techniques will make the most out of this unique visual experience. So we want to spend some ink here covering what we believe to be the best of them.

Use Graphic Design Principles for the Printed Page as a Guideline

Because most extranet applications are sparing on the graphics, making sure that the graphics chosen "work" is even more essential. Since no "Fish Cam" will be around to be a wow factor, the page has to speak for itself. (The exception is, of course, the extranet designed for video applications and/or graphic applications, such as an image database. Those applications notwithstanding, this section applies more often than not.) Here's a rundown of a few good graphic design tips. Consult a professional for a more personalized approach.

Top 10 Indicators that a Webmaster Needs to Hire a Graphic Designer:

No. 10: The Webmaster doesn't know the difference between coral pink and fuchsia.

No. 9: The Webmaster believes that text that runs to the margins is efficient use of space.

No. 8: The Webmaster prefers the Courier font.

No. 7: The Webmaster emphasizes important text with exclamation points.

No. 6: The home page features a picture of the Webmaster's dog.

No. 5: Every page has a different banner.

No. 4: HTML supports 256 colors and the Webmaster has used all of them.

No. 3: The Webmaster has placed a spot graphic on every third line of text.

No. 2: The Webmaster thinks that italics are stylish.

And the No. 1 indicator that a Webmaster needs to hire a graphic designer is that the Webmaster chose a red and purple paisley print as the site's background .GIF.

Tips for Effective-Looking Written Communications

Be consistent in fonts, placement of banners, image maps, and so on. The visual design should prepare users for what they will see elsewhere. In an extranet especially, the object is to create a natural, intuitive environment, which can *only* be achieved with a consistent visual image. Construct a template that will apply to your whole site. A sample is shown in Figure 4.2.

Choose a readable font. Most browsers default to the Times New Roman font. However, it is now possible to set the font using the HTML language, and more and more browsers are supporting this new HTML extension, including Navigator 3.0 and Internet Explorer 3.0. We recommend using this new extension for better control of the end user's experience. However if you do use it, just a hint: Courier, the typewriter font, is *bad* for pages read onscreen.

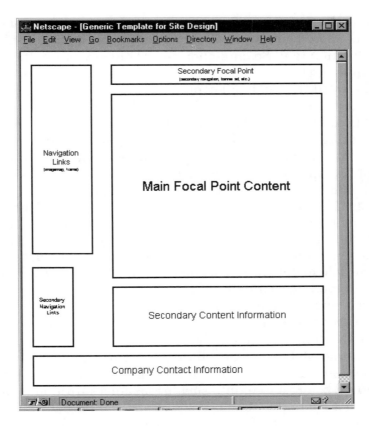

Figure 4.2 A generic template for site design.

So is just about any type of serif font—fonts with a lot of elaborate extra strokes on the ends of letters, such as Times New Roman. (It always surprises us how many software applications come with Times New Roman as the default font, as it is much harder to read onscreen than any sans serif font, like Arial.) In print, a serif font can be effective, but that is due, at least in part, to the increase of leading (space) between lines of published material versus onscreen material. Onscreen leading can be much tighter (12 points) than it is in most books (around 14 points). This, however, makes it essential that the fonts used be clean looking, rather than elaborate.

Use variety in fonts sparingly, and only for emphasis, not as a matter of style. The visual effect of a change of consistency is to draw attention to it. So, an italicized or bolded word in the middle of the sentence will be read in a person's mind with emphasis, as will a word written in all capital letters. Of the three, italics are the hardest to read onscreen, while the all-capped words are the easiest (and they also represent the strongest emphasis, like someone shouting). You should never use all capitals for regular information on your pages—it strongly contradicts one of the basic rules of "netiquette." Many companies have a policy of using all capital letters for every mention of the company's name or its products. This is tacky because it is an overt abuse of visual emphasis. We strongly recommend avoiding such tactics. At the same time, changes in fonts can be a great way to draw attention to some text within a longer passage. For instance, a *sidebar* in an online article might warrant a change in font, to visually underscore that the information is an aside to the main story, or the word *new* might be bolded and enlarged.

White space is good. Text is actually pretty ugly, even with an attractive font. Too much of it is even uglier than a server error message at 4:59 P.M. So, go easy. Margins should be wide onscreen—at least 1 to 1.5 inches on either side. Every screen of text should be broken up into smaller sections surrounded by white space. Definitely one passage of text should not run more than a screen and a half without white space. This means that the page will avoid exceptionally long paragraphs. Long paragraphs that go on for fifty lines or so can always be broken into smaller ones. Literary great James Joyce aside, more than the occasional use of long paragraphs indicates poor writing and should be avoided on that count alone. White space allows text to be the eye's focal point. It is a Webmaster's friend.

Make sure that body text centers on the page. We are talking about the block of text, not centering every line. Sometimes, when too many very short paragraphs are used (like one-sentence paragraphs) text winds up bunched up at the left of the screen. This is visually unappealing. As with extremely long paragraphs, too many short ones also indicates poor writing.

TIP *HTML tutorials abound on the Internet. Use your favorite search engine with the text "HTML Tutorial" and you will probably find the answer to every possible question you can think of concerning HTML including tricks and techniques to make text look beautiful on the screen.*

When it comes to supplemental graphics, go for quality, not quantity. We've pretty much pounded this idea in at every plausible moment, so it's not much of a surprise that it's shown up here as well. However, we do want to emphasize the word *quality* in this tip. Make sure that your graphics are legible on systems that fall below the capabilities of the average screaming PentiumPro.

Avoid cryptic icons—pictures should be self-explanatory. This is one of Julie's pet peeves. The graphical user interface was supposed to represent a huge leap in computing because it played on human intuitive visual responses. However, icons got carried away somewhere in the late eighties and no one could figure them out. Icons were then imbued with little text pop-up tags next to them to explain what the pictures meant. *Excuse me,* but isn't that nasty old text exactly what the icons were supposed to replace? A picture with the text pop-up is fine for applications such as MS Word because a user will get used to the application and soon know what the button does. But it simply doesn't work for Web pages because you have so many first-time users who don't want to learn the buttons. So, if icons are not going to be self-explanatory on the page, make the text the point and a graphic the accompaniment. While Internet Explorer 3.0 does automatically show a pop-up tag indicating the name of an HTML element, not every browser will be using that browser and it doesn't excuse mystic graphics anyway.

Avoid cartoons. Generally speaking, cartoons give an impression of lack of sophistication. If this is the image the company wants, then cartoons are a good choice. Otherwise, use photo images, word art, more detailed drawings, and so on.

Graphic Tips that Apply Especially to Web Sites

Use only one focal point per screen (which is going to be about two per printed page). A focal point is an item that draws a person's attention. On the Web, these tend to be multimedia stuff such as .GIF files, Virtual HTML images, photographs, .JPEG files that beckon to be played, and so on. Web sites that have a lot of interesting interactive or visual files all over the first screen tend to be overwhelming. The user doesn't have a single focal point that draws attention. The effect is more like a headache than an attraction.

Turn a home page into an easily understood directory. This isn't a magazine. Don't make users wait for a big background .GIF, a beautiful photograph of the Webmaster, then give them only a vague clue as to what's inside. Visuals should offer concrete content. For instance, list the page's contents in an image map right up front. The home page should also set the stage for consistency throughout all the Web pages. For instance, an image map that jumps to other sites, servers, or pages within is a great choice on a home page. Then be sure that each page also uses the *same* image map in the *same* spot inside, so a user can navigate through a site without having to reorient to each new page.

Put at least two screens of meaty text on every internal page. Less than that, and the visual effect will make the person wonder why the Webmaster bothered to put up such an informationally thin page. The page could hold the winning numbers to next week's lottery, but the visual effect is that there is nothing important here. The exception would be a specialty page, such as a home page, index page, contact information page, and so on. These should *not* be bogged down with a bunch of extraneous stuff—just an image map, search engine, selected links, or other means to draw folks to other parts of the site.

Link Management

Probably the single most tedious aspect of managing any Web-based application is link management. Pages must be altered, moved, updated, renamed, and so forth on a frequent basis. That is, after all, one of the major advantages of using an electronic medium over a printed one—easy, on-the-fly changes. Often such changes lead to broken links. Link management will therefore be an issue even with an extranet site, where, presumably, fewer links exist compared to a public Web site. Furthermore, bad links, like any performance issue, are far less acceptable on an extranet than they are on the Web.

Link management should be considered at the design phase and then administered on an ongoing basis. Here we've compiled a number of tips to help the Webmaster perform this potentially monotonous task.

Architect links. Use an automated process to verify and change the links that appear throughout the site. For instance, if the contact page information was moved or the file updated and renamed, that new link must be updated on every page. In Unix it can be done with the "sed" command. A number of commercial HTML "grinders" are also becoming available for Windows and Mac link control. At the same time, when a user surfs upon a broken link, have that link activate a page that will notify the Webmaster of its existence. Instead of the usual SERVER NOT FOUND, a CGI script can offer an apology, send an e-mail notice of the problem to the Webmaster, and allow the user to send an e-mail as well so that service to the partner can continue.

Don't go link crazy. Be selective regarding what you link to on every page for the extranet. Remember, this application probably has a different goal than a public Web site. Most published Web sites exist to provide information (although they may also perform other tasks, like electronic commerce). However, this may not be the primary goal of the extranet. Therefore, links, while still useful, should be qualified according to the goal. For example, if an extranet application is to provide order status information to customers, it might also link to an online catalogue, a reference page of sales contacts, or service contract information. But too many links on a page can be extremely frustrating to users—they might feel that they don't know where to begin or that they are missing something by not visiting every link.

Use relative links. This is similar to architecting links. In the HTML code you can give a link either a relative URL or an absolute URL. An absolute URL gives the full address of the link (for example, http://www.mycompany.com/somedir/somehtml.html). A relative URL simply gives the directory and filename of the link (for example, somedir/somehtml.html). When the browser sees that there is no "http" in the front of the URL it assumes that the address is the same as the page you are currently viewing, therefore the full URL is not needed. The main advantage here is that if you move directories or move servers you can often avoid that step of changing, or "grinding" links. Since the links are relative they should work regardless of what directory or server they are placed on. Set up a structure that works for you and be consistent. Create a "root" directory for your site and plan out the files or directories that will reside beneath the root. Often it is not possible to do this fully, since you may be dealing with certain CGI applications that require an odd remote directory, in which case HTML grinding may become necessary. But many developers are recognizing the inconvenience of the proprietary directory and are adjusting accordingly. For example, Allaire's Cold Fusion originally required a strange API URL address for their template files, which made it difficult to link to. But their latest release allows you to place the template files right in the document directory and the server will process them correctly.

Segregate links from the application. If a company wants to offer its partners a lot of linked sources to other sites, pages, or whatever from the extranet application, it may be better to offer a *resource page,* rather than sprinkling a large quantity of links throughout every page. What's wrong with links (we are talking about a Web application, after all)? The issue is that links take people away from where they are. If you've built this application to serve them, and then put in a bunch of distractions, guess what? Users are likely to get distracted. Let them accomplish their tasks first, then guide them to linked resources.

Note an "off-site" link as such. This is a nice touch. Because a company's page will be designed with consistency, including links back to a home page or to the interactive application's start page, users tend to feel that they can wander at leisure around the site and still get back in one jump (rather than backtracking with the back button). So, if a link will take the surfer off-site (and away from the consistent banner or image map), a warning icon on the link is a courtesy. It also helps to remind users to stay focused on achieving what they came to the site to do, and explore links afterward.

Employ same-page (relative) links for long documents. As little as a year ago, the choice for long documents was to either force surfers to scroll through page after page, or break them up into a bunch of links and force users to wait while the pages loaded. A better solution that has cropped up recently is the relative link for use in this circumstance. This puts an index at the top of the page of links that all point to sections of the same document. The result is that POTS surfers can begin reading the document while it continues to load. When they are ready to read another section, it's there and waiting. No lag time occurs because a new page has to load, and users still get the benefits of hyperlinks. Be careful with the graphics here—these types of pages are much better off being mostly textual. If users want to view another section before the page is done downloading then the plan has backfired, since they now have to wait *longer* for some other unwanted section to load its graphics before they can view the desired section. Remember: as far as file size is concerned, text is *nothing* compared to graphics.

Consider engaging a document management system for HTML. Document management vendors such as PC Docs, Inc., of Burlington, MA (www.pcdocs.com), Novasoft Systems, Inc., of Burlington, MA (www.novasoft.com), Interleaf, Inc., of Waltham, MA (www.ileaf.com), and Documentum, Inc., of Pleasanton, CA (www.documentum.com) have jumped on the Web bandwagon with systems that automate this task. Document management offers features such as check-in/check-out of documents, automatic revision matching and updating, and myriad others. Such systems are ideal for extranet applications where a large number of documents will be served, or where accuracy is imperative. Consider the company that is using an extranet application to automate the bidding process for a custom bolt. The specifications of that bolt change from product to product and from model year to model year. If someone unknowingly posts an outdated specification, the company will receive inaccurate bids at best, and at worst, inaccurate bolts. Document management systems have features that ensure that the right version of a document is where it's supposed to be. Also, many of these systems include dead link finders to aid you in link management.

Database Integration

We end this chapter with a brief look at how the database fits into the back-end picture, should an existing database be used. Among the biggest questions is whether the database back-end will be replicated or live data will be used. The more secure choice is, of course, replication. But then that carries some management issues. How does an administrator make sure that the extranet database remains accurate? If changes are made to one database application, they must then be ported to the other. For companies with distributed networks, these problems are old issues. However, if the extranet application is the first-time database replication and will become part of the company's architecture, we urge you to seek knowledgeable help in establishing the back-end management.

Issues involved include:

◆ When does replicated data get dumped (hourly, daily, weekly)?

◆ If discrepancies among databases appear, what will be considered the "gold" source of accurate data?

◆ Where will the database physically reside? Ideally, from a performance standpoint, it should reside close to the extranet application. However, this may mean that it no longer resides physically close the database administrator. Will the administrator manage the database remotely (in which case strong access control mechanisms must be in place) or will someone on site be trained in its care?

Introducing a database into the extranet adds an extreme level of complication and deserves in-depth analysis. We mention it here only to alert extranet developers to the potential difficulties. We highly recommend further research in this area.

Summary

Performance issues can be defined as how the extranet behaves toward the people using it. Back-end management is how it behaves toward those who created it. The two behaviors can vary dramatically. That is, the extranet may function and perform well for users but be a maintenance pig for administrators. This chapter suggested numerous tips and solutions for an easy-going extranet, concentrating mainly on HTTP, as it has emerged as the monarch of all Internet technologies.

One of the biggest issues for extranet developers is overcoming the Web's inherent static nature. Cookies are a popular solution for this. Cookies work well and are easy to create and brainless to use. However, cookies have an enormous and unearned security stigma associated with them that makes them somewhat politically incorrect. Developers are sometimes forced to ignore an effective problem-solving technology when using it runs counter to some partner's security policies (hence the application may be rejected).

Another back-end development choice centers on applet development tools. The two contenders are Sun Microsystems' Java and Microsoft's ActiveX. Each has distinct and competing advantages and disadvantages. It is becoming possible to integrate the two technologies, as standards for doing so are being hammered out.

Graphic design and link management both remain issues of back-end development. Sound graphic design must be built into an extranet from the beginning. Link management is an ongoing issue, but one that can be automated with a bit of forethought and the right tools. Finally, we end the chapter with a plea to consider database integration deeply, seriously, and with the help of someone with experience. Database integration with Web sites can be done easily with the many tools available, but this can create real maintenance headaches later if it is not well planned.

## PART TWO

Applications

## chapter five

Java "Bridge to Suppliers" Application

Java, over the past year, has become increasingly common to the everyday Web page. Last year, predictions bordered on mania as to how popular the new language would become. We have to admit there was a lot of merit in those claims. Furthermore, we think that Java's popularity will only continue to increase as a broader segment of the developer population learns to master its complexities and its power.

At present, Java applets and applications are primarily used to spruce up Web pages, with animation and fancy visual effects. But people are realizing more and more that Java is capable of higher, more complex tasks. Because of its well-designed object-oriented features and its adaptability on the Web, Java is leading the wave of creating an open distributed environment and will indeed benefit business processes in the long run. Searching the Internet will provide a vast amount of information about Java, along with sample applications and demonstrations. The latest information about the language itself can be found at http://java.sun.com. One of the best resources for Java examples can be found at Earthweb's Gamelan site at http://www.gamelan.com.

Here we present an example application that helps demonstrate some of these abilities. Specifically, the goal of the "Bridge to Suppliers" example application is to allow a company to carry out business with its suppliers. Suppliers can visit the site, at which point they are presented with a list of the available jobs or products that the company needs. This information is extracted from a database, possibly even the same database that a company uses on a day-to-day basis to handle this information, or a replicated version of it, rather than a newly developed supplier information database. By reusing the current materials ordering systems, a company increases its return on investment and significantly lessens the development load.

Information on desired services, products, or raw materials (which we lump together under the term "job") is placed into the database by the company using its regular method (such as an intranet application or database data entry front end). Suppliers then view the specifications of these jobs, which can include a diagram, if appropriate. Finally, the supplier submits a bid for the job they are interested in. The bid is stored directly into the database, and can be reviewed at the company's convenience. Here is another opportunity for an intranet application—reporting on submitted bids.

The approach taken with this application merits some discussion. For example, if Java is unable to write to a local hard drive, what are the security concerns? When a bid is submitted, how do you use Java to connect to a real database?

Applets versus Applications

First, let us distinguish between a Java applet and a Java application. An applet is what the browser is sent by the Web server. The applet is what appears on the screen of the Web browser. It is a chunk of compiled binary code that the browser can interpret, regardless of the platform that the client browser employs.

An application, on the other hand, is similar to an application written in any other language, such as C or Perl or C++. It is compiled and *stands alone* on a system that has a Java Developer's Kit (JDK) installed. In the case of our application, it is the behind-the-scenes worker that users never really see, like a regular CGI script.

What most people are interested in is creating applets, for Internet use. The reason for this is that applets can far exceed the capabilities of standard HTML programming. This has its price, however, taking its toll in terms of the speed of the applet and the ease of development. Some Java applets can take what seems like years to load, and the time it takes to create an applet is infinitely greater than the time it takes to create an HTML page. Both of these issues, however, are being attacked by companies that realize the potential of Java. Microsoft, for example, offers their *just-in-time* (JIT) Java interpreter (in their own Internet Explorer browser, of course) that may help speed up the time for a Java applet to execute (see http://www.microsoft.com/kb/articles/q154/5/80.htm for some information, or search the Knowledge Base at www.microsoft.com). Other vendors are also attempting to ease Java performance issues. These include products such as Symantec's Visual Café Pro (www.symantec.com) and Aimtech's Jamba (www.aimtech.com), both of which allow developers to easily create applets by providing an interface to the lower-level Java language. This is along the lines of Visual Basic or C++, which provides a form editor, allowing the programmer to design the layout of the page (including buttons and lists and panels, etc.) and then plug in the interactive events that occur behind the scenes. We realize that these types of products are a recent addition to the world of Java, and therefore need some maturing before they can approach the polish of C++ tools, but their emergence in the market at this early juncture in Java's evolution bodes well for the Java development community. Furthermore, they are popping up in abundance and improving rapidly.

Connecting to the Database

This application brings up one of the most interesting questions about using Java as a development tool. Let us look at some general methods for connecting to a database over the Internet.

Early in the creation of this type of Java application, the developer realizes that the task of simply creating a Java applet that will connect directly to some database is not that straightforward. A database server must exist somewhere to act as a *mediator* and pass information back and forth between the database and the requesting application. Essentially, two methods are available to Java developers by which they can create a Java applet that will connect to a database.

The first is a two-tier design, as shown in Figure 5.1. Here the Java client communicates directly with the database server. This is rather difficult to pull off, as the programmer needs to drop down

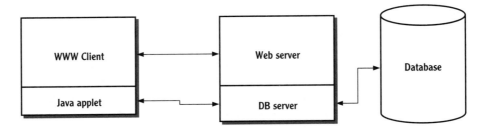

Figure 5.1 An example of a two-tier database architecture using Java.

to the database protocol level in order to communicate. It is much more work than it is worth, in our opinion.

The alternative is a three-tier solution, as shown in Figure 5.2. A separate application acts as a gateway between the client and the remote database server. This allows communication to the database server in native client/server protocols, as well as user-defined communication to the client Java applet. This is the approach used in our example application in this chapter. A more in-depth discussion of client/server database design on the Internet is available at http://www5conf.inria.fr/fich_html/papers/P23/Overview.html.

For our sample application, we have employed the three-tier model. This requires that a *separate* application is in place that runs on the server as a CGI process in order to connect and inter-

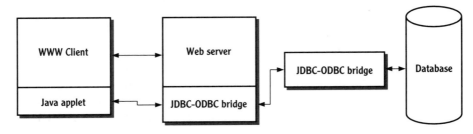

Figure 5.2 An example of a three-tier database architecture using Java.

act with the database. Now here's a stray thought: this application certainly does not need to be written in Java. It could be written in any language of choice, as long as that language had the capabilities to connect with the database. We could have even used proprietary products such as Allaire's Cold Fusion to perform these functions.

However, because we wanted to give you the maximum Java experience with these sample applications, we decided to do the whole deal in Java, simply to demonstrate as much of its functionality as possible. We therefore have two Java "applications." One is the *applet* that gets sent to the browser, which includes the user interface form. The other is the Java *application* that runs as a CGI process on the Web server.

The database applet was written to use the JDBC API for Java. Like ODBC, JDBC provides a way for programmers to connect to databases using Java. JDBC is available from Javasoft (part of Sun Microsystems, Inc.) at http://splash.javasoft.com/jdbc/index.html. JDBC is not necessarily a Java version of ODBC—it is actually a way to bridge Java to ODBC (you will also need the JDBC-ODBC bridge, available from Javasoft). Since we are firm believers that a wheel invented is worth using, we want to point out that simply providing the translation from Java to ODBC calls allows programmers to connect to any ODBC database necessary for use with the application. At the time of publication, JDBC was certainly the most prominent of Java database connectivity tools. In fact, several vendors are getting their feet wet in this new market, including many of the Java development vendors listed in Chapter 8. The best approach is to browse the Web pages of those listed as well as spending some time surfing the Web to find a tool that best suits your needs. We outline some strategies for finding and evaluating tools in Chapter 8 as well. As does the Order Status application in Chapter 6, this application uses a Microsoft Access database.

As an end note, Remote Method Invocation (RMI) deserves some discussion. One central problem that must be overcome by applets connecting to a database is the World Wide Web's inherent statelessness. Each request made by a client establishes a new connection to the server. RMI solves this problem by maintaining a connection between client and server. This persistent connection is also socket independent; therefore you do not need to program for a specific UDP or TCP socket. An excellent discussion of RMI can be found at Bill Bilow's Web World, http://www. geocities.com/SiliconValley/Park/9841/. The reason why RMI has not gained much popularity is that no major browsers support it (at the time of publication). Look for RMI to dramatically gain popularity as soon as it gains support in the major Web browsers.

The Application

We assume that the developer has a general understanding of the Java language, although expert-level knowledge is not required. Furthermore, this example application, like the other sample applications in this book, is certainly not meant to be the ultimate solution to a company's needs. It is merely presented as a starting point for further development and fine-tuning. Specifically, the example applet and CGI application demonstrate many of the fundamentals of Java as well as some of the more interesting advanced features.

Upon loading the applet, a window is established that represents the interface to the applet. A list of available jobs is initially retrieved from the database, and presented in the list box. A user can then browse the list of available jobs, retrieving more information about each job with a single click of the mouse (Figure 5.3). One advantage here is that this interface is the sole screen involved. Unlike standard Web interfaces, there is no need to jump to a separate Web page to view other details. Also, a user can view a diagram of the available job with another mouse click. This brings up a separate window with the diagram in it. The additional window shows off another useful interface feature of Java.

When users find a job that they feel is worthy of a bid, they can fill in the required information, including the actual bid price, and submit that bid. Upon submission, a new entry in the database is created. Separate modules can then be created (using Java or any other type of Internet database integration method) on the company side that allow for viewing and processing of these bids. The job and bid database used here is extremely simple, as shown in Figure 5.4.

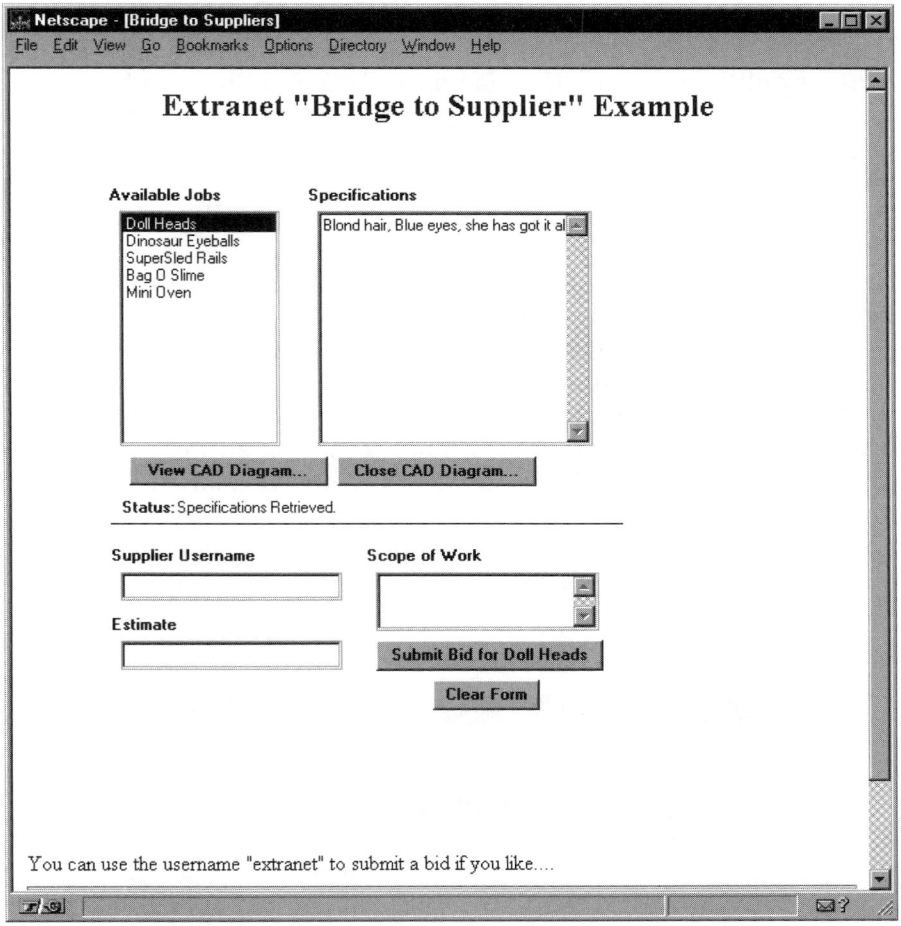

Figure 5.3 The "Bridge to Suppliers" Java applet interface.

Installation

The JDK is available from http://java.sun.com. This is the fundamental kit that is used to compile the source code into Java class files. Full instructions are available at the Web site. Most programmers who will venture into this application will probably know all about this, so there is no need to go into details.

The JDBC Database Access API and the JDBC-ODBC Bridge Driver are available from http://splash.javasoft.com/jdbc/. At the time of publication, the Bridge was only available for a few platforms—check our Web site for updates at http://www.wiley.com/compbooks/bort. Useful information about installation of these packages can be found at Bill Bilow's Web World (http://www.geocities.com/SiliconValley/Park/9841) and Intelligent Software's home page (http://www.hooked.net/~gturner/).

You can obtain the source and class files from our Web site as well, again at http://www.wiley.com/compbooks/bort, and then compile the Supplier.java file and the SupBridge.java files. The Supplier class is the application that resides on the server, while the SupBridge class is the applet that is delivered to client browsers by the Web server. Place the compiled applet files in a directory served by the Web server (see your Web server's documentation for more specific information on how to "serve" Java applets). Place the application class in a directory that will be accessible to the wrapper script—usually this directory is a subdirectory of the location of the JDK.

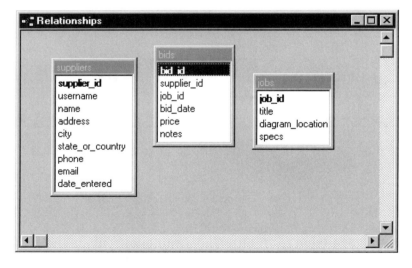

Figure 5.4 Simple database tables to store job, bid, and supplier information. You can expand them to fit your needs.

Also obtain the Perl wrapper script (or use your own) and install that in a Web server–accessible area. Since you cannot run a Java script from a CGI call, it is easiest to call a Perl script that will in turn call the Java application. Be sure to edit it to reflect the correct settings for your system. The Java application presented here was developed on a Windows NT 4.0 platform. You may have to make adjustments to the wrapper script if you are running a different operating system.

Now let us browse the code to point out key features and methods as to how this thing works.

The Code

Our applet starts with the standard class and references to library functions:

SupBridge.java

```
import java.net.*;
import java.awt.*;
import java.io.*;
import java.applet.*;

public class SupBridge extends Applet {
     Frame nwindow;
     String url_string;
```

We then go on to set up the user interface, and add those elements to our form. Please see our site (http://www.wiley.com/compbooks/bort) for the full code.

As mentioned earlier, we can use a user-defined protocol to communicate with the CGI application. So for this applet we pass codes to the CGI application to tell it what to do. Here we pass in the number "1" to tell the application that the applet is starting, and we need to retrieve the list of available jobs. The following routine shows how to communicate with the CGI Java application. Later in the chapter you will find the corresponding functions in the CGI application to handle this user-defined protocol.

```
url_string = "command=" + URLEncoder.encode("1");

    try {
    GETjobs(url_string);
    } catch (MalformedURLException e) {
       statusMsg.setText("Could not connect at this time.");
    } catch (Exception e) {
       statusMsg.setText("An error occurred.");
    }

public void GETjobs(String url_string) throws Exception {
    URL url = new URL(getDocumentBase(), "/Extranet/cgi-
            bin/javawrap.cgi");

    try {
       URLConnection con = url.openConnection();

       statusMsg.setText("Connecting...");
       con.setDoOutput(true);
       con.setDoInput(true);
       con.setUseCaches(false);

       con.setRequestProperty("Content-type",
          "application/x-www-form-urlencoded");
       con.setRequestProperty("Content-length",
          url_string.length()+"");

       PrintStream out = new PrintStream(con.getOutputStream());
       out.print(url_string);
       out.flush();
       out.close();

       statusMsg.setText("Retrieving Available Jobs...");
       DataInputStream in = new
          DataInputStream(con.getInputStream());
       String s;
       while ((s = in.readLine()) != null) {
          // set list items for available jobs.
          list1.addItem(s);
       }
       in.close();

       statusMsg.setText("Jobs Retrieved.");

    } catch (MalformedURLException e) {
       statusMsg.setText("Bad URL: " + url);
    } catch (Exception e) {
       statusMsg.setText("An error occurred while retrieving the
          job list.");
    }
}
```

Now users have a list of the available jobs in front of them. If they want to see more details about a job, they simply click on it. For this we use a code number "2" to tell the CGI Java application to retrieve the specifications for the selected job from the database. The GetSpecs routine is very similar to the GETjobs routine shown above.

```
if (evnt.id == Event.LIST_SELECT) {
    // clear certain fields
    notes.setText("");
    price.setText("");
    // Set the other label to this value.
    submit_bid.setLabel("Submit Bid for " +
    list1.getSelectedItem());
    // Retrieve specs information from database.
    url_string = "command=" + URLEncoder.encode("2") + "&"
        + "job=" + URLEncoder.encode(list1.getSelectedItem());
    getSpecs(url_string);
}
```

Finally, if users decide to place a bid, they can do so by filling in the information on the form, and clicking the Submit Bid button. Again, the SENDbid routine resembles the GETjobs routine shown above. The following is the event-handling code. Note the URL encoding routines, used just in case there is information that the user filled in that contains spaces or other odd characters.

```
public void sendBid_Clicked(Event event) {

    String url_string;

    try {
        url_string = "command=" + URLEncoder.encode("3") + "&"
        + "username=" + URLEncoder.encode(company_id.getText()) +
        "&" + "price=" + URLEncoder.encode(price.getText()) + "&"
        + "title=" + URLEncoder.encode(list1.getSelectedItem()) +
        "&" + "notes=" + URLEncoder.encode(notes.getText());

        SENDbid(url_string);

    } catch (Exception e) {
        statusMsg.setText("An error occurred.");
    }

}
```

The last part of this applet is the small subclass, NFrame. This is the window that pops up when a user clicks on View CAD Diagram. Essentially, it retrieves a URL image and "paints" it in the new window (using the popular Java paint(Graphics g) routine). A user can then view the diagram and close the window, all the while never having to leave the main form interface. The beginnings of the subclass follow.

```
class NFrame extends Frame {
 Label lab;
 String get_url;
 Image image;

 public NFrame(String title, Applet applet) {
      super(title);
 …
 }
```

Supplier.java is the standalone application that runs on the Web server that communicates with our ODBC database. The following shows the beginning of the main class, illustrating some of the database functions. It also shows the `switch` statement that interprets our user-defined code that was discussed earlier.

Supplier.java

```
public static void main(String args[]) throws Exception {

    // Load the JDBC-ODBC bridge driver
    Class.forName ("sun.jdbc.odbc.JdbcOdbcDriver");

    // Open the database
    open();

    // Obtain CGI variables.
    CGI cgi=new CGI();

    cgi.read();

    // Determine action to take.
    cgi.outInit("text/html");

    // Do some converting - Java is finicky about object types
       versus primitive types.

    Integer commandInt = new Integer(cgi.valueOf("command"));
    int realInt = commandInt.intValue();
```

```
    switch (realInt) {
    case 1:
       select();
       break;
    case 2:
       select(cgi.valueOf("job"));
       break;
    case 3:
       insert(cgi.valueOf("username"),
       cgi.valueOf("title"), cgi.valueOf("price"),
       cgi.valueOf("notes"));
       break;
    default:
       cgi.sendln("An error has occurred.");
    }

    /** Open a database connection */
    static void open() throws SQLException {

    // ODBC data source name
    String dsn = "jdbc:odbc:SupplierBridge";
    String user = "admin";
    String password = "";

    // Connect to the database
    con = DriverManager.getConnection(dsn, user, password);

    // Shut off autocommit
    con.setAutoCommit(false);

    }

    /** Commit all pending transactions and close the database
       connection */
    static void close() throws SQLException {

    con.commit();
    con.close();

    }
```

Now let us look at the routines that handle our user-defined protocol. The routine corresponding to code "1," which is to retrieve all available jobs from the database, calls the following routine, `select()`. This demonstrates how to use the SQL statements in the application to retrieve the desired information from the database. The second procedure, retrieving specifications of a job, is very similar.

```
static void select() throws SQLException {

    Statement stmt; // SQL statement object
    String query;   // SQL select string
    ResultSet rs;   // SQL query results
    boolean more;   // "more rows found" switch

    query = "SELECT * FROM jobs";

    stmt = con.createStatement();
    rs = stmt.executeQuery(query);

    // Check to see if any rows were read
    more = rs.next();
    if (!more) {

        System.out.println("No jobs found.");
        return;

    }

    // Loop through the rows retrieved from the query
    while (more) {

        System.out.println(rs.getString("title"));
        more = rs.next();

    }

    rs.close();
    stmt.close();

}
```

The last code ("3") allows users to submit a bid. Again, this is similar to the above routine, except we are inserting instead of querying.

```
// Insert into database.
    sql = "INSERT INTO bids (supplier_id, job_id, bid_date,
        price, notes) VALUES " + "(" + supplier_id + ", " + job_id
        + ", '" + bid_date + "', '" + price + "', '" + notes +
        "')";

    stmt = con.createStatement();
    rows = stmt.executeUpdate(sql);
    con.commit();
    stmt.close();

    System.out.println("Thank you - Bid submitted.");
```

The application also utilizes another class called CGI that contains all of the necessary routines to handle CGI activities, such as sending information, reading information, and parsing command lines. Many thanks to Bill Bilow (http://www.geocities.com/SiliconValley/Park/9841) for help with this.

From here, the application can be customized any number of ways until it is the ideal application to enhance your company's extranet. Again, a visit to our site (http://www.wiley.com/compbooks/bort) will demonstrate the working example and display the full source code.

Summary

Java's gain in popularity has started to make it feasible to develop valuable applications for extranet use. Some interesting problems occur when developing an application entirely in Java; among them is database integration. The JDBC specification has been released to serve this need, and of course, it may not be necessary to have every aspect of the application developed in Java if another method will serve the purpose.

However, for this book we have presented a sample application written in Java that performs a common extranet function: Bridge the gap between customer and supplier. The application is set up as a three-tier approach, utilizing a separate applet for the client and a full standalone application as a CGI link to the database, to demonstrate how Java would be used in such a case. We have more goodies available for you online and invite you to visit the Extranet Demo Site for full source code and downloads, at http://www.wiley.com/compbooks/bort.

## chapter six

Sample Extranet Applications for Customers

In this chapter we will present to you two sample applications that demonstrate how to open your business to your customers. Essentially, customers undertake two primary activities in any business: (1) placing orders, and (2) reviewing the status of those orders later on. Therefore, we have divided these two actions into two separate applications. The first application allows a customer to engage in electronic commerce, that is, customers may submit orders over the company's extranet. The second allows them to review the status of orders, which could have been placed electronically or by more traditional means.

These two applications also represent different levels of development complexities. The first application, our electronic commerce shopping cart app, uses the Perl language and simply reads and writes to a normal text file, thereby representing a fairly simple level of involvement in the development process. The second application uses Visual Basic, which connects to a real ODBC database. This is certainly more involved and appropriate for bigger systems that need the functionality and performance of interactive information.

Please visit our home page at http://www.wiley.com/ compbooks/bort to view and download the full source to these applications. Working demonstrations are also available.

Many people agree that the best way to learn programming is by example. So without further ado let us jump right into the applications.

Perl Shopping Cart/Order Entry Application

Perl has become a popular World Wide Web programming language due to its powerful capabilities to manipulate text. Its powerful text scanning features allow it to process much of the common data found on the Internet at a very high speed. Perl combines some of the best features of some other common languages and Unix utilities, such as C, sed, awk, and sh. One of the best of these features is its run-time compilation. Unlike C, Perl compiles at run time (rather quickly we might add), thereby avoiding the sometimes annoying and time-consuming "compile and test" programming tasks. The latest information about Perl can be found at http://www.perl.com. Perl for Win32 machines can be found at http://www.perl.hip.com. Perl is intriguing because it is rather picky regarding line syntax, but very flexible in that a programmer can usually do the same routine or function in several ways.

The Application

The function of the application is to allow a Web user to continuously add predetermined "products" to an electronic version of a shopping cart (Figures 6.1 through 6.4). A user can have the program automatically recalculate charges due to changes in quantities and shipping methods (Figure 6.5). The program stores the products until the user wishes to "check out" and purchase the products. This avoids the problem of the user only being able to purchase one product at a time, or having to fill in the desired multiple products on a form and submit it. Instead, with a click of a mouse, a user can bring up all the information about a product, and have the application calculate subtotals, shipping charges, taxes, and so on automatically.

Cookies provide the central working protocol for the application. A cookie is a piece of information that is sent by a Web server and stored client-side on a user's browser. This can be any sort of information, usually in name=value pairs. When the browser then retrieves another page on the correct server and in the correct directory, that information is passed back to the

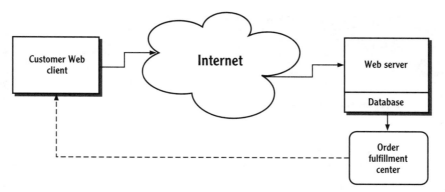

Figure 6.1 A sample Extranet Order Fulfillment System utilizing the Internet.

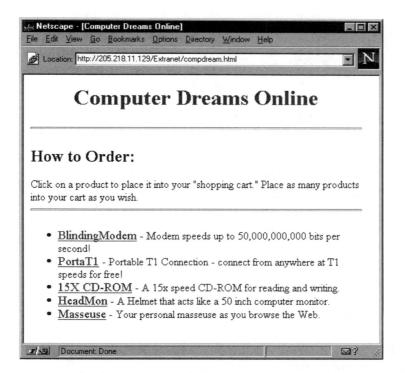

Figure 6.2 The home page of the Order Entry Application. Each hyperlink here links to the shopping cart CGI in order to add that product to the virtual shopping cart.

Figure 6.3   Viewing the virtual shopping cart after adding a product from the home page.

Web server from the browser. The server-side CGI program can then process this extra data in whatever way necessary. A good source of information on cookies can be found at http://www .illuminatus.com/cookie.fcgi. Netscape also offers preliminary specifications of cookies at http://home.netscape.com/newsref/ std/cookie_spec.html. Issues have arisen concerning the security of cookies—we believe that as long as the data being sent back and forth as cookie name=value pairs does not give away secrets such as customer account numbers, then cookies represent no real

Figure 6.4 The virtual shopping cart after a second product has been added from the home page. All information about the first product is retained, using cookie technology. Subtotals and shipping charges are automatically calculated.

security threat in a shopping cart application. Cookies and their pros and cons are discussed more thoroughly in Chapter 4.

In terms of this application, if the extranet developer or its customers remain concerned over the real or imagined security risks of intercepted data or storage of cookies on the client side, it is really not too much of a project to do without them. Developers can con-

Figure 6.5 The virtual shopping cart after a user increases the quantity and recalculates. Subtotals and shipping charges are automatically recalculated.

vert the code to store shopping cart information within simple files on the Web server itself, rather than the client. This can be done by creating a random session ID for each user, and sending it back and forth from the client in the URL or POST action. But it is plainly obvious that using cookies makes life much easier.

Some people are also concerned with browser support of cookies. Cookies have been supported in nearly all of the popular browsers such as Netscape and MS Internet Explorer for some time now.

For this application we have kept the product database approach very simple. Product information is stored in a simple ASCII text file on the server. We have done this to provide a means for those who do not have access to fancy databases but still want to make use of the shopping cart application. Other applications show how to connect to a real database. See the Perl documentation to determine how to connect a Perl script to a heavy-duty database (one of Brad's favorites is http://www-cgi.cs.cmu.edu/cgi-bin/perl-man). Here we have set it up as a comma-delimited file called prices.dat with the following fields: Product Code, Product Description, Price, Shipping Code. A sample prices.dat file follows:

```
ABC101,Grade A Rib-Eye Steaks 16 oz,29.95,1
DEF203,New York Strip 8 oz,31.99,2
GHI330,Beef Jerky 20 oz,35.00,
JKL456,Bone-In Rib Roasts 40oz,55.35,1
```

The last field is a code representing shipping information. Since we are selling food, certain products must be shipped overnight. Others may be shipped two-day air, and still others may be shipped via ground transport. In the codes above, the "1" indicates the product must be shipped next day air. A "2" indicates that a minimum of two days is required. No entry means that there are no shipping requirements. The application can then process these codes accordingly.

The point of these shipping fields is to demonstrate that even an unsophisticated text file can be used to expand the application in functional and significant ways. In fact, as many fields and/or codes and be added as needed, and the application can then modified to correctly process those fields.

Installation

This application has been tested on both an Windows NT 4.0 server running O'Reilly's WebSite Pro webserver, and on a BSDi

2.1 Unix server running an Apache 1.1.1 Web server. One important note on crossing platforms and Web servers is the possible difference in the code for retrieving the cookie information. Some Web servers parse incoming CGI data with what is known as the NCSA extra header format while others do not. Some Web servers have the ability for both. Basically the difference is that the cookie information might be stored in a variable called COOKIE (with no extra headers) or it might be in a variable called HTTP_COOKIE (with the extra header). Simply adjust the code accordingly.

Setting up the scripts is relatively simple. Visit our Web site at http://www.wiley.com/compbooks/bort to download the source code. Install the scripts to the appropriate directory on your server. Edit the scripts to reflect your server's settings, such as the correct Perl executable location (for Unix systems). For example, the correct first two lines of every script may look like this:

```
#!/usr/bin/perl
#
```

Also check file permissions to make sure that the scripts are executable and that the prices.dat file is readable by the correct user and group.

Next construct a prices.dat file that stores the product information. Install that file in the same directories as your scripts.

Activate your products on their display pages by linking them to the correct executable script. For example, you can add the following HTML code snippet:

```
<A HREF="/cgi-bin/shopcart.cgi?status=additem&prodcode=ABC101">Purchase</A>
```

This snippet provides the URL to the CGI script, then tells the script that you are adding an item to the shopping cart, and that the product code to be added is ABC101. Of course, it is easy to customize this to use a "purchase" image as the link instead of the word "Purchase." Developers can use imagination with such details, as long as the HREF anchor protocol remains constant.

Now let's walk through the code. The code itself is strewn with comments to help you along. There are also certain security features in the code which are worth looking at.

Here is the initiation of the script:

```
#
# Set up Permitted referrers array for security -
# only these domains will be allowed to call
# this script.  This prevents hackers from trying to
# use other servers to gain access to
# these scripts and gleaning protected product information.
#
@referers=('www.yourcompany.com','yourcompany.com');

# This is the root directories of where files will be.
$root_dir = "/www/docs/yourcompany/cgi-bin/";
$root_html_dir = "/www/docs/yourcompany/";

# This is the location of the product price data file.
$product_file = $root_dir . "prices.dat";

# This is the script that processes order data later on.
$processorder  = "procorder.cgi";

# Use this library for Cookie functions.
require $root_dir . 'cookies.lib';

# Check the referring URL for security
&CheckUrl;

# Parse the incoming URL fields
&ParseUrl;

# Load the product prices.
&LoadPrices;

# Now check to see if they are a return shopper.  This
# is done by getting the cookie information.

# Retrieve all Cookies.
&GetCookies;
```

The first line shows one of the security features. Extranet developers can set up the script so that it is only able to be called from a specific server(s). The first line represents the array of addresses that the developer decides are valid to call this script (the server name that your products are listed on). This prevents hackers from somehow calling it from their own servers with their own special set of destructive commands. This can easily be checked with the following:

```
sub CheckUrl {
#
   if ($ENV{ 'HTTP_REFERER'}) {
      foreach $referer (@referers) {
         if ($ENV{ 'HTTP_REFERER'} =~ /$referer/i) {
            $check_referer = '1';
                last;
         }
      }
   }
   if ($check_referer != 1) {
      &error('bad_referer');
   }
}
```

After checking the referrer for security, we parse the incoming CGI data, initiate some constants that make life easier, load up the prices.dat file into memory, and finally retrieve all cookie values from the client, if any.

The rest of the main routine determines which action to take. This is dependent on a variable called "status." Earlier we saw that when linking your product to the script we assigned the status variable to equal additem. Obviously, this tells the script that we are adding an item to the shopping basket. The other options include recalculating the shopping basket and checking out. Finally, if no status variable is present, we send back an error message.

```
# Check the status variable to decide which action to take.
if ($PARSE{'status'} eq 'additem') {
  &AddFormCookieAdd;
  &AddItem ();
  exit (0);
}

if ($PARSE{'status'} eq 'Recalculate') {
  &AddFormCookieRecalc;
  &Recalculate ();
  exit (0);
}

if ($PARSE{'status'} eq 'Check Out') {
  &AddFormCookieRecalc;
  &CheckOut ();
  exit (0);
}
```

```
# If we get this far it is probably because the browser
# does not support cookies or something else went wrong.
# Print out a notice.

print "Content-type: text/html\n";
print "\n";

print "<BODY BGCOLOR=ffffff>\n";
print "<H3 ALIGN=CENTER>Whoops! There has been a problem.</H3>\n";
print "<P>It is most likely that this problem occurred because
    your browser does not\n";
print " support the use of cookies.  Any recent version of
    <A HREF=\"http://www.netscape.com\">\n";
print "Netscape</A> or <A HREF=\"http://www.microsoft.com\">
    MS Internet Explorer</A>\n";
print " support cookies.\n";
print "<P>You can still <A HREF=\"/home2.html\">browse</A>
    and purchase products\n";
print " using one of our other purchasing methods\!\n";

exit;
```

Cookie-related routines are located in a separate library file, which was obtained from Matt's Script Archive (http://www .worldwidemart.com/scripts). These routines allow easy retrieval and setting of all aspects of cookie variables.

Upon checking out, the exact back-end events that will occur are determined by you, the developer. Normally a page is returned prompting for some sort of payment information. If the application will only be dealing with certain customers then it may be more appropriate to ask for a customer ID, account number, and so on. In this case, some sort of secure session, such as SSL, should have been activated prior to the submission of this type of sensitive information. The secure session could have been activated from the initial logon to the system or it can occur immediately before customer payment information is input. It is also possible to modify the application to require the user to log in, in which case the application would already know who was placing the order and would not have to prompt for payment information at all.

When the customer finally submits the confirmation for the order, what happens? The order information needs to be recorded in some form of a database. The simplest solution is to write it out to a text file, but developers can also choose to insert information directly into the corporate database. The company's size and needs will determine which method is best.

Another popular feature is to send an e-mail to the person who is responsible for fulfilling the order. When this option is employed, extranet developers must take pains to ensure that order information remains secure. For example, if an e-mail is sent over the Internet that contains the full order, customer identification, and so on, the e-mail should be encrypted using PGP or a similar encryption algorithm, otherwise it runs the risk of being viewed in the clear by a sniffer (which completely bypasses the security measures put in place on the Web side of the application). Information about PGP can be found at http://www.pgp.com.

Of course, another solution is to simply limit the information in the e-mail message to something innocuous, such as a generic message that an order has been received, sans details. The e-mail recipient can then go directly to the server or database that contains the order information, access it through the normal network authentication procedures already in place, and virtually eliminate the threat of unwanted prying eyes on the Internet.

This suite of routines, adding an item to the shopping cart, viewing the shopping cart, and calculating correct shipping charges, is available on our Web site at http://www.wiley.com/compbooks/bort.

Visual Basic Order Status Application

Visual Basic has gained immense popularity over the past few years for general application development. It is now starting to play a role in the Internet as a development tool. Therefore, we felt that an application for your Extranet written in Visual Basic might be advantageous. VB programmers are a populous breed—therefore resources to write these extranet applications may be more readily available (perhaps already within the company) than those written in less popular languages.

Admittedly, this application could have easily been written using one of the many specialized web database applications available today, such as Allaire's Cold Fusion. However, due to Visual Basic's widespread use and its potential future in push technology, we felt Visual Basic was an appropriate choice.

Microsoft continues to develop VB, gearing it more towards Internet use; however, to date, CGI obviously does not need VB forms—there's no GUI in CGI. So, by writing code in VB, a developer gains a greater understanding of how the database integration programming works. With that understanding, a developer could then opt to use higher-level Web/database integration tools, such as Cold Fusion. Information about Visual Basic can be found from Microsoft at http://www.microsoft.com/vbasic/.

The Application

Once orders are submitted to your company, electronically or not, why not allow your customers to check on the status of that order electronically? The success of such automated order status Web applications has been demonstrated by several international shipping companies, such as Federal Express (http://www.fedex .com) or United Parcel Service (http://www.ups.com). Both of these companies provide Web applications that perform a similar function—allowing people to check on the status of package delivery based on their shipment order numbers. Obviously, a similar application can be appropriate for virtually any business.

The application presented here provides customers with a few options. First they can view orders that are pending (i.e., ordered, but not yet shipped) (Figures 6.6 and 6.7). This gives the average customer a quick way of determining if that crucial shipment has left your warehouse, without having to call your company on the phone every twenty minutes. The other significant customer option is to review their order *history.* Here a customer can enter a date range, and submit a query to the database that will retrieve all orders placed within that date range (Figure 6.8).

For both of these options, customers can view the details of the order, including information such as the date and time ordered and shipped, shipping method, which products were ordered, and

Figure 6.6 The main menu of the Order Status application, shown after a user logs in.

so on (Figure 6.9). The application includes a link into your online product "catalog" where customers can go and browse and purchase other products. Your catalog can then be written in Visual Basic or you can perhaps link this into your Perl shopping cart application, discussed earlier.

The application uses a Microsoft Access database as an example. Visual Basic provides a robust set of tools to connect to almost any type of common database. Refer to the Visual Basic documentation for more information about how to connect to other databases.

The database itself consists of a simple setup of the appropriate tables for storing order information. The flowchart is shown in Figure 6.10.

Figure 6.7   Upon "Viewing Order Status," only pending orders are displayed.

Figure 6.8   Users can select a date range from which to view their order history.

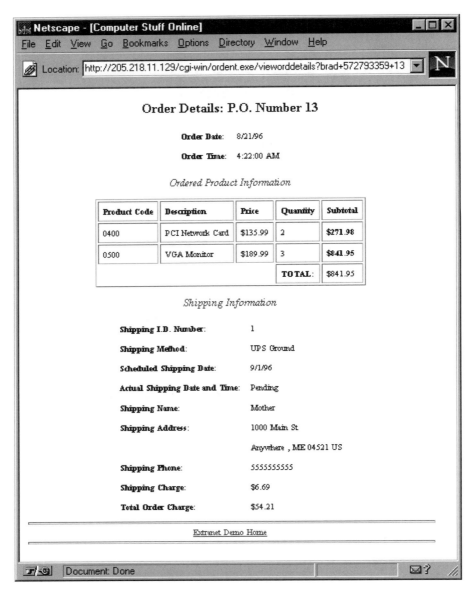

Figure 6.9   Viewing the details of an order.

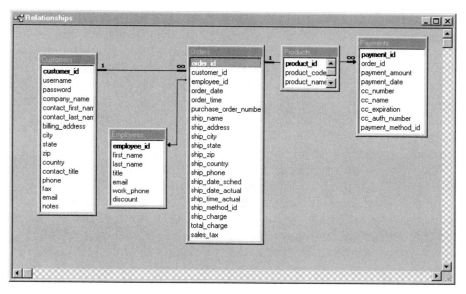

Figure 6.10   Tables to store information in the Order Entry application database. You can add to or customize these to fit your needs.

One important feature of the Order Status Application is the ability for a customer to log in and use *session IDs.* A customer enters a username and password into a form and submits the form. The code then generates a session ID for that customer. It is often a large random number that would be very difficult to guess. This session ID is used to track and verify every action that customers take once they have logged in. The session ID performs two major functions: security and tracking. Upon each new page that the customer visits, the session ID is cross-checked to make sure that the customer did indeed log in successfully to your system. Since the session ID is difficult to guess, it prevents a hacker from simply plugging in the basic URL into a browser and illegally accessing information. The URL changes every time a customer logs in. Often the session IDs are thrown back and forth from server to browser in the URL query string.

These session IDs must expire. The amount of time that they remain active is up to the developer. The choice of how long to allow session IDs to remain active is essentially a balance between how much time a customer is expected to be inactive at a browser, versus how much time the developer thinks a hacker needs to get the session ID after the real customer is finished. It is also possible to create a log-off routine, but it might be difficult to get customers to use it consistently. Developers should certainly not place any optional security responsibilities upon the user.

Two general methods exist for getting session IDs to expire. One is to build into the current code a command that checks the last time accessed, does the math, erases the ID if it is past the time allotted, and returns an error to the user. Of course, if the access time is within the time allotted, the routine should update the access time stored in the database. The other is to create a *daemon* process that routinely scours the database and deletes entries that are old. When users try to use an invalid session ID they are denied access. Either way will work—experimentation will show the better approach.

Session IDs are by no means a strong security measure. For example, if an authorized customer is browsing an order history when a disgruntled employee passes by and sees the session ID, that malcontent can immediately go to another computer, punch in the same URL, and gain access. Since the authorized customer and the hacker are accessing the information at the same time, the session ID has not expired. However, since session IDs are typically several numerals long, they are difficult "capture" in a glance, excepting hackers with photographic memories. We also assume that customers do not have hoards of malicious people floating around trying to snag session IDs.

The same concerns apply to the Internet as the communication medium. A sniffer can be used to intercept session IDs if they are sent unencrypted. Hackers can then use these IDs for access. It is therefore recommended that, when using the Internet, session IDs (and therefore the entire application) be protected by an Internet security protocol such as SSL (discussed in Chapter 2).

However, despite their weaknesses, session IDs do offer a heaping dollop of security for virtually negligible effort or expense.

Furthermore, the session ID can be also be useful in tracking a user's activity on the system. This is useful for reporting routines that indicate hits as well as the paths taken by users. Session IDs also can provide general logging information that can be used in cases of disputed activity. More extensive logging routines and reporting routines can easily be added to the code to accommodate using session IDs in this manner.

Installation

Visual Basic, being a Microsoft product, requires operation on a Windows 95 or Windows NT server (at least at the time of publication). Due to the nature of the operating system, performance has, not surprisingly, been shown to be significantly better on the Windows NT platform (information available at http://www.microsoft.com/ntserver/default.asp).

Furthermore, one problem that developers may encounter is that there has been little standardization of Visual Basic CGI interface routines for Windows Web servers. In other words, the API for each Web server package is usually different. Microsoft promotes their Internet Information Server, which utilizes ISAPI, while O'Reilly's WebSite Web server utilizes WSAPI and Netscape's servers still another. Depending on the server you are running you must obtain a solid CGI interface module. This application happens to be utilizing O'Reilly's WebSite Pro Web server and therefore could use a module called CGI32.bas, which was written as a CGI interface for WebSite Pro users by Robert Denny, one of the chief engineers of the O'Reilly Web server (more information is available at http://website.ora.com/).

Instead, there exists a standard CGI interface that utilizes the "standard-in" and "standard-out" generic pipes, thereby avoiding Windows temp files and APIs. It is also rumored to boost performance, since the temp files are unnecessary. It was written by Kevin O'Brien, and should run on any Windows Web Server (see http://pw2.netcom.com/~obrienk/index.html). The application included here uses this CGI interface.

To install the code, first browse through to get an understanding of what it does. Edit necessary pieces, such as the path to the database file. Compile the code and place the corresponding executable(s) into the appropriate CGI directories on your Web server. Be sure to also have whatever run-time libraries are necessary for database access (for example, Microsoft Access has some run-time libraries that must be installed to access the database—one easy way to install them is to simply install the entire Access application on the Web server). Once you are up and running it becomes easier to go back and customize the code to suite your needs.

The code is provided all inclusive in one Visual Basic project. You can divide up the code into numerous .EXE files, or develop appropriate .DLL files, or keep it all as one .EXE file. Again, experimentation is the best approach to determining what will provide the best results concerning performance and efficiency.

The code itself is populated with comments. The available Microsoft Access database is also populated with some sample data. Please visit the Extranet Demonstration Web site at http: //www.wiley.com/compbooks/bort to download the database file.

The Modules

Now let's take our tour of the code to point out features of how it works. The code is divided into four modules. The first is the CGI-to-VB interface, here being the general STDIN-STDOUT version that should work with any Web server (on a Windows platform). There were some minor changes done to it, but you will also have to do some customization if you start with this interface, as its main routines must be customized for your application. Descriptions of the rest of the modules follow.

ordent.bas

Here is where some variables get set, such as the path to the database file:

```
Global Const DB_FILE = "c:\Work Docs\Intranet\OrderStat.mdb"
```

Also, we are going to use a proprietary protocol for our URL. Instead of doing the standard "name1=value1&name2=value2 . . ." we are just going to use "value1+value2. . . ." The name is determined by the position in the URL query string and values are delimited with the plus (+) character. In other words, "value1" is the value of name1, since it is in the first position in the URL. For example, your URL would look something like this:

```
http://www.whatever.com/thisprogram.exe/dothis?value1+value2+value3
```

This was done to demonstrate that you can develop your own (albeit simple) protocol, and for applications that do not place tons of textual information in the URL it is easier to deal with. You can develop your own protocol that best suits your needs, or you could also easily use the standard one. Here is the function that parses the data with the new protocol:

```
Function ParseURL(ByVal x_string As String, ByVal x As Integer)
  Dim z As Integer

  For z = 1 To x
    If InStr(x_string, "+") = 0 Then
      ParseURL = x_string
      Exit Function
    End If
    ParseURL = Left(x_string, InStr(x_string, "+") - 1)
    x_string = Right(x_string, Len(x_string)-InStr(x_string, "+"))
  Next

End Function
```

Each time the application is called, the user's login is checked for validity. Each function therefore contains a call to the following:

```
Function CheckPostLogin(ByVal username As String,
        ByVal session_id As String) As Boolean

  Dim ds_login As Recordset

  Set ds_login = db!user_locks.OpenRecordset(dbOpenDynaset)

  ds_login.FindFirst "username = '" & username & "' and
                     session_id = '" & session_id & "'"

  If ds_login.NoMatch Then
    CheckPostLogin = False
  Else
    CheckPostLogin = True
  End If

  ds_login.Close

End Function
```

This routine checks the username and session ID in the user_ locks table of the database. There is another similar one for GET operations. If the username/session ID combination is not found, the system kicks you out. You can expand these routines to provide a check for the last access timestamp, and include that in the check (thereby providing a timeout feature for user activity).

order.bas

This module handles most of the actual order-processing features. For example, when users select the option to view their current orders, the following routine processes that request and displays the result. Users can then select the order of interest to view the details of that order. See the Demo site at http://www.wiley.com/ compbooks/bort for a working example.

```
Sub ViewOrderPending()
    Dim cust, order As Recordset   ` Recordset is a result set
                                     from an SQL query.
    Dim c_username As String
    Dim c_session_id As String

    c_username = ParseURL(CGI_QueryString, 1) ` retrieve the
        username from position #1 in the URL
    c_session_id = ParseURL(CGI_QueryString, 2) ` retrieve the
        session ID from position #2 in the URL

` check their username/session ID pair.
    If CheckLogin(c_username, c_session_id) Then

        Set cust = db.OpenRecordset("SELECT * FROM customers WHERE
            username = '" & c_username & "'")
        If cust.BOF Then   ' no records exist
            PageHeader
            Send ("<H1 ALIGN=CENTER>There was an error</H1>")
            Send ("<P>The application encountered an error with
                your username.")
            HTMLfooter
            cust.Close
            Exit Sub
        Else
            cust.MoveFirst
        End If

' SQL here selects orders that have a blank "ship_date_actual"
' field in the database.
```

```
    Set order = db.OpenRecordset("SELECT * FROM orders WHERE
        customer_id = " & _
        cust("customer_id") & " AND ship_date_actual = Null" & _
        " ORDER BY order_date")

    If order.BOF Then   ' no records exist
        PageHeader
        Send ("<H1 ALIGN=CENTER>No Orders Exist</H1>")
        Send ("<P>There are no orders pending at this time ")
        Send ("for customer " & c_username & "</P>")
        HTMLfooter
        cust.Close
        order.Close
        Exit Sub
    End If

    order.MoveFirst
    PageHeader
    Send ("<H1 ALIGN=CENTER>Current Orders:</H1><HR>")
    Send ("<CENTER><TABLE BORDER=1 CELLPADDING=5>")
    Send ("<TR><TD><B>P.O. Number</B></TD><TD><B>Order
            Date</B></TD><TD><B>Scheduled Ship
            Date</B></TD><TD><B>Shipping
            Name</B></TD><TD><B>Details</B></TD></TR>")

    Do While Not order.EOF
        Send ("<TR><TD ALIGN=CENTER>" &
            CStr(order("purchase_order_number")) & _
            "</TD><TD>" & CStr(order("order_date")) & _
            "</TD><TD>" & CStr(order("ship_date_sched")) & _
            "</TD><TD>" & order("ship_name") & _
            "</TD><TD><I><A HREF=""" & "/cgi-
            bin/ordent.exe/vieworddetails?" & _
            c_username & "+" & c_session_id & "+" & _
            CStr(order("purchase_order_number")) & _
            """>Details...</A></I></TD></TR>")

        order.MoveNext
    Loop

    Send ("</TABLE></CENTER>")

Else

    PageHeader
    Send ("<H1 ALIGN=CENTER><FONT COLOR=ff0000>Security
            Violation</FONT></H1>")
    Send ("<H3>Please login again.</H3>")

End If
End Sub
```

The next routine displays the detailed information about an order.

```
Sub ViewOrdDetails()
    Dim cust, order, ordprods, prods, shipmeth As Recordset
    Dim c_username As String
    Dim c_session_id As String
    Dim c_po_id As String
    Dim c_subtotal As Double

    c_username = ParseURL(CGI_QueryString, 1)
    c_session_id = ParseURL(CGI_QueryString, 2)
    c_po_id = ParseURL(CGI_QueryString, 3)

    If CheckLogin(c_username, c_session_id) Then
        Set cust = db.OpenRecordset("SELECT * FROM customers WHERE
            username = '" & c_username & "'")
        If cust.BOF Then  ' no records exist
            PageHeader
            Send ("<H1 ALIGN=CENTER>There was an error</H1>")
            Send ("<P>The application encountered an error with your
                    username.")
            HTMLfooter
            cust.Close
            Exit Sub
        Else
            cust.MoveFirst
        End If

        Set order = db.OpenRecordset("select * from orders where
            purchase_order_number = '" & c_po_id & "'")
        order.MoveFirst ' we know this one exists
        Set ordprods = db.OpenRecordset("select * from
            ordered_products where order_id = " & order("order_id"))
        If ordprods.BOF Then  ' no records exist
            PageHeader
            Send ("<H1 ALIGN=CENTER>There was an error</H1>")
            Send ("<P>There were no products matched to this
                    order.")
            HTMLfooter
            cust.Close
            ordprods.Close
            order.Close
            Exit Sub
        Else
            ordprods.MoveFirst
        End If

        PageHeader
        Send ("<H2 ALIGN=CENTER>Order Details: P.O. Number " &
            CStr(c_po_id) & "</H2>")
```

```
Send ("<CENTER><TABLE BORDER=0 CELLPADDING=5>")
Send ("<TR><TD><B>Order Date:</B></TD><TD>" &
    CStr(order("order_date")) & "</TD></TR>")
Send ("<TR><TD><B>Order Time:</B></TD><TD>" &
    CStr(order("order_time")) & "</TD></TR>")
Send ("</TABLE></CENTER>")

Send ("<H3 ALIGN=CENTER><FONT COLOR=ee0000><I>Ordered
    Product Information</I></FONT></H3>")

Send ("<CENTER><TABLE BORDER=1 CELLPADDING=5>")
Send ("<TR><TD><B>Product
    Code</B></TD> <TD><B>Description</B></TD>
    <TD><B>Price</B></TD> <TD><B>Quantity</B></TD>
    <TD><B>Subtotal</B></TD></TR>")

Set prods = db!products.OpenRecordset(dbOpenDynaset)

' Order Information
c_subtotal = 0
Do While Not ordprods.EOF
    prods.FindFirst "product_id = " &
        ordprods("product_id")

    c_subtotal = c_subtotal + (prods("product_price") *
        ordprods("quantity"))  ' calculate subtotal

    Send ("<TR><TD>" & prods("product_code") & _
        "</TD><TD>" & _
        prods("product_name") & "</TD><TD>" &
        Format(prods("product_price"), "Currency") & _
        "</TD><TD>" & CStr(ordprods("quantity")) &
        "</TD><TD><B>" & _
        Format(c_subtotal, "Currency") & "</B></TR>")

    ordprods.MoveNext
Loop

Send ("<TR><TD COLSPAN=3></TD><TD><B>TOTAL:</B></TD>" & _
    "<TD>" & Format(c_subtotal, "Currency") &
    "</TABLE></CENTER>")
' Shipping Information
Send ("<H3 ALIGN=CENTER><FONT COLOR=ee0000><I>Shipping
    Information</I></FONT></H3>")

Set shipmeth = db!shipping_methods.OpenRecordset(dbOpenDynaset)
shipmeth.FindFirst "shipping_method_id = " &
    order("ship_method_id")

Send ("<CENTER><TABLE BORDER=0 CELLPADDING=5>")
```

```
Send ("<TR><TD><B>Shipping I.D. Number:</B></TD><TD>" &
    CStr(order("ship_method_id")) & "</TD></TR>")
Send ("<TR><TD><B>Shipping Method:</B></TD><TD>" &
    shipmeth("shipping_method") & "</TD></TR>")
Send ("<TR><TD><B>Scheduled Ship Date:</B></TD><TD>" & _
    CStr(order("ship_date_sched")) & "</TD></TR>")
If order("ship_date_actual") <> "" Then
    Send ("<TR><TD><B>Actual Shipping Date and
        Time:</B></TD><TD>" & _
        CStr(order("ship_date_actual")) & " at " & _
        CStr(order("ship_time_actual")) & "</TD></TR>")
Else
    Send ("<TR><TD><B>Actual Shipping Date and
        Time:</B></TD><TD>" & _
        "Pending</TD></TR>")
End If
Send ("<TR><TD><B>Shipping Name:</B></TD><TD>" &
    order("ship_name") & "</TD></TR>")
Send ("<TR><TD><B>Shipping Address:</B></TD><TD>" &
    order("ship_address") & "</TD></TR>")
Send ("<TR><TD></TD><TD>" & order("ship_city") & " , " &
    order("ship_state") & _
    "  " & order("ship_zip") & "  " &
    order("ship_country") & "</TD></TR>")
Send ("<TR><TD><B>Shipping Phone:</B></TD><TD>" &
    CStr(order("ship_phone")) & "</TD></TR>")
Send ("<TR><TD><B>Shipping Charge:</B></TD><TD>" &
    Format(order("ship_charge"), "Currency") &
    "</TD></TR>")
Send ("<TR><TD><B>Total Order Charge:</B></TD><TD>" &
    Format(order("total_charge"), "Currency") &
    "</TD></TR>")

Send ("</TABLE></CENTER>")
HTMLfooter

cust.Close
ordprods.Close
order.Close
prods.Close
shipmeth.Close

Else

PageHeader
Send ("<H1 ALIGN=CENTER><FONT COLOR=ff0000>Security
    Violation</FONT></H1>")
Send ("<H3>Please login again.</H3>")

End If

End Sub
```

Note that with Visual Basic developers can perform database queries in a number of ways. The previous routine uses both SQL statements for recordset variables, as well as the built-in FindFirst and FindNext methods.

The CancelOrderDB routine in this module also demonstrates another variation of using SQL in Visual Basic. Note that in your application you may not want to actually allow a user to delete all information about an order. The code snippet here is shown for example purposes.

```
' First must get the order_id from the orders table
        Set order = db.OpenRecordset("SELECT * FROM orders WHERE
            purchase_order_number = '" & c_po_id & "'")
        c_order_id = order("order_id")
        order.Close

    ' Create the criteria string.
    ' SQL here deletes the po order that we have passed in.
        SQLQuery = "DELETE * FROM orders WHERE
            purchase_order_number = '" & c_po_id & "'"
        db.Execute SQLQuery ' Execute the query.

    ' SQL here deletes all of the ordered products.
        SQLQuery = "DELETE * FROM ordered_products WHERE order_id =
            " & c_order_id
        db.Execute SQLQuery ' Execute the query.
```

Users can also select a date range from which to view order history. Upon selecting and submitting that range, here is a code snippet that will process the query and return the result to the user.

```
' Compile dates into one variable
    begindate = DateValue(GetSmallField("beginmonth") & " " &
        GetSmallField("beginday") & _
        " " & GetSmallField("beginyear"))
    enddate = DateValue(GetSmallField("endmonth") & " " &
        GetSmallField("endday") & _
        " " & GetSmallField("endyear"))

' Retrieve Order History with some funky SQL
' This SQL statement will actually allow the selection to work
' backwards, i.e.
' a user can enter an ending date before the begin date and it will
' still work.
' This is because of the BETWEEN parameter.
' This is not necessarily a good thing, just thought I would share
' it.
        Set order = db.OpenRecordset("SELECT * FROM orders " & _
```

```
                "WHERE customer_id = " & cust("customer_id") & _
                " AND order_date BETWEEN #" & CStr(begindate) & _
                "# And #" & CStr(enddate) & "# ORDER BY order_date")
        If order.BOF Then   ' no records exist within date range
                PageHeader
                Send ("<H1 ALIGN=CENTER>No Orders Exist</H1>")
                Send ("<P>There are no orders within the selected date
                        range ")
                Send ("for customer " & c_username & "</P>")
                HTMLfooter
                cust.Close
                order.Close
                Exit Sub
        End If

        order.MoveFirst

        PageHeader
        Send ("<H1 ALIGN=CENTER>Order History:</H1><HR>")
        Send ("<CENTER><TABLE BORDER=1 CELLPADDING=5>")
        Send ("<TR><TD><B>P.O. Number</B></TD><TD><B>Order
                Date</B></TD> <TD><B>Scheduled Ship Date</B></TD>
                <TD><B>Shipping Name</B></TD>
                <TD><B>Details</B></TD></TR>")

        Do While Not order.EOF

            Send ("<TR><TD ALIGN=CENTER>" &
                CStr(order("purchase_order_number")) & _
                "</TD><TD>" & CStr(order("order_date")) & _
                "</TD><TD>" & CStr(order("ship_date_sched")) & _
                "</TD><TD>" & order("ship_name") & _
                "</TD><TD><I><A HREF=""" & "/cgi-
                bin/ordent.exe/vieworddetails?" & _
                c_username & "+" & c_session_id & "+" & _
                CStr(order("purchase_order_number")) & _
                """>Details...</A></I></TD></TR>")

            order.MoveNext
        Loop

        Send ("</TABLE></CENTER>")

        cust.Close
        order.Close
```

user.bas

Only one routine in this last module is actually used in the application. The module is provided as an example for administration of your users. Routines in this module are used to add, view, edit, and delete users from the database. You can incorporate these routines into a separate maintenance/administration application if desired.

The routine that is used is to log in a user. It will assign a session ID for the customer for the current session, as well as write the session ID to the database for subsequent login checks.

```
Sub LoginUser()
    Dim random_long As Long

    Set ds = db!customers.OpenRecordset(dbOpenDynaset)

    ds.FindFirst "username = '" + GetSmallField("username") + "' and
        " + "password = '" + GetSmallField("password") + "'"

    If ds.NoMatch Then ' user not found

        PageHeader
        Send ("<H2 ALIGN=CENTER>" & GetSmallField("username") & "
            login un-successfull, no such username and
            password.</H2><BR>")
        Send ("<P>Please check to make sure you have entered your
            information correctly, and ")
        Send ("<A HREF=" + Chr(34) + "/Intranet/login.html" + Chr(34)
            + ">try again</A>.<BR>")
        ds.Close

    Else  ' assign session ID

        Randomize
        random_long = CLng((999999999 - 100000000 + 1) * Rnd +
            100000000)

        Set ds = db!user_locks.OpenRecordset(dbOpenDynaset)
        ds.AddNew

        ds("username") = GetSmallField("username")
        ds("session_id") = CStr(random_long)
        ds("create_date") = Date
        ds("create_time") = Time
        ds.Update
        ds.Close

        PageHeader
        Send ("<H2 ALIGN=CENTER>Welcome " & GetSmallField("username")
            & "!</H2>")
```

```
        UserMenu (random_long)

    End If

End Sub
```

Summary

We have presented two useful example applications for use within your extranet. The first one, written in Perl, allows users to "shop" your site and place items they wish to purchase into a dynamic shopping cart.

The second application, written in Visual Basic, allow customers to review the status of orders that have previously been placed with your company. Visit the Extranet Demonstration Site at http://www.wiley.com/compbooks/bort for working examples of these applications as well as to obtain the source code and sample data.

Both applications are intended to be working examples for extranet developers to customize as they wish. We've explained some of the choices we made when developing these applications and pointed out issues that developers will face when they evaluate similar choices for their applications.

## PART THREE

Practical Advice

## chapter seven

Calculating ROI for an Extranet

Throughout this book, we have alluded to a tremendous potential return on investment (ROI) for companies engaged in an extranet. Our belief in these high ROIs stems from the fact that an extranet usually leverages the infrastructure and knowledge a company already has. So it requires very little capital investment or training, but can save a company significant amounts of money, particularly by increasing the efficiency of the workforce and by cementing business relationships. The effect is similar to what can be achieved with an intranet. In fact, in the fall of 1996, International Data Corporation, one of the world's premier technology market research companies, released a preliminary report (commissioned by Netscape) that examined the ROIs of intranets. In a comprehensive study of four companies, IDC found that the typical return was over *1,000 percent.* Granted, four companies is hardly a representative sample of the entire corporate world, yet, the study's author told us other research has confirmed that returns of 200 to 1,000+ percent seemed to be the norm. (The study can be found on Netscape's Web site, www.netscape.com.) This is astounding because many financial analysts consider a sound investment one that offers returns of 20 percent or more.

The elements that make intranets such a strong project for companies are the same ones that apply to extranets. They use standard software and hardware, most if which is already in place, and they require very little training of developers, administrators, or end users, as most people have crested the learning curve from using the Internet. They offer tremendous increases in productivity, allowing end users to have real-time access to data and applications in a way that was achievable only by expensive, time-intensive solutions before, such as custom-developed data warehouses.

But, it's not enough just to exclaim that an extranet will have an ROI of 1,000+ percent; a company needs to examine its own particular circumstances. In this chapter, we aim to help you do that. First, we'll give you a basic overview of how to calculate how much an extranet will cost you and what that investment will net you. This will be a simplistic view of what can become very complicated procedures, so financial analysts forgive us. The idea is to give extranet developers a rough idea of the budgets required for an extranet, and what that money will gain the company if spent on an extranet project, not to provide a comprehensive tutorial on corporate financial planning. We strongly advise that companies have their financial analyst calculate the ROI, rates of return, cash flows, and so on once the parameters of the project are established. In fact, we recommend that companies develop a standard model for calculating ROI that can be used to make decisions on any project.

What Is a Return On Investment (ROI)?

ROI has become a critical part of doing business today. Many methods have been developed for calculating ROIs such as the Payback Period, Net Present Value, and Internal Rate of Return. Briefly, the Payback Period calculates how much time is involved for an investment to break even. It is derived by dividing the initial cost of the investment by the net annual cash flows it will bring back into the business. It is communicated in "number of years" and assumes that benefits will rise steadily over time.

Net Present Value (NPV) is the result of subtracting net costs from net revenues to get a profit number. It ignores many of the other elements that contribute to a more detailed analysis of ROI, such as correcting for inflation on a return that is achieved over a number of years. However, it is among the most common and the simplest returns to calculate and can give a company an idea of the potential returns on a given project, even if the ROI is being performed at a preliminary stage.

Internal Rate of Return is where ROI calculations get quite complex. This is the act of determining the rate of the return on the investment, while including many more factors than the NPV considers. (Specifically, it calculates the discount rate at which the NPV is $0.) It is useful in comparing various business opportunities, but because it returns a percentage rate, it does not give a company an absolute profit figure.

A great explanation of ROI can be found at the Web site http://www.lotus.com/ntsdoc96/22de.htm.

This chapter will focus on the simplest measure of ROI, NPV. Since our intent is to assist a company in determining an initial financial impact for an extranet, NPV is adequate for our purposes. We did however, want to point out that many other factors contribute to a project's ultimate financial success, and should be evaluated by the company.

Whereas, in other chapters, we have offered information and recommendations, here we supply a series of worksheets, filled with lots of questions. Answer the questions, and you should have a handle on the budgetary concerns and the potential payback for this project.

Chances are, your company has a financial department well versed in the algebra required to calculate return on investment. Still, in this chapter we want to cover a few basics that are often specific to technology investments. So, before we jump into worksheets, let's take a brief look at what we mean by ROI, as we use the term, and some of the factors involved.

ROI Primer

ROI is how companies evaluate where they should spend their cash (or what projects are worth borrowing for). It helps companies navigate through choices. Should we build an extranet or upgrade our desktop PCs to Pentiums? Should we pursue a project that will cost us $100,000 and pay back $20,000 or a project that will cost $1 million and pay back $30,000? Although the latter project generates more cash, it actually returns a smaller percentage against the funds invested. (Only 25 percent compared to 11 percent.) The choice of which investment to pursue becomes obvious when stated in this form.

The challenge, of course, is to convert all of the variables that make up an "investment" and all of the variables that make up a "return" into numbers that can be compared against each other. The trick to this, at least in part, is to set up a standardized ROI model which can then apply to any potential expenditure. This model would use standardized quantities to represent intangibles. For instance, one hour of executive management time saved might be worth $100. That figure could then be used as part of a company's ROI model. With a uniform method of calculating ROI, the company is in a much better position to evaluate what types of investments it can make. Still, some general methods of calculating ROI apply to most businesses. Costs must be determined, even those that don't take money out of the pocketbook immediately. Savings must be calculated, even those savings that hide in the cracks of a project, and earnings must be estimated or included.

What Are Costs?

Costs include both the up-front outlay for equipment or consultants and the intangible outlay of resources such as time spent for in-house development, training, or maintenance. Allocating costs can be tricky for a technology project such as an extranet. Not every expenditure incurred should be included dollar-for-dollar in an ROI analysis of an extranet. A general rule of thumb when allocating costs is as follows:

- If the cost is directly associated with the project, allocate 100 percent of the cost to the project.
- If the cost is associated with several specific projects, split the allocation of the cost between them.
- If the cost is a part of the overall strategy of the company—if it is a cost associated with infrastructure—do

not allocate any part of the cost to the project. The reason for this is that infrastructure costs are part of the cost of doing business and should already be included in the company's overhead budgets.

Here's how the rule works. If a company is planning an extranet and needs to buy a new $10,000 server to host the site and that server will perform no other function, the entire $10,000 is allocated to the cost of the extranet. If a company is planning an extranet and needs a $10,000 firewall to be part of the project, but will also use that firewall to partition the marketing department away from the rest of the company, and each use of the new firewall will account for 50 percent of the firewall's total usage, split the allocation equally between the two projects. Therefore, only $5,000 of that new firewall should be allocated to the extranet. If the company will be using the new firewall 75 percent of the time to partition the marketing department and 25 percent of the time to allow partners onto the marketing department's intranet, then the company would allocate $2,500 of the cost to the extranet.

However, if the company plans to put up an extranet, but first needs to spend $10,000 upgrading its network to handle the extra traffic it anticipates will be created with the extranet, none of the cost will be allocated to the extranet. This is because the network is part of the company's infrastructure and not a direct cost of the extranet. Instead, it is the foundation of virtually all of the company's technology uses. Upgrading and maintaining infrastructure is necessary for a business to stay competitive, just like installing carpets is necessary for building maintenance.

An extranet is in a unique position. In most cases it will almost completely leverage the existing investments a company has made with its intranet. For that reason, it should have fewer costs allocated 100 percent to the project than would be the case when analyzing other new technology projects, such as data warehouses. It may share some of the costs associated with an intranet, if both are being installed together. However, if the company has put in the intranet and is merely adding an extranet, few if any of the costs of the intranet would be allocated to the extranet project as they are already part of the intranet budget.

Intangible Costs

Of course, the above example of a $10,000 piece of equipment is easy to work with. But it is also extremely important to consider both up-front worker hours and ongoing maintenance, the latter being the hardest to calculate.

Up-front worker hours will include items such as the training of the development team in learning new technologies, the time it takes them to code and prototype, and the time it takes end users to learn the new system. However, like the allocation rule of thumb for capital expenditures, the same holds true for calculating the cost of worker hours. If the company has made a strategic decision to use Visual Basic for its primary application development platform, and the extranet project is created in VB, the training of developers in VB should *not* be counted. However, if the team must specifically learn a tool for the extranet project, such as a secure Web server, the entire cost of that training should be allocated to the project. If the time spent learning was done on a previous project, none of the cost of that previous training should suddenly wind up allocated to the extranet. If the time spent learning was to create two new projects, say an extranet and an electronic commerce site on the Web, the costs will be split between projects, based on the percentage each used the resource.

Intangible costs can be accessed according to job function and pay scale. The time executives spend in training costs a company both in the actual time that they are paying them and in the loss of productivity. For instance, take a sales manager that earns $100,000 a year and typically brings in $50,000 worth of business a week. Based on a 40-hour workweek, if she spends eight hours training on a new system, that training costs the company $48 (per hour) × 8 hours or $384 in hard dollars, but also a potential additional $10,000 in lost revenue for the day the sales manager trained instead of sold. Of course, it may not actually cost the company this in hard costs, because of the roller-coaster nature of sales, so the company should do its best to correct for true loss of productivity, rather than potential loss of productivity.

If training takes place during a slow cycle of sales, such as the first week of the year, or a Saturday, the company may actually lose minimal, if any, additional revenue. Or that phenomenal sales manager could have still managed to pull in the full $50,000 that week. This is one of the values of conducting an ROI. It provides an opportunity for a company to think through the financial consequences of various choices and use that as a basis of decisions.

Again, in some cases, the users of an extranet are the partners, which means that the training of end users may not even be a cost for the company at all. However, if the extranet is a new application that will be shared by partners and employees, such as new communications tools for collaboration, training will have to be considered a cost.

Estimating Costs

We understand that it can be difficult to gage the costs of intangible items before the project has begun. However, since this chapter is about giving a company a preliminary ROI to use for approval and budgetary purposes, some guesswork is required. Try to base guestimates such as training and development time on empirical data from similar projects. Then try to correct for the part of the learning curve that programmers/developers have already achieved. For instance, it may have taken a half-day training session to teach users how to use their Internet e-mail and browser. Then it may have taken only a one-hour seminar to show them the wonders of the company phone directory on a brand new intranet. An extranet tool based on the Web that uses those same browsers would probably require training of the latter nature, while one based on the Mbone and using a videoconferencing interface might take another half-day seminar.

What Are Some of the Costs and Investments Involved in Our Extranet?

It's time for our first worksheet. In our Types of Costs worksheet you will find a list of questions that should guide you through the items that will be allocated as costs.

Types of Costs	Yes/No	Price per Unit	Total Cost
Equipment			
Will the company have to pay for a separate server(s) for the extranet?			
Will the company have to pay for additional phone lines?			
Will the company have to pay for Web server software?			
Will the company have to pay for document management software?			
Will the company rely on lesser-used Internet protocols such as IP6SEC, UDP, IP multicast, that might require the installation of special client software at the partner site? If so, who will pay for it (company/ partner)?			
Will the company pay for the software licenses of this specialized client software?			
Will the project require new development tools such as database integration tools, ActiveX controls, etc.?			
Security			
Will the company need to purchase additional firewalls?			
Will the company hire outside security consultants to audit/assist in the development of a secure system?			
Will the company need to purchase other types of security products?			
Development			
Will the extranet be developed with in-house developers? How many hours?			
Will the extranet be developed with contracted resources?			
Training			
Will programmers need training classes or significant training time?			
Will end users need training seminars? How many hours?			
Will the company hire outside consultants to assist with development and training?			

Types of Costs	Yes/No	Price per Unit	Total Cost
Management			
Will resources be assigned to ongoing management of the extranet? How many in terms of worker hours and equipment?			
Will the extranet software be upgraded as new versions become available? How often are upgrades planned?			
Support			
Will the company pay for a third party to perform the installation of client software, or perform it itself?			
Will the company offer support for the extranet application, such as a helpdesk? How many helpdesk resources will be dedicated to extranet support in terms of worker hours and equipment?			
Taxes			
Will the extranet have depreciable components? How much will any capital expenditure depreciate?			
Totals			

What Are Savings?

Until this point, we've talked about the types of costs involved in an extranet and how to allocate them to uncover the true cost of the project and given you a checklist of them. Now, we'll cover savings. Like costs, savings can be broken into two parts, hard savings and soft savings.

Hard Savings

Hard savings is money that a CFO can deposit in the bank as a result of this project. For instance, there are savings associated with paper when an extranet is used to provide documentation or support that used to be printed. Say a company sells software products and it wants to offer its customers a choice of online access to a support database or paper documentation and a quarterly mailer. For each customer that chooses the extranet application, the company saves the cost of printing and the cost of postage.

Other examples of hard savings for extranets would be the money saved by taking a project in-house that used to be outsourced before the project migrated to the Web. For instance, a company would experience savings if it ceased to outsource for mainframe-based EDI services and now offered similar electronic payment using an extranet. A company might experience hard savings if the extranet is used for communications purposes, such as voice calls, video training, video conferencing. The company would save money over using long-distance carriers on such projects. It might also save travel costs associated with in-person meetings.

Soft Savings

Conversely, soft savings are the intangible savings that occur because the new process is more efficient, easier to use, reaches to a broader audience, and so on. True savings can be misleading so it's important to have an agreed-upon model for how much certain types of intangible savings are worth, such as time savings. In fact, time savings is one of the most difficult of all soft savings to quantify, particularly for technology projects. This is for two reasons: (1) it can be difficult to determine how much time is being saved and (2) it can be difficult to determine exactly how much time saved actually translates into dollars for the company.

Let's examine the first problem. For most extranet projects, time savings will turn out to be a big benefit. For vendor-related projects, the time saved might be that of the purchasing department employees who will have readily available online information, rather than calling for prices and order numbers. For a customer application, time savings might be on the part of the sales team or the after-market support team.

How do you determine exactly how much time is saved? Basic legwork. The ROI analyst must interview people and ask them how much time it took them to perform tasks before the extranet was available, then time them or ask them how much time they now spend doing their tasks. Time savings are best calculated after the new system has been in place a while and users are fully trained on it. Except for those of us who love technology for its own sake, people have a natural tendency to resist new systems, even if they are faster, better, and easier. It takes anywhere from 30 days to six months before a new system is fully integrated into the daily work habits of employees. This chapter is about getting a handle on ROI including time savings at an early stage of extranet development. So interviewers must simply do their best to guestimate how much time could be saved. It may not be as hard as it sounds. For instance, if an end user spends 15 minutes a day sending out a large fax to business partners (baby sitting the fax machine to be sure papers don't get jammed, etc.), and the extranet would allow that information to be posted to a Web site in one minute, the interviewer can assume that 14 minutes will be saved. Of course, verifying how close to mark these original estimates hit after the system is in place becomes imperative at a later date.

An inkling of this type of data can be gathered at the prototype stage. If the project is only in the planning stages, the ROI analyst must make an educated guess. (This guess and others must be verified with empirical data when the project comes online, and the ROI recalculated.)

When evaluating time savings, be sure to consider both the first-tier and the second-tier effects. First-tier savings would be the time saved by the person who is using the extranet instead of performing the task the "old" way. Second-tier savings would be the time saved by people who ordinarily assist the user during the "old" way. The classic example is the executive and the administrative assistant. The executive needs a document, and calls the assistant who then searches for and faxes the document to the executive. If an extranet is in place that allows the document to be retrieved quickly by the executive alone, time savings have occurred on two tiers, those of the executive and the administrative assistant.

Another area that is considered time savings is the time it takes programmers to produce an extranet compared to the time it takes them to create other IS systems. It may take a matter of days to get an extranet up and running, but months for a client/server system that performs similar tasks. Similarly, there are time savings of training new employees in how to operate an extranet system versus how long it would have taken them to learn the processes the old way. A case in point is a salesperson, operating an extranet system from a client site to place an order. If the salesperson could learn that system in two hours, but needed two months to learn how to place orders the "old" way, which meant filling out myriad paper forms, the savings are tremendous, and should be included in an ROI analysis.

The second problem when quantifying time savings is a problem called the "inefficient transfer of time," according to technology ROI expert Ian Campbell, director of Collaborative and Intranet Computing for IDC. Specifically, if the company saves an employee 15 minutes of time, it doesn't necessary translate to 15 minutes more of work. Time savings can be squandered by employees, or can be used to reduce burdensome workloads, or might actually be used to increase productivity by doing other work. When calculating soft savings based on time savings, it's important to apply an appropriate correction factor that will account for the discrepancy between time saved and increases in productivity.

A good rule of thumb for the correction factor frequently used by Campbell is to quantify by category: production workers, white-collar middle management, executives, and so on. The lowest correction factor is achieved by production workers or anyone whose work is a continuous flow. That is, if an assembly line worker can save ten minutes of time, 100 percent of that ten minutes saved is allocated to work. Another example is a counterperson at a fast-food place. If that person saved two minutes per order, 100 percent of that time saved would be allocated to doing more work. Other types of jobs that qualify are data entry workers, telesales personnel, customer support representatives, and others who do continuous and/or repetitive tasks.

For white-collar or middle-management workers, time savings is typically 50 to 60 percent allocated to work. Oddly enough, the highest correction factor is often applied to top-level executives who work long workweeks. When executives who put in 60 hours a week save six hours a week, they are likely to allocate 0 percent to work and go home. Among the white-collar crowd, the lowest correction factor is applied to those who are paid by billable time, such as consultants. For these people, time saved is literally money they can make.

The key to understanding the correction factors for the employees at your company is to ask them what they do when they save ten minutes, 30 minutes, an hour, and so on. Of course, it's important to have the questioner not be in a position to fire these people—otherwise results might be skewed.

The Type of Savings worksheet should help you consider most of the savings factors for your extranet.

Type of Savings	Yes/No	Savings per Unit	Total Savings
Hard Savings			
Will the extranet reduce the cost of offset printing?			
Will the extranet reduce the general consumption of paper?			
Will the extranet reduce the cost of postage?			
Will the extranet offer a cheaper means of voice communications?			
Will the extranet offer a cheaper means of visual communications such as video training or video conferencing?			
Will the extranet reduce the amount of billable time a partner must charge the company to perform its tasks?			
Will the extranet reduce the number of worker hours currently associated with the process?			
Will the extranet provide for other types of hard savings?			
Soft Savings			
Will the extranet save the time of production workers? (100% of allocation to work)			
Will the extranet save the time of middle-tier workers? (50–60% of allocation to work)			
Will the extranet save the time of top executives? (0–20% of allocation to work)			
Will the extranet save the time of IS personnel? (60–100% of allocation to work)			
Will the extranet reduce the amount of equipment or other resources now used to perform its tasks?			
Totals			

Earnings

Of course, the final area that should be calculated into an ROI is earnings from the project, if the extranet is intended to be a revenue generator. For instance, if a company has its entire product catalogue on its intranet, and it allows selective customers to browse the online catalogue and make purchases, the extranet will be earning revenue. If an extranet is used so that business partners can collaborate on the same document using whiteboard software over the Web, it may produce savings, but it isn't producing revenue.

The key to this is to determine whether earnings generated are additional or incremental revenue earned solely by the merits of the extranet system or whether it is merely shifting the revenues from other sources. The above example might be a case of the latter category, one in which the revenue is shifted. As long as the cost to pursue the sale is less when customers use the extranet than it is with other sales means, the company winds up in a better position. This is almost certainly guaranteed, because customers who place orders on the extranet may need no human interaction in order to complete the order. (However, they may need such interaction in the form of technical support, if they experience problems with the system—so costs versus earnings must be carefully considered.)

An extranet in which a company charges partners to access an incredible database on U.S. import/export information, such as the extranets created by Trade Compass Inc. (www.tradecompass .com), clearly belongs to the category of additional revenue. In fact, as in the case of Trade Compass, the selling of information via an extranet may even become an entire business in itself.

Soft earnings may also factor in, but in a manner different from soft costs or savings. Soft earnings represent user satisfaction with the extranet and the general goodwill it produces. An extranet that allows its biggest customers to check the status of an order 100 times a day, 24 hours a day, builds significant goodwill. However, performance factors in greatly here. If a system provides the features users want and need and is speedy and responsive, it will positively make them glow. If it is also intuitive to use, pleasant to look at, secure, and available, customers will use it more frequently and recommend that others do so as well (if such recommendations are appropriate for the extranet application). If the system fails on one or more of these points, soft earnings will wind up becoming soft costs. Users will require higher levels of support or simply won't use the system at all—which doesn't bode well for a healthy ROI, no matter how it's calculated.

Anticipating Demand

Again, in order to derive a preliminary ROI, some attempt has to be made at anticipating the revenue that will be generated from an income-producing extranet. The marketing department should assist in this.

It may be wise to create a smaller test case of any electronic commerce extranet to gain insight into some preliminary empirical figures. This will also help determine some of the other factors that will make the business a success, such as the psychological prompts that encourage people to shop online. Even though the target of such efforts is a business partner customer who is already motivated to purchase the company's products and services—and not the masses—providing a positive shopping experience remains necessary. For instance, an office supply company may want to offer its electronic commerce extranet to its few top customers to see what kind of products they buy online and whether it affects the types of products they buy through the catalogue or in person. The company that is using an extranet to sell information not available anywhere else may want to poll its potential client base to see how much they are willing to pay.

In any case, we have provided an Earnings Worksheet to help extranet developers think through some of the issues involved, as they pertain to ROI.

Results

With a list of projected costs, savings, and earnings, the company can determine a rough Net Present Value. Simply add the savings and earnings together and subtract the costs. What remains is the

Earnings Worksheet	Yes/No	Price per Unit	Anticipated Demand	Total Annual Revenue
Will the extranet sell original products?				
List products:				
Product 1				
Product 2				
Will the extranet sell products available in other ways? If so, will the use of the extranet diminish the revenue generated by these other means?				
Will the extranet be a sellable service itself?				
Is there a potential for revenue every time a user logs on? What is the maximum number of concurrent users the current planned system can support?				
Will use of the extranet be billable to clients in other ways?				
Totals				

NPV or profit of the project. By converting this figure to a percentage of the total costs, the company will have the return on investment. A figure of 20 percent or more is considered an acceptable risk for most projects, generally speaking. However, because these types of projects usually have extremely low costs associated with them, figures approaching 200 percent are common. Should your ROI be lower than 50 percent, the project may need to be reanalyzed. Is the company spending too much on custom development? Should the company hire outside consultants, rather than train internal people? Can the company shrug off installation and support of client components to the partner entirely?

Tips for Realizing High ROIs

It may not be enough just to produce a great extranet application that costs little to create, requires virtually no training, and performs well. The application must also be integrated into the routines of the people who will use it. If an extranet is to be offered as an alternative to other means by which partners work together, designers may want to offer incentives for the extranet to be the choice. Incentives could be as simple as access to information not available any other way or it can be a trip to the Bahamas for the person responsible for the most hits. The point is, developers may want to bait the hook rather than expecting partners to automatically accept their offer.

Don't aim to satisfy 100 percent of the functionality that partners on an extranet may want when dealing with your company. Aim for 80 percent of the situations, then offer a way for an extranet user to connect with a human being. This may be automated, such as an e-mail to an administrator. Or it could be a phone number to a support desk. Remember the lesson learned in the late 1980s when voice mail became popular? It was soon termed "mail jail." Don't trap extranet users into the same situation with the extranet. In this way, usage of the system is likely to remain high for the most common tasks, off-loading the need for human intervention in accomplishing these. This means including voice phone numbers on Web pages, for example. Numbers should not be made prominent, tempting users to call constantly. However, they should not be so buried that a user becomes frustrated trying to find them.

We've said this before but it bears repeating: include partners in the development process so the net result is what they want. This is one of the best ways to ensure that the system will be highly utilized and realize its potential ROI.

Segregate the management of the project to the people best able to perform the tasks. For instance, if an extranet will be providing a lot of information, automate the content submission as much as is securely possible. This alleviates routine tasks such as updating a page on the Web site from having to be managed by two or more people: the person responsible for the data and an IS person responsible for updating. The result is to lower the ongoing cost of maintenance and improve ROI.

ROIs for Different Industries

Some industries will have a naturally higher ROI for extranet projects than others because these industries cater to customers (or use vendors) with characteristics that lend themselves more easily to electronic interaction. Part of the ROI research should include an analysis of the partners. This will help determine the level of customization that is needed. Do your business partners need to be treated differently from one another and an extranet is a way to provide that specialization? For instance, do you want to provide personalized service to a customer, offering an electronic look at accounts? Perhaps your business partners fundamentally need to be treated the same way and a standardized extranet is the right choice. For instance, do vendors need a standardized way to submit invoices or bid on new projects?

Customers

Customers are a major target of extranets. For extranets aimed specifically at them it helps to analyze an entire customer base. Customers can be graphed on two axes: (1) what each customer needs from the company, and (2) the value that each customer has to the company.

When it comes to determining the needs of customers, those needs may be diverse or similar. For instance, a grocery store's customers have extremely diverse needs. Each has a different list of food they want the store to supply them. On the other hand, a school bus maintenance company has customers that all have similar needs, reliable school buses.

The value the customer has to the company allows them to be classified as strategic partners, important partners, or practical partners as defined in Chapter 1. Generally, customers who spend or influence the most revenue are strategic. Those who consistently purchase services are important and the rest are practical.

In-depth information such as demographics, transactional histories, and so forth may be needed to determine where on the graph a particular customer falls on either axis. But it may not be necessary to analyze every customer. An overall analysis of the customer base will help a company determine what kind of extranet will be the best received, and for which customers it should provide this type of project. For instance, companies may discover that their customer base falls squarely on one axis or the other, both, or neither. The grocery store, for example, has a customer base that falls heavily into one end of the diversification axis of the graph, but its revenues are pretty evenly dispersed among customers, with no one customer accounting for the bulk of the company's profits. The school bus company, on the other hand, falls on the other end of the diversification axis, but may have only one customer, accounting for 100 percent of its profits. A coffee shop, on the other hand, has customers with similar needs plus customers of roughly equal value.

In between are companies such as manufacturers, which may have several customers that account for 80 percent of profits over half a dozen product lines. A service industry, such as a computer consultant that creates custom solutions for each client, would find that its customer base falls into neither side of the graph (Figure 7.1).

Once a company has analyzed its customer base, it can develop an extranet that will have the best ROI. If it discovers that 20 per-

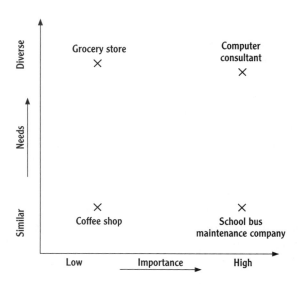

Figure 7.1   Examples of where certain businesses may fall in terms of importance and needs.

cent of its customers are 80 percent of the value, it may want to tailor the entire extranet to the needs of these customers, even if it offers access to this extranet to other customers. If it discovers that every customer is completely different, and equally important, it may want to create extranet applications that are customizable.

The ROI will depend greatly on how well the company has targeted its extranet toward those who are its most important customers.

A similar analysis can be done with vendors and joint-venture partners. By assessing what they need from the company along with their value to the company, aiming an extranet at the ones most likely to provide a high ROI becomes more feasible.

Summary

Return on investment is an increasingly important tool that businesses use today to make decisions on which projects to pursue and to judge the success or failure of a project. ROI essentially reveals to a company the "interest" it earned on any investment. As such, its role is to quantify as many elements of a project as possible, turning these elements into costs, savings, or revenue figures. A full ROI also corrects for a full range of factors such as cash flow, inflation, the inefficient transfer of time saved, and more.

In this chapter, we offer parameters for conducting a simple, basic Net Present Value ROI of elements that will be present in many extranet implementations. The NPV will give a company a net profit figure and can easily be converted to a percentage that represents the interest earned on an extranet. Extranets, like intranets, can have extremely high NPV, equally returns of 1,000+ percent or more. This is because much of what is needed to produce an extranet is already in place as the infrastructure or was acquired during previous projects, such as intranets. Yet an extranet can be expected to offer significant savings, particularly of time, and possibly even generate additional revenue for the company.

Companies should conduct a preliminary ROI on extranet projects, both as a gage to the financial benefits a company offers and also as a basis for budgets. Companies should also conduct more in-depth ROIs after the extranet has been in place for several months and users have integrated it into their daily work habits.

## chapter eight

Tools for Building an Extranet

In this chapter, we've given you a great start for finding the perfect tools to build and maintain an extranet. Yet, the sheer numbers of vendors and products aimed at the Internet, particularly the Web, make it impossible to list every conceivable extranet tool here (nor would anyone but the most diehard market lovers want to read such a thing). But we did our best to give you a good cross-section of what a typical extranet might use. We avoided certain categories of tools that didn't seem appropriate for an extranet, such as software that was aimed more at the "wow" factor than practical use. We tried to include most of the major players in each category as well as some lesser-known, harder-to-find prospects.

To make up for any deficiencies in this list, we've included the URLs of sources where a company might dig up more entries in a particular category. We've also included some information on how to evaluate tools against each other. And, of course, most vendors listed here offer numerous products that might be worth considering for your extranet project. So, be sure to allow yourself some time to browse through Web sites when you are shopping.

Also, to maximize the use of space, we didn't go on at length about every tool, but instead presented a basic description, URL, and other pointers that will allow an extranet developer to gather more information. We excluded pricing information as this information is so volatile prices printed here might not reflect current street prices. We strongly advise you to verify prices with your own sources before disqualifying (or including) any item because of cost. Chances are you can find a better deal than what has been listed here.

Finally, a quick disclaimer. This list is intended as a resource guide and not an endorsement of these tools. We strongly advise extranet developers to run any prospective tool through a thorough evaluation process before implementing it. We further recommend contacting the company's current vendors to see if they offer Internet/intranet retrofits of products you may already own. Many companies not listed in this chapter are scurrying to add HTML components to their wares. Such companies include Computer Associates (www.cai.com), PeopleSoft (www.peoplesoft.com), SAP America (www.sap.com), Informix (www.informix.com), and Sybase (www.sybase.com).

How to Evaluate Tools

Before extranet developers whip out the corporate pocketbooks, they should know the answer to the following question: "How is this tool different from any other tool I could buy or obtain free to perform this task?" Unfortunately, sifting fact from marketing fantasy is often a problem when shopping for computer tools, particularly in the hot and quickly mutating industry of Internet technologies.

If a tool is fairly inexpensive, say $49, the risks of making the wrong choice are pretty low. But many of the enterprise-level or development tools top $2,000, plus significant worker hours in the learning curve. Hardware can run $10,000, plus the worker hours of configuration (not exactly pocket change, except for the largest companies). The extranet developer needs to be confident that this tool will be functional, perform well, and have top-notch support from the vendor after the sale. How can the developer be sure? The answer lies in good old-fashioned legwork. Thorough research should uncover the major players in the category, what parts of the tool should be evaluated (speed or integration?), what each tool does best and worst, and costs both tangible and intangible. Research consists of three legs: preresearch, interviews, and evaluation.

Preresearch

Preresearch is the gathering of background information that will allow a shopper to identify vendors and the issues on which they compete. Generally speaking, for PC-level technologies, the older and more mature the tools and technologies, the more likely those tools have become commodity markets. This means that vendors have consolidated into only a handful of major players and prices have stabilized. The points of competition between players will be price, followed by service. The personal computer itself is a prime example of this. Although several dozen vendors may exist, only a handful control most of the market (Compaq, Dell, IBM, Gateway 2000, Packard Bell, etc.). Most use a CPU from a single company, Intel, and hard disks from the same handful of companies; they use the same operating system, and bundle in many of the same technologies. All of their ads feature prices, since that is the single most important shopping criterion of buyers.

On the opposite side of the pendulum swing is new technologies. Generally speaking, these technologies can be characterized as a market in which hundreds of players may compete, with no reigning monarch controlling the market. Since technologies are less defined, vastly different tools can claim to be part of the new technology and service the new area. Comparing apples to oranges is often stark reality. An example of this is the intranet. Dozens of new products for the intranet are being introduced daily, many from startup companies. Tools that perform similar functions, say electronic commerce, may have very different features. Prices are all over the place, not only between competing companies but within a company itself. Price also isn't an indicator of features and quality, because until a market turns the corner from infantile to established, vendors haven't yet figured out exactly what prices the market will bear for what types of products. For example, a year or so ago when the secure Web server was introduced, Open Market, Inc. (Cambridge, MA) priced it at about $5,000. A year later the price was cut to around $1,000. Now the company doesn't even really promote it anymore (mainly due to Netscape and Microsoft's dominance).

Even in this chapter, some tools with immense feature sets will be less than $100. Others with seemingly less to offer will be over $1,000. (The intranet management market is a prime example of this.)

Preresearch, then, will help a shopper identify the maturity of the market, the areas of differentiation among tools, and the trade-offs of each. In the Internet/intranet/extranet market today, one of the common trade-offs is ease-of-use for functionality. Generally speaking, the more graphical and drag and drop the interface is, the less the developer can fully take advantage of the underlying technology. (Some may argue that such is the case for all development. That's true to some extent. But our response to that is, how many companies perform all of their custom development quite satisfactorily with Visual Basic?)

When it comes to preresearch, the more time spent on this area of the evaluation process, the more time saved on the evaluation process, and the more confident you will be that you made the right choice.

The first step is to see what has been written about a specific product category, say, Web-to-database integration tools. Get on the net and any online services you have access to and read up on these tools. Computer magazine databases are rich sources of this type of information. One good one is ZD Net, an online service in its own right and also accessible through several commercial online services, such as CompuServe. ZD Net also has a terrific Web site that offers much of this type of trade information for free (http://www5.zdnet.com/). This site offers full-text back issues of most of the top computer publications, including all the Ziff-Davis news weeklies, such as *PC Week.* Another good one is InfoSeek, a Web-based search engine that also sports a subscription service which archives back issues of *InfoWorld* (www.infoseek.com). *InfoWorld* also archives many of its stories on its Web site (www .infoworld.com) and posts current reviews from its test center there as well. In fact, probably every major computer magazine that performs reviews will have a backlog of great product information on its Web site. The point here is to read a few generic articles on the tools themselves, such as roundups, rather than many articles on specific tools. These articles will also offer lots of names of tools to pursue. Category reviews are particularly good because they will offer objective performance metrics on a category. We've found that individual reviews tend to be much more positive about the tool being reviewed than the comparative roundup.

Follow this up with a visit to the Web sites of potential vendors. Often these sites have posted press releases—short papers intended for use by the press—which will have a lot of information about products probably not available anywhere else on the site. For instance, press releases frequently have a product's price and ship date. (For some vague reason that we cannot fathom, many sites strip this information out of their press releases and refuse to list pricing information on their sites. Yet they readily make this information available to the press who print it in their roundups.) Press releases present a fairly concise description of the product.

Another good source of information, albeit more expensive, is market research companies, such as IDC (www.idcresearch.com), the Gartner Group/Dataquest (www.gartner.com), Giga Information Group (www.gigweb.com), and the Aberdeen Group (www.aberdeen.com) to name a few. These companies produce massive compilations of statistics and/or review information about various markets, such as Internet/intranet, computer security, hardware servers, you name it. Expect to pay a premium for one of these reports (typically $1,000 or more); however, scaled-down versions or executive summaries are often available for less.

Industry trade groups are another source of information. The security industry, for example, has several, such as the Computer Security Institute (www.gocsi.com) and the National Computer Security Association (www.ncsa.com). Industry organizations often have extensive market research information, data on specific products, and numerous other tidbits helpful to the shopper. We've listed some of the many trade groups involved with various aspects of Internet technologies in Chapter 9.

Articles, press releases, and other Web information will give an extranet developer a good background, but should also lead to questions about specific tools, such as:

- What platforms do they support?
- What security features do they offer?
- Is there an objective test or stamp of approval that products can obtain, such as the NCSA certification process for firewalls? (See the "Note" in the Firewall category.)
- Have they been tested with encryption products?
- What performance metrics are used to compare these products with one another?
- What are the products' limitations?

Finally, search the newsgroups or forums where other users of this product are likely to be online. Subscribe yourself to their mailing list. Is the list very active with messages from a wide variety of people, or does it consist of messages from a select few? The former would suggest that the tool has garnered some marketplace popularity; the latter, the converse. What kinds of questions are posted? If users are dissatisfied or frustrated with the product, this is a surefire way to find out. It's also a great way to find consultants and others who may be willing to offer their experience during the learning curve phase.

Also, search for the product's name, plus the word "sucks" (as this vernacular is often used on the Internet to express displeasure) on some of the many Internet search engines today.

Search Engines

It seems that the only thing growing faster than the net itself is the number of search engines available to search it. It may seem that they are all alike, but they may use different approaches to scanning a Web site and update at different times. So failure with one search engine doesn't necessarily mean that the information you're looking for—even obscure product categories—doesn't exist.

Each search engine catalogs differently. For instance, Alta Vista (www.altavista.com) scans individual Web pages, rather than entire Web sites, including Usenet discussion groups. This makes it one of the largest repositories of Web information on the Net.

Excite reviews Web sites and displays a summary of each. Excite (www.excite.com) also searches Usenet discussion groups and classified ads. Infoseek (www.infoseek.com) tosses in links to other Web pages that might be of interest. Yahoo organizes sites by category and includes a link to the category with its search results.

Some, like Yahoo and Webcrawler (www.webcrawler.com), start you off with a list of categories. Others, such as Excite and Net-Guide (www.netguide.com), offer national and special-interest news from leading sources such as CNN (NetGuide) and Reuters (Excite) from the home page. Some use fancy new technology. For instance, Magellen (http://searcher.mckinley.com) offers a "Voyeurs" page which lists searches the other visitors are performing, and automatically refreshes the page.

If you've always used the same search engine, try a new one every so often. You may be surprised at the types of information that other sources have available. In addition to the engines listed here, two other good lists of available search engines are on the Microsoft page (www.microsoft.com/search/) and at the bottom of each Yahoo search result page.

Interviews

With a list of questions at the ready, it's time to talk to a human being at each potential company. Make sure that your list includes some generic questions that will be asked of everyone. This is one of the best ways to uncover differences in products and also get feel for the character of the company. We've supplied a standard list of questions that we find are almost always useful, no matter what kind of product is being researched. Talk to a salesperson or marketing representative. Now, don't groan: the idea here isn't to digest endless hours of company propaganda, but to conduct an interview of a knowledgeable source who can answer specific questions. If the person turns out to be useless in answering technical questions, try to speak to someone who knows the product extremely well, such as an engineer or a product manager.

Here are some questions that might be useful:

Questions for Vendors

1. What is your company's definition of the category (extranet, for example)? (Note: this may seem unnecessary, but it's amazing how many vendors bend a definition of a category so that their product will fit in. That's a valuable bit of knowledge, and indicates if they really belong, of if they are retrofitting themselves to cash in on a trend.)

2. Who is your primary target market for this tool? why?

3. Who are your company's biggest customers of this product? Will they speak to me about the product? Can you give me a list of contact names and phone numbers?

4. Who are your major competitors?

5. What differentiates this product from those competitors?

6. What specific types of technical problems was the product developed to solve?

7. What areas are beyond this product's capabilities?

8. What are some indications that this product is of higher quality than its competitors? Is it faster? Does it offer more features? Does the company have any objective performance data it can give me? (Try to get specifics about the product here, not just that it's being used by some hotshot big-name customer. Shady companies often play the name game, even if that company only bought a evaluation copy.)

9. What platforms does it support?

10. Do any standards exist for this industry that the product supports?

11. How can I tell if those standards were implemented properly? Does some kind of independent testing exist for standard-compliant products? Who performs it?

(Continued)

12. What kind of after-sale support do you offer? free telephone technical support, for how long? online access to updates or bug fixes? access to an engineer if the problem is complicated?

13. How long has this company been in business? How many other products does it sell, and in what areas? (A warning flag should go up over the startup company with only this one flagship product. Unless this company has a significant market share, odds are they won't be around for the long haul to upgrade and support this product. This guideline isn't absolute, though. Some startup companies start by providing many products, realize that one or two are going places, then drop the losers and focus on the winners.)

14. How long will it take me to install and configure this product? (This and an evaluation copy are a good "lie detector" test. If the vendor says "five minutes" and the evaluation unit takes all day, chasing down errors, red flags are waving.)

15. How long will it take me to learn how to use this product at a master level? What kinds of training options do you offer?

16. Are there any computer consultants (VARs) trained with this product in my area? What types of training do they obtain before they are an authorized reseller of yours? (Many companies offer levels of "partnership" with VARs and some require *no* training to become authorized. It's good to know if the person you're about to hire can really help.)

17. If I decide to evaluate the product before purchase, can I get a free 30-day evaluation unit? Is this evaluation unit a fully functional copy or is it lacking from the commercial version in some ways? what ways?

18. If I decide to evaluate the product before purchase, what areas do you recommend I test for?

(Continued)

19. How much does the product cost? Can a volume discount be negotiated?

20. For development tools: does the software license include run-time fees or does the company expect to be paid separately for the tool and the applications developed from it?

In addition to interviewing the company, it is important to talk to some of the company's user references, which the company should be able to supply to you. Here's a list of questions that are almost always helpful when talking to references. Presumably, these references are all the company's clients that are satisfied with the product and company and will give it a good review. However, even customers who are essentially happy will usually offer candid and objective information about the product and the other choices in the marketplace. Hindsight is 20/20.

Product Evaluations

At this point, the company should have boiled down the contenders to four or fewer prospects. It should have eliminated, right off the bat, any products that didn't support the necessary platforms, whose customer references gave it lukewarm or outright bad reviews, and so forth.

It's time to evaluate the products. If a product is expensive and difficult to learn, ask the vendor to come in and demonstrate. However, nothing beats a hands-on experience. Fortunately for today's extranet developers, tools based on Internet protocols were born in a free society. Although most tools that you'll use today are not going to be free, the commercial Internet vendors have often upheld this tradition by offering free demonstration tools on their sites. Typically, the tool is a working version, maybe even a full-fledged one, with a limited run time. This makes evaluating tools fairly easy. Download the tool and run it.

Questions for Customer References

1. How long have you used the product?
2. What are you using it for?
3. Why did you choose this one?
4. Did you evaluate other types of products besides this one? which ones?
5. What were your opinions on those other products?
6. What areas did you test for when you evaluated?
7. What do you especially like about the product?
8. What do you especially dislike?
9. Did you find that the product held up to the vendor's claims? Which claims were accurate and which inaccurate?
10. If you could change the product in any way, what would you change?
11. Was the product intuitive or did it have a steep learning curve? What was the most difficult aspect to master?
12. Does the product scale well?
13. Have there been any quality issues with it since you've been using it?
14. Has the company offered good technical support?
15. Would you recommend that other people use this product?

You specifically want to look for any quality-related issues that you uncovered during your preresearch and interviews. For example, if the vendors were all touting some kind of standard compliance, you should try to test each product in that area. Likewise, if one was touting scalability, try to test for it.

Areas in which each product should be evaluated include:

◆ Ease of installation and use.
◆ Competent documentation and technical support. (Call tech support with a question and see what kind of queue times you get and if the person answering is knowledgeable.)
◆ Quality: does the product perform reliably?
◆ Scalability: will it handle 1,000 hits as easily as 10 hits?
◆ Compatibility with existing systems.

Of course, it doesn't make sense from a worker-hours point of view to do this kind of intensive product evaluation for low-cost, commodity tools. A good scan of the computer trade databases plus a scan of the newsgroups on the tool will suffice. Remaining questions can be fired off in an e-mail to the company and an evaluation unit downloaded and checked out. Or you can download the demo as one of the first steps, and see what happens there. You might find that none of your programmers have any interest in it. This will save you the time of going out to do the interviews. You may also find that they pick up the product, and before you know it you are developing with it. That is a good sign to start interviewing.

Hardware

Internet Servers in a Box

Easy Web Server

Digital Equipment Corp., Maynard, MA, 508-493-5111, 800-344-4825 (www.digital.com/info/internet/resources/servers). An Alpha/NT solution which uses Netscape Communications for Windows NT as the Web server.

HP 9000 Web Server

Hewlett-Packard Co., Palo Alto, CA, 800-752-0900 (www.hp.com). An HP 9000 Server bundled with Open Markets WebServer software for HP's Unix.

Internet Server Solution 6150/66

Apple Computer Corp., Cupertino, CA, 408-996-1010 or 800-776-2333 (www.apple.com). PowerPC server with WebStar from StarNine Technologies, a division of Quarterdeck Corp. WebStar is the commercial version of StarNine's popular shareware program, MacHTTP.

InterServe Web-300, Web-610, and Web-630

Intergraph Computer Systems, Huntsville, AL, 205-730-2000, 800-763-0242 (www.intergraph.com). A Pentium/NT box Microsoft's Internet Information Server.

WebForce Indy

Silicon Graphics, Inc., Mountain View, CA, 415-960-1980 or 800-800-7441 (www.sgi.com). A high-performance Unix box based on SGI's Irix operating system and using Netscape Fast-Track Web Server as the Web server.

NOTE   *A company may want to source hardware servers and Web servers separately, to get greater control of security and other features. Hardware servers are available for Windows NT from most of the major PC manufacturers as well as Tandem Computers (www.tandem.com). Hardware servers for Unix are available from the large Unix manufacturers, such as Sun Microsystems (www.sun.com), IBM, Hewlett-Packard (www.hp.com), and Digital Equipment Corp. (www.digital.com).*

IP Switches

GRF 400

Ascend Communications Corp., Alameda, CA, 800-621-9578 (www.ascend.com). An IP switch designed for exceptionally busy IP networks.

IP Switch ATM1600

Ipsilon Networks, Inc. (www.ipsilon.com). The IP switch that made router vendors, such as Cisco and Bay Networks, scramble to compete.

Tag Switching

Cisco Systems, Inc., San Jose, CA, 408-526-4000 or 800-553-6387 (www.cisco.com). Cisco's version of IP switching will be available first on the Cisco 7500 series routers in the first half of 1997 and the Cisco StrataCom BPX later in 1997.

NOTE   *Bay Networks has announced plans to include IP switching technology in its Centillion Switches (http:// www.baynetworks.com/Products/Switches/Centillion/) and currently offers a combination of Frame Relay switching and IP routing in its BayStream multiservice software.*

Internet-Specific Clients

NOTE   *Ideally, the clients used in an extranet belong to the partners, not the company. So, clients won't be part of most extranet expenditures. However, in certain situations, a company may want to provide its partners with dedicated clients. Obviously, a PC would do for this. However, the less expensive Network Computer (NC), also known as thin clients, might also be a solution. These are devices that shift most or all of the processing power to network servers, and also have little if any hard disk storage. (Sounds an awful lot like a dumb terminal to us.) So, we've included a short list of thin clients for this reason.*

JavaStation

Sun Microsystems, Mountain View, CA, 800-786-0785, ext. 475 (www.sun.com). A diskless NC powered by a microSPARCII CPU and operating on the JavaOS or legacy terminal operating systems such as SNA or VT220.

Netstations 400

Tektronix, Dept. 613, 800-547-8949 (http://www.tek.com/Network_Displays/). Billed as an upgrade to text terminals, this RISC-based NC supports access to Windows, Unix, and therefore, intranet-based applications.

NOTE   *Oracle Corp. (www.oracle.com), Apple Computer Corp. (ww.apple.com), and Boundless Technologies, formerly SunRiver Corp. (www.sunriver.com), will also release network computers in 1997.*

Web Software

Secure Web Servers

For Unix

Apache SSL-US

Community ConneXion, Inc., Berkeley, CA, 510-601-9777 (www.apache-ssl.com). A popular secure freeware server. A commercial version, called Stronghold, is also available from UK Web (http://www.ukweb.com/). [Free].

Enterprise Server

Netscape Communications Corp., Mountain View, CA, 415-937-3678 (www.netscape.com). Netscape's bread-and-butter secure server, which is bundled into its SuitSpot suite of servers and is the basis of many other products.

FastTrack Server 2.0

Netscape Communications Corp., Mountain View, CA, 415-937-3678 (www.netscape.com). Also available on other platforms.

NCSA HTTPd

National Center for Supercomputing Applications, University of Illinois, Champaign, IL (http://hoohoo.ncsa.uiuc.edu/). The popular freeware Web server. Does not support SSL yet, but does support other types of encryption and Kerberos authentication. [Free].

For NT

Enterprise Server

Netscape Communications Corp. See listing For Unix.

FastTrack Server 2.0

Netscape Communications Corp. See listing For Unix.

Internet Information Server 2.0

Microsoft Corp., Redmond, WA, 800-426-9400 (www .microsoft.com/infoserv/iisinfo.htm). Microsoft's entry into the Web server market. Supports SSL and is available with Windows NT or from the Microsoft Web site. [Free].

Internet Transaction Processing Messaging Server

Tandem Computer, Inc., Cupertino, CA, 408-285-6000 or 800-482-6336 (http://www.tandem.com/). A secure server specifically designed for business-to-business transaction processing such as EDI over the Internet.

Web Commander for Windows NT

Luckman Interactive, Inc., Los Angeles, CA, 213-614-1758 (www.luckman.com). Extensive use of wizards and feature-packed server including support for SSL, S-HTTP, and RSA encryption.

WebSite Professional for Windows NT and 95

O'Reilly & Associates, Inc., Sebastopol, CA, 800-998-9938 (software.ora.com). A popular and robust Web server that supports SSL and S-HTTP.

Wildcat Interactive Net Server

Mustang Software, Inc., Bakersfield, CA, 805-873-2500 or 800-663-7310 (www.mustang.com). Includes a real-time chat server and support for secure electronic commerce. It includes a freeware browser optimized for Win Server. [Free personal edition.]

For Other Environments

Domino

Lotus Development Corp., Cambridge, MA, 800-828-7086 (http://domino.lotus.com). Domino is a secure Web server for the Lotus Notes platform that also performs workflow and other interactive functions.

Secure Web Server

HiTecSoft Corp., Scottsdale, AZ, 602-970-1025 or 888-970-1025 (www.hitecsoft.com). A secure server for the NetWare network operating system that supports SSL and RSA encryption.

Web Server

Novell, Inc., Provo, UT, 800-554-4445. An SSL-compliant Web Server, for NetWare.

Secure Browsers

HotJava Views

JavaSoft (a unit of Sun Microsystems), Cupertino, CA, 408-523-2797 or 800-288-0443 (www.javasoft.com). A suite of tools designed network computers, particularly the Java-Station as well as X terminals and PCs. Includes a web browser, contact directory, calendar, and e-mail.

NOTE *The JavaSoft Web site is evidence that Java applets don't have to be a ticker tape or obtrusive and slow to be of value. The site uses Java pop-up menus to assist in navigation, for instance.*

Internet Explorer 3.0

Microsoft Corp., Redmond, WA, 800-426-9400 (www.
microsoft.com/ie/default.asp/). Internet Explorer is one of
two leading 32-bit browsers that supports SSL and other
security features, such as Authenticode. Its features are
roughly comparable to Netscape's Navigator 3.0.

Mosaic

National Center for Supercomputing Applications
(http://www.ncsa.uiuc.edu/SDG/Software/XMosaic/). Still
the most popular browser for Unix/X-Windows systems.
Although it does not support SSL yet, it can be configured to
encrypt data with an HTTPd server. An add-on called Shared
Mosaic gives the browser support for collaboration, Mbone,
and other goodies found in commercial browsers. [Free].

Netscape Navigator 3.0/Netscape Communicator
(the upgrade to the Navigator line)

Netscape Communications Corp., Mountain View, CA, 415-
937-2555. Navigator is the premier client 32-bit browser
whose only major competition is Microsoft's Internet
Explorer 3.0. Navigator 3.0 will be replaced by Communicator in 1997. Communicator will include Navigator 4.0 and
other applications such as an HTML authoring tool, messaging, collaboration, and group discussion software.

Wildcat! Navigator for Windows

Mustang Software, Inc., Bakersfield, CA, 805-873-2500 or
800-663-7310 (www.mustang.com). A browser designed
specifically for Mustang's secure Web server but that can be
launched from Internet Explorer or Navigator. [Free].

HTML Editors/Web Development

Backstage Internet Studio

Macromedia, Inc., San Francisco, CA, 800-326-2128 (www.
macromedia.com). An HTML editor with some powerful
backend capabilities, such as database connectivity and
image editing.

FrontPage

Microsoft Corp., Redmond, WA, 800-936-3500. FrontPage 97, now an adjunct to Microsoft's popular application suite, Office 97, is an HTML editor that allows Office documents to easily be converted to HTML. Of course, it also can create original HTML documents.

HAHTsite

HAHT Software, Inc., Raleigh, NC, 919-786-5100 or 888-GET-HAHT (www.haht.com). Develops, maintains, and deploys secure, interactive intranets over existing IT infrastructures and can integrate with existing databases. HAGTsite engine.

HotMetal

SoftQuad International, Inc., Toronto, 416-544-9000 (www.softquad.com). By far among the most popular and robust tools for creating Web pages. Includes drag and drop, support for Java, ActiveX, frames, VRML, and more.

HTML Transit

InfoAccess, Inc., Bellevue, WA, 206-747-3203 (www.infoaccess.com). Converts existing documents and graphics into HTML format automatically. Supports most of the more popular formats such as Word and WordPerfect files, the generic Rich Text Format, and a slew of image files.

Intranet Genie

Frontier Technologies Corp., Mequon, WI, 414-241-4555 or 800-929-3054 (www.frontiertech.com). A suite of tools designed to create and manage an intranet on NT, including a secure Web server and secure e-mail server.

LiveWire

Netscape Communications Corp., Mountain View, CA, 415-937-2555 (www.netscape.com). A sophisticated tool for creating interactive Web pages, including database connectivity. NT and Unix versions available.

Net-It Now

Net-It Software Corp., San Francisco, CA, 415-988-6961 (www.net-it.com). Net-It Now is a unique HTML editor because it takes documents created by popular Windows applications, such as Word or WordPerfect or an assortment of image files, and turns them into Java files that maintain original layouts in which interactive elements can be added.

NetObjects Fusion for Windows

NetObjects Inc., Redwood City, CA, 415-482-3200 or 888-449-6400, ext. 922 (www.netobjects.com). NetObjects Fusion offers drag-and-drop HTML editing and supports plug-ins, ActiveX, auto frame creation, and other interactive technologies. A Macintosh version is also available.

Prolifics

Prolifics, a subsidiary of JYACC, New York, 212-267-7722 (www.prolifics.com). A development tool for creating enterprise transactional applications on the Web.

Studio

NetDynamics Inc., Menlo Park, CA, 415-462-7600 (www .netdynamics.com). A development tool for creating transaction processing applications on the Web.

VisualWave

ParcPlace Digitalk, Sunnyvale, CA, 408-481-9090 or 800-759-7272 (www.parcplace.com). VisualWave is an object-oriented development tool that creates integrated client/server/Web applications. It provides automatic session management for Web applications, offers database connectivity, supports the latest Web technologies, such as Java, ActiveX, and VRML, and is useful for putting traditional client/server database applications on the Web, such as inventory planning, customer service, or order entry applications.

WebBatch

Wilson WindowWare, Inc., Seattle, WA, 206-938-1740 or 800-762-8383 (www.windowware.com). A CGI scripting tool for Windows 95 or NT Web servers.

WebEdit Pro 2.0 for Windows 95

Luckman Interactive, Inc., Los Angeles, CA, 213-614-1758 (www.nesbitt.com). Created by Ken Nesbitt and recently sold to Luckman, this product offers an exceptionally large feature set for creating HTML pages, including drag-and-drop files, frames, and HTML tags directly onto Web pages.

WebFactory Pro Image

Thunder & Lightning Co., San Diego, CA, 619-643-5550 or 800-826-3520 (www.tlco.com). WebFactory Pro is a full-featured HTML editor that does images and graphics exceptionally well. A lite version with fewer graphics capabilities is also available.

WebSpeed

Progress Software Corp., Bedford, MA, 800-477-6473 (http://webspeed.progress.com). A development tool for creating and deploying Internet transaction processing applications. It allows extranet developers to create self-service automated applications for use by business partners.

Business-to-Business Electronic Commerce Development Tools

Amazon

Intelligent Environments, Inc., Burlington, MA, 617-272-9700 (www.ieinc.com/Products/Amazon/a database). An NT database integration development tool specifically for creating extranet sites and business-to-business electronic commerce. Links to legacy backend data including DB2 and ODBC.

iCat Electronic Commerce Suite

iCat Corp., Seattle, WA, 206-623-0977 or 888-533-8800 (www.icat.com). ICat is a suite of tools for creating interactive catalogs and then electronic commerce sites and CD ROMs based on them. For Windows and Macintosh.

OM-Transact

Open Market, Inc., Cambridge, MA, 617-949-7000 (www .openmarket.com). A backend transaction management infrastructure for secure business-to-business Internet commerce.

Pecos.net

Elcom Systems, Inc., Westwood, MA, 617-407-5000 (www .elcom.com). Pecos.net is an electronic commerce system specifically for handling large-volume catalog orders, such as distributors' and manufacturers' transactions, over the Web. Passwords, authentication, encryption, and EDI interfaces are supported, as is Java.

PurchasingNet

American Tech, Inc., Holmdel, NJ, 908-946-8844 (www .purchasingnet.com). An intranet or Internet extension to any purchasing or accounting system which can link to or provide the requisition, purchase, and electronic payment process.

Trade'Ex Market Maker

Trade'Ex Electronic Commerce Systems, Inc., Tampa, FL, 813-222-2050, (www.tradeex.com). This company, an online computer product distributor for high-volume customers, licenses its Java-based transaction software which creates similar business-to-business electronic commerce sites. Includes modules for wholesaling, payment and fulfillment, procurement systems, and more over the Web and linking browsers to EDI systems.

Database Integration Tools

Cold Fusion

Allaire Corp., Cambridge, MA, 617-761-2000 (www.allaire.com). One of the more popular tools for producing Web sites with database backends on Windows. Proprietary HTML allows easy connections to backend databases.

DataSite

NetScheme Solutions, Inc., Marlborough, MA, 508-480-0877 (www.netscheme.com). This Windows product constructs a server-based navigation model and a complete set of hyperlinked Web page templates from the database automatically. This allows users to "mine" the backend database, because DataSite translates these automatic hyperlinks into SQL queries.

DB/Text WebServer

Inmagic, Inc., Woburn, MA, 617-938-4442 or 800-229-8398 (www.inmagic.com). A search engine tool that also manages Web site data within the framework of a DBMS rather than static HTML documents, for Windows.

Globetrotter Web Publisher for the Macintosh

Akimbo Systems, Inc., Someville, MA, 800-375-6515 (www.akimbo.com). A feature set is mapped to HTML tags so that users can publish a site without any knowledge of HTML.

IntranBuilder Professional for Windows 95 and Windows NT

Borland International, Inc., Scotts Valley, CA, 408-431-1000 or 800-523-7070 (www.borland.com). A complete toolkit for creating Web-based database applications and editing database entries.

JetConnect

XDB Systems, Inc., Columbia, MD, 410-312-9300 or 800-488-4948 (www.xdb.com). A set of Java classes for allowing access to databases via JDBC and ODBC. Free for single license. For Windows and Unix.

Livewire

Netscape Communications Corp. See entry in HTML Editors/ Web development tools.

Sanga Pages

Sanga International, Inc., Burlington, MA, 617-272-8500 or 800-627-2642 (www.sangacorp.com). A database integration tool which allows Java access to relational databases by using the Java Database Connectivity Standard.

SaphireWeb

Bluestone, Inc., Mount Laurel, NJ, 609-727-4600 (www .bluestone.com). A sophisticated visual Web database integration tool that provides automatic code generation and visual views of databases, and can integrate with other, popular HTML editors, such as FrontPage.

SiteMill for the Macintosh

Adobe Systems, Inc., San Jose, CA, 408-536-6000 (www .adoble.com). Manages complex Web sites with a drag-and-drop interface similar to Adobe's PageMill authoring software.

Universal Web Architecture

Informix Software, Inc., Menlo Park, CA, 415-926-6300. A middleware technology composed of the Universal Web Connect database, the Web DataBlade module, Java Anywhere, JWorks, and Web tools from other vendors to provide services such as extranet electronic commerce which creates both interactive Web applications and transaction-based applications.

WebFocus

Information Builders, Inc., New York, NY, 212-736-4433 or 800-969-INFO (www.ibi.com). This company has brought its data-mining background to the Web with WebFocus. This reporting tool turns backend SQL databases into Web-based decision support systems, much like a data warehouse or data-mining system.

WebObjects

Next Software, Inc., Redwood City, CA, 415-366-0900 or 1-800-TRY-NeXT (www.next.com). A drag-and-drop application development tool allows developers to choose HTML-based forms or browser-based applets to connect to server applications and databases. The product can balance CPU loads between client and server, allowing developers to fine-tune client performance. For Windows, Nextstep, Openstep and Solaris.

Management/Grinding Tools
(Tools that Search Out and Repair Bad Links)

SiteMill for the Macintosh

Adobe Systems, Inc., San Jose, CA, 408-536-6000. Manages complex Web sites with a drag-and-drop interface similar to Adobe's PageMill authoring software.

Visual SourceSafe 5.0

Microsoft Corp., Redmond, WA, 206-882-8080 (www .microsoft.com/ssafe/). Visual SourceSafe, a version control product that has been enhanced for the Web. It now performs grinding and also allows collaborative development over the Web.

Tools that Customize the Web Site

Arrive

Fusion Com Corp., New York, NY, 212-352-4500 (www .ifusion.com/). Arrive is similar to BackWeb in that it is a client/server product that broadcasts information to clients who tune into "channels" to receive that information. Content can be personalized, depending on who is viewing it.

BackWeb

BackWeb Technologies, Inc., San Jose, CA, 408-437-0200
(www.backweb.com). A client/server system for NT and
Solaris that allows companies to "broadcast" customized
information to BackWeb clients on "channels." Clients support Windows and Macs. The server is based on UPD to better deliver video, and the client receives information in the
background while connected to the Internet. Client is [Free].

Intermind Communicator

Intermind, Seattle, WA, 800-625-6150 (www.intermind.com).
A tool for Windows 3.1, 96, and NT that performs customized
searches for designated information on specified Web sites
and creates a database of that information.

RightSite for Enterprise Document Management System

Documentum, Inc., Pleasanton, CA, 510-463-6800 or 888-362-
3367 (www.documentum.com). RiteSite allows Web pages to
be customized depending on the user logon or password. It is
an adjunct the company's document management system.

Intranet Platforms

IntranetWare

Novell, Inc., Provo, UT, 800-554-4445 (www.novell.com/
intranet_ready/). A 32-bit operating system designed specifically for intranets, scaleable for multiprocessors. It integrates
with various Novell products such as Netware and Groupwise and uses Novell's directory service, NDS. It includes
Novell's NetWare Web Server 2.5. Novell asserts that the
product is C-2 network security compliant.

LiveLink Intranet

Open Text Corp., Waterloo, Ontario, 519-888-7111 (www
.opentext.com). An intranet development platform that provides a search engine, workflow, and document management.

Notes

Lotus Development Corp., Cambridge, MA, 800-828-7086 (www.lotus.com). Notes, the quintessential groupware development platform, has been refitted for intranet/extranet support.

Web Communication Tools

Emaze WebThread

Emaze Software Corp., Reisterstown, MD, 410-526-1298. A Web discussion software that stores all messages in each thread on a single page. Can run conferences secured to a variety of access levels. For NT, Mac, or Unix.

Infinite InterChange

Infinite Technologies, Owings Mills, MD, 410-363-1097 or 800-678-1097 (www.ihub.com). An e-mail program that can map LAN-based e-mail packages to standard Internet protocols such as IMAP4, POP3, and SMTP so that users can access their LAN e-mail from the Web, even remotely.

Internet Phone

VocalTec, Inc., Northvale, NJ, 201-768-9400 (www.vocaltec .com). One of the more popular products that allow live voice transmissions over the Internet, much like a telephone. Also supports video conferencing, with upgrade. For Windows and Mac.

NOTE   *About a dozen Internet telephone products exist on the market today. In addition to VocalTec, other manufacturers include NetSpeak Corp. (www.netspeak.com), Quarterdeck Corp. (www.webtalk.qdeck.com), Intel Corp. (http://connectedpc.com), 408-765-8080, and Netscape CoolTalk (www.netscape.com).*

NetMeeting Software Developers Kit

Microsoft Corp., Redmond, WA, 800-426-9400 (www.microsoft.com/intdev/msconf). A developer tool for use with Microsoft's browser-based videoconferencing and whiteboard tool, NetMeeting. Also useful for Web sites that use Visual Basic Scripting, JavaScript, and ActiveX live-interaction applications. [Free].

netT.120 Conference Server

DataBeam Corp., Lexington, KY, 606-245-3500 or 800-877-2325 (www.databeam.com). Multipoint whiteboard conferencing over the Web. Any browser can view a conference but a client-side conferencing product, such as DataBeam's Far-Site, is required to participate. For NT or Solaris.

Web Crossing

Lundeen & Associates, Alameda, CA, 510-521-5855. Server software which provides online discussion forums for NT, Unix, and the Mac.

Xpound

DigitalFacades, Inc., Santa Monica, CA, 310-581-4100 or 800-501-7695 (www.xpound.com). Xpound is a Web-based discussion group for Unix that supports cookies and frames.

Other Cool and Useful Tools

Common Ground

Hummingbird Communications Ltd., North York, Ontario, 416-496-2200 (www.hummingbird.com). A product that preserves document formats in a secure way, a process the company calls Digital Paper, yet allows annotation and searching.

InfoPress

Castelle Inc., Santa Clara, CA, 800-655-8818 (www.castelle.com). Maintains a library of documents which can be automatically converted to HTML on request from a browser, or can be faxed or e-mailed to recipients instead. Fax-on-demand information from this same database can also be requested by phone. For Windows NT.

I-Server

PointCast, Inc., Cupertino, CA, 408-253-0894 or 888-564-6726 (www.pointcast.com). I-Server broadcasts data, such as industry headlines, stock prices, or competitive pricing details, to a desktop automatically. For Windows 95; also integrated with Lotus Notes.

PowerMedia Pro 3.0

Radmedia Corp., Palo Alto, CA, 415-617-9433 (www .radmedia.com). A presentation tool that is optimized for Web delivery by allowing users to embed Java applets into presentation slides and post the presentation on the Web. For Windows and Unix.

UWI Masque Business Forms

UWI Unisoft Wares, Inc., Victoria, B.C., Canada, 604-479-8334 (www.uwi.bc.ca). Software for distributing electronic business forms over an intranet.

WebCal Intranet Edition

WebCal LCC, New York, NY, 212-226-1563 (www.webcal .com). An HTTP-based group calendar product for NT, Unix, and Mac WebCal also sponsors EventCal, a World Wide Web calendar service of industry events.

NOTE   *Other companies that have Web calendar/scheduling software include Lotus Development Corp. with Web Calendar (www.lotus.com), Oracle Corp. with Interoffice (www.oracle.com), and Novell, Inc., with GroupWise (www .novell.com).*

WebTheater

Vxtreme, Inc., Palo Alto, CA, 415-614-0700 (www.vxtreme .com). Products for client, server, and production that integrate video into ordinary HTML pages that remain of high quality even when pages are downloaded over modems. For NT, Solaris, and IRIX.

WiseWire

Empirical Media, Pittsburgh, PA, 412-688-8870 (http:// www.empirical.com). WiseWire is billed as a "personal surfing assistant." It combs Web sites looking for information of interest to the surfer and learns from feedback.

TCP/IP Stacks and Utility Suites

Iware Connect4

Quarterdeck Corp., Marina Del Rey, CA, 310-309-3700 or 800-225-8148 (www.quarterdeck.com). Iware Connect enables NetWare networks to connect to the Internet at the server level, rather than installing TCP/IP on every client.

OnNet32

FTP Software, Inc., 800-282-4387 (www.ftp.com). VIP OnNet32, a suite of client TCP/IP utilities for Windows such as a newsreader, Mosaic browser, chat tool, and TCP/IP stack and e-mail that supports SSL, PGP encryption for e-mail, CheckPoint's VPN, and Ipv6 security standards. FTP Software has recently declared that extranets—which it calls the Virtual IP Network—are its strategic focus and that it will align all of its products to support extranets.

SuperTCP Suite 96

Frontier Technologies Corp., Mequon, WI, 414-241-4555 or 800-929-3054. Over 40 TCP/IP applications including complete Internet access.

tcpConnect4

Intercon Systems Corp., Herndon, VA, 703-709-5500 or 800-468-7266 (www.intercon.com). An integrated suite of net tools for both Windows and Macintosh platforms in one box, such as TCP stack, e-mail, Gopher and Web clients, and other Unix utilities.

Security Tools

Firewalls

> **N**OTE   *The National Computer Security Association offers a firewall certification process in which it offers its stamp of approval based on functionality and performance. Although certifications are not the ultimate in shopping criteria, they do offer some objective guarantee of performance. We therefore advise companies to verify whether their potential firewall product has earned the NCSA certification before purchasing the product. The firewalls listed here qualify.*

Unix Firewalls

BorderWare

Secure Computing, Roseville, MN, 612-628-2700 or 800-692-5625 (www.sctc.com/borderware/). Another immensely popular Unix firewall that combines several methods of firewall protections including application gateways and network address translation—the hiding of internal IP address.

Eagle

Raptor Systems, Inc., Waltham, MA, 617-487-7700 or 800-9-EAGLE-6 (www.raptor.com). A popular and powerful Unix firewall that supports encryption for VPNs, bidirectional control for managing internal users' privileges.

FireWall-1

CheckPoint Software Technologies Ltd., Redwood City, CA, 415-562-0400 (www.checkpoint.com). An extremely popular and versatile Unix firewall and one that supports encryption for VPNs and authentication. It can also scan for malicious applets and viruses.

Guantlet Internet Firewall

Trusted Information Systems, Glenwood, MD, 301-854-6889 (www.tis.com). A popular, application proxy-based firewall that supports encryption for virtual private networks and offers all of the features of a top-notch firewall.

Sidewinder

Secure Computing, Roseville, MN, 612-628-2700 or 800-692-5625 (www.sctc.com/borderware/). A unique firewall that employs a concept called "typecasting" which separates Internet services, such as e-mail and HTTP, and prevents access from one to another, even if a service is compromised.

NT Firewalls

Eagle for NT

Raptor Systems, Inc. See entry under Unix Firewalls.

FireWall/Plus for Windows NT

Network-1 Software and Technologies, Inc., New York, NY, 800-NETWRK1. An unusual firewall originally created for government use. It filters traffic at any layer of the communications architecture for any protocol or application, not just IP. [Cost varies, depending on edition and configuration].

Gauntlet Internet Firewall for NT

See entry under Unix Firewalls.

Products for Virtual Private Networks

> **N**OTE   *In addition to these hardware products, NT server and most firewalls can create VPNs.*

Black Box VPNs

NetFortress

Digital Secured Network Technology, Inc., Englewood Cliffs, NJ, 201-568-3232. A pair of black boxes that encrypts/decrypts at the Network layer, using the Diffie-Hellman key exchange protocol (not RSA).

VSU-1000

VPNet Technologies, Inc., San Jose, CA, 408-445-6600 (www.vpnet.com). When used in pairs, these boxes encrypt/decrypt at the network layer.

Routers that Support Virtual Private Networks

Ascend MAX family of IP routers

Ascend Communications Corp., Alameda, CA, 800-621-9578 (www.ascend.com). Ascend supports VPNs by incorporating Microsoft's Point-to-Point Tunneling Protocol, a feature of Windows NT.

BayStream

Bay Networks, Santa Clara, CA, 800-231-4213 (www.baynetworks.com). Frame Relay/IP Routing multiservice software that runs on a number of Bay router families, including the BLN and BCN product lines; also provides support for VPNs.

Cisco 1600 series routers

Cisco Systems, Inc., San Jose, CA, 408-526-4000 or 800-553-6387 (www.cisco.com). Routers specifically designed for small office Internet/intranet use, including support for end-to-end encryption, otherwise known as VPNs.

Auditing Tools

> **N**OTE   *Several tools exist that perform automated auditing, the act of verifying that security policies are working and are implemented correctly. However, the highest degree of audit a company can perform would be done by a human being, preferably a security professional. Professional security audits can be expensive, though, often costing several thousand dollars. We therefore have listed a few products that can assist a company to audit itself.*

Bindview EMS

BindView Development Corp., Houston, TX, 713-881-9100 (www.bindview.com). A network management system for NetWare that includes intensive security auditing, both policies and audit logs.

Kane Security Analyst

Intrusion Detection, Inc., New York City, 212-348-8900 (www.intrusion.com). A product whose sole mission is to uncover security flaws in NetWare and NT networks.

SQL<>SECURE Policy Manager and Audit Manager

BrainTree Technology, Inc., Norwell, MA, 617-982-0200 (www.bti.com). Tools that provide policy testing and then audit trail management for Oracle databases.

> **N**OTE *Numerous freeware security testing/auditing tools are available for Unix. Among the most famous are the following: SATAN (ftp://ciac.llnl.gov/pub/ciac/sectools/unix/satan) and COPS (ftp://ftp.cert.org/pub/tools/cops), both of which look for specific security loopholes that hackers commonly use; ARPWatch, which detects bogus host systems pretending to be trusted hosts (ftp://coast.cs.purdue.edu/pub/tools/unix/arpwatch); Crack, which tests for safe passwords (ftp://sable.ox.ac.uk/pub/comp/security/software/crackers); and Tiger, a more recent version of COPS (ftp://cert.org./pub/tools/tcp_wrappers).*

Access Control Tools

Access Key II

Developed jointly by TriNet Services, Inc., Raleigh, NC, 919-833-2247 (www.trinet.com) and VASCO Data Security, Inc., Lombard, IL, 630-932-8844 (www.vasco.com). A very cool Java applet access control device that replaces smart card readers with an onscreen reader.

Kerberos 4.0

MIT (http://gost.isi.edu/info/kerberos/). One of the many versions of this encryption authentication system. Other information about Kerberos can be researched via Kerberos newsgroups, such as kerberos@mit.edu (send subscriptions to kerberos-request@mit.edu.). [Free].

> **N**OTE *Commercial versions or commercial support of Kerberos are available from companies such as CyberSafe Corp. (206-391-6000, sales@cybersafe.com); Cygnus Support (415-903-1400, network-security@cygnus.com); and Digital Equipment Corp. (DECathena and CySecure, 508-952-4350, info@athena.tay.dec.com).*

ProGuard

Vasco Data Security, Inc., Lombard, IL, 630-932-8844 (www.vasco.com). An access control, data security, and virus protection product for notebook computers from one of the developers of the Access Key.

RB-I Token

CryptoCard Corp. (www.cryptocard.com). A highly secure challenge-response token-based authentication product that does not require a separate token reader.

SecurID Tokens

Security Dynamics, Bedford, MA, 800-SECURID (http://www.securid.com/). Certainly among the most popular security tokens on the market today. Most major firewall vendors and other security products have partnered with this company to offer integrated support. Security Dyamics also offers soft tokens.

Other Security Tools

InterScan VirusWall

Trend Micro Devices, Inc., Cupertino, CA, 408-257-1500 (www.trendmicro.com). A virus scanner that works on HTTP, e-mail, and FTP traffic at the Internet gateway. It is currently being bundled with a number of Web servers, including Netscape's Proxy Server, Sun's Netra Server, and Worldtalk, Inc.'s Netjunction, and is available separately. For NT and Unix.

Webster Control List

Secure Computing Corp., Roseville, MN, 612-628-2700 or 800-692-5625 (www.sctc.com/borderware/). Webster Control List is a URL-filtering application that allows access to specific Web site categories to be restricted, such as sex, job search, entertainment.

Entrust

Entrust Technologies, Inc., Research Triangle Park, NC, 919-992-5525 (www.nortel.com/entrust/). A spinoff of Northern Telecom, this company makes one of the most popular certificate management software available on the market today. It is specifically designed for business-to-business transactions and for companies who do not want to source out their certificate generation and management to third-party services such as Verisign.

Java Tools

Development Tools

HP-UX Developer's Kit for Java

Hewlett-Packard Co., Palo Alto, CA, 415-857-1501 or 800-472-4772 (http://www.hp.com/gsyinternet/hpjdk/). Freeware from HP that allows developers to create Java applications for HP-UX. It includes a Java Virtual Machine and various programming tools, such as a compiler, debugger, and applet viewer. [Free].

Jamba

Aimtech Corp., Nashua, NH, 603-883-0220 or 800-289-2884 (http://www.aimtech.com). Jamba is uses a prebuilt Java class library which allows Web designers to quickly develop applets and applications in a WYSIWYG environment, using drag and drop.

Java WorkShop

SunSoft, Inc., Mountain View, CA, 800-SUNSOFT (www.sun.com/developer-products/). One of the best debuggers in terms of functions, but often criticized for being slow.

JetConnect

XDB Systems, Inc. See entry, Database Integration.

Layout Mill

Ignite Technologies LLC., New York City, 212-339-2890 or 888-446-4834 (www.ignite.com). A development tool for creating Java interfaces written entirely in Java, so developers can use them on any platform, and created expressly with intranets in mind.

Liquid Motion Pro

Dimension X, Inc., San Francisco, CA, 415-296-0100 (www.dimensionx.com). A full-featured Java development tool written entirely in Java.

Mojo

Penumbra Software, Inc., Norcross, GA, 770-352-0100 (www.penumbrasoftware.com). Mojo is an integrated development environment for use on Windows or Windows 95 with an extensive library of Java components for drag-and-drop development.

Sanga Pages

Sanga International, Inc. See entry, Database Integration.

Visual Café

Symantec Corp., Cupertino, CA, 408-253-9600 (www.symantec.com). A popular Java development tool, known for speed and ease of use for the difficult, quirky Java language. NT and Mac.

Visual J++ Professional Edition

Microsoft Corp., Redmond, WA, 206-882-8080 (www.microsoft.com/visualj). A Java development tool that allows developers to integrate Java applets into the ActiveX framework. It includes hundreds of tests to ensure applets comply with Sun's Java logo program, an extensive Java class library, animation tool, and more.

Applets/Java Components

Access Key II

Developed jointly by TriNet Services, Inc., and VASCO Data Security, Inc. See entry, Access Control.

Interactive Org Chart

DTAI, Inc., San Diego, CA, 619-281-2292 (www.dtai.com). A Java applet that builds complex organizational charts. It includes numerous reusable Java classes for handling dialog boxes, mouse events, and more.

NetResults

Innotech Multimedia Corp., North York, Ontario, 416-492-3838 (www.netresults-search.com). A Java Web search engine.

Peak Net.Jet

Peak Technologies, Inc., Bellingham, WA, 360-733-6010 (www.peak-media.com). A Java applet that works with Internet Explorer 3.0 and Navigator 3.0 and increases the speed at which browsers work by downloading the text and graphics of each link displayed. When users click on a link, they can view the contents immediately because the linked page has already been cached.

The Café del Sol

Sun Microsystems Computer Corp., Mountain View, CA, 415-960-1300 (www.xm.com/café/). A collection of applets developed by the creators of Café. Free runtime licenses, but the source code is not available. Applets range from particle, such as buttons and scrolling, animated images to fun, such as a comic strip applet.

Management Tools

Castinet

Marimba, Inc., Palo Alto, CA, 415-328-5282 (www.marimba
.com). A Java-based software distribution that uses a "channels" metaphor which allows Java applications to "upgrade
themselves" to run from a hard drive, sans browser (thanks to
the Java Virtual Machine embedded in the client portion), and
otherwise seem to be regular applications.

OrbixWeb Java

Iona Technologies, Inc., Cambridge, MA, 617-679-0900 or
800-orbix4u. An object request broker (ORB) which supports
Java objects using the OMG's CORBA Internet Inter-ORB protocol. For NT and Unix.

ActiveX

Development Tools

ActiveX SKD for the PC and for the Mac

Microsoft Corp., Redmond, WA, 800-426-9400 (www
.microsoft.com/activex/). The quintessential ActiveX development tool, which now includes some beta code for developing for RISC platforms, but has been optimized for Intel to
date. Requires the latest version of Internet Explorer and the
Win32 SKD. [Free].

Explorer X-ponents

MicroHelp, Inc., Marietta, GA, 800-847-8488 (www
.microhelp.com). A suite of programming objects that
allows developers to create Windows 95 and Windows NT
"Explorer-like" applications using Visual Basic. Includes
an extensive library of Active-X controls.

SQA Suite 5.1

SQA, Inc., Burlington, MA, 800-228-9922 (www.sqa.inc).
SQA tests and fine-tunes a variety of objects, including those

generated in HTML and Java, and can simulate Web server traffic on NT.

Controls

> **N**OTE   *According to Microsoft, over 1,000 controls are available for ActiveX.*

Communications Library

MicroHelp, Inc., Marietta, GA, 800-847-8488 (www .microhelp.com). Communications Library is an ActiveX control for LAN/Host connectivity and communications. Micro-Help has created numerous other controls as well.

Novera System Software

Novera Software, Cambridge, MA, 617-492-8538 (www.novera.com). ActiveX controls for business-to-business electronic commerce, customer management, database connectivity, and more.

RealAudio Player/Control for ActiveX

Progressive Networks, Inc. (www.prognet.com). A control for Progressive Networks' popular "hear-as-it-downloads" streaming audio player.

Surround Video SKD

Black Diamond Consulting, Inc., Portsmouth, NH, 603-430-7777 (www.bdiamond.com). A control that shows a 360-degree video image.

> **N**OTE   *CNet offers Activex.Com (http://www.activex.com/), a source for researching, locating, and downloading the latest ActiveXTM controls.*
>
> *Freeware ActiveX components are becoming more available. One good library is Microsoft's "gallery," a Web page where developers can download hundreds of ActiveX demos (www.microsoft.com/activex)—protected by Authenticode certificates.*

Performance Evaluation Tools

Aria

Andromedia Inc., San Francisco, CA, 415-278-0700 (www .andromedia.com). Hit analysis that captures Web traffic as it happens, which allows Webmasters to gauge peak/off-peak times.

Astra SiteTest and Astra SiteManager

Mercury Interactive Corp., Sunnyvale, CA, 408-523-9900 (http://www.merc-int.com). SiteTest tests CGI scripts and API calls to databases, emulates real-life loads by generating millions of hits to test for scalability/performance issues. SiteManager Maps sites, monitors usage, analyzes links, and includes an open API, so its management features can be customized.

Insight

Accrue Software, Inc., Mountain View, CA, 415-969-9031 (www.accrue.com). Insight monitors performance data over multiple sites allowing Webmasters to identify problems in download times, visitor connections, and other areas. Java applets allow Webmasters to graph performance elements visually, such as CGI response times. For Solaris.

Intersé Market Focus 3

Intersé Corp., Sunnyvale, CA, 408-732-0932 (www.interse .com). Performs hit analysis, configures complex multiple sites and their logs, provides database tracking and database management.

Interactive Network Dispatcher

IBM, Raleigh, NC, 1-800-IBM-1822 (http://www.ics.raleigh .ibm.com/ics/issfact.htm). Automatically load balances Web queries over clustered pools of servers and monitors how busy each server is to determine which one can handle a given query.

Keynote Perspective

Keynote Systems, Inc., San Mateo, CA, 415-524-3000. A service/software combination product using a Java-based agent that offers Web server response times from a client's perspective, including denials of access, because a portion of the product resides at the ISP. Available in 96 cities at launch. For Windows, Unix, Novell, and Macintosh.

ManageWise

Novell, Inc., Provo, UT, 800-554-4446 (www.novell.com). ManageWise is a network management tool that supports NetWare and NT Servers and Novell's intranet operating system, IntranetWare. It detects over 400 network problems and offers other performance statistics for intranet servers (provided they are on NT or IntranetWare) such as CPU utilization and packet throughput.

net.Commander

Tivoli Systems, Inc., Austin, TX, 512-794-9070 (www .tivoli.com). Provides administrators with enterprise-wide management for a range of intranet services from HTTP to e-mail.

Optimal Internet Monitor

Optimal Networks, Inc., Palo Alto, CA, 415-845-6333 (www .optimal.com). Internet Monitor provides statistics on how fast an NT or Windows 95 Web site is performing as well as data on access attempts by networked users to unauthorized sites.

Resonate Dispatch

Resonate Inc., Mountain View, CA, 415-967-6500 (http:// www.resonateinc.com). Automatically balances the load of incoming traffic against multiple, clustered Web servers.

Webpest

Thomson Technology Services Group, Rockville, MD, 301-548-4000 (http://ttis.thomtech.com/~suresh/webpest/

paper.html). A freeware tool from extranet consultants that evaluates the performance of Web servers running on a variety of Unix platforms. [Free].

WireTap

Platinum Technology, Inc., Oakbrook Terrace, IL, 630-620-5000 or 800-442-6861 (www.platinum.com). WireTap dishes up various resource utilization data, such as response time and statistics for network service requests and page requests. For Solaris.

NOTE   *Many network management tools that offer performance metrics can be configured to support Web sites as well. For companies that already use an enterprisewide network management tool, we highly advise checking with the vendor to see if Web servers can be monitored as well. Typically, these tools won't do a lot of analysis of hits. However, that trade-off may be acceptable for an extranet, especially when gaining the benefit of having the extranet manageable with a well-known tool already employed. We have not included such network management tools in this resource list unless they have a specific Web component, according to the vendor.*

Freeware/Shareware Tools Appropriate for Extranets

AppFoundry

Netscape Communications Corp., Mountain View, CA, 415-937-2555 (www.netscape.com). AppFoundry is a database of freeware tools appropriate for the Web, intranet, and extranet. Most of the tools are scaled-down versions of commercial products. Often security features are sacrificed for the price. Still, AppFoundry is a great way to evaluate, or even implement, a Web application without a big capital expenditure.

Cookie Master

Ziff-Davis Publishing will be available for free at the Software Library (www.hotfiles.com). The program provides users with a list of the cookies that reside on their hard drives and lets them see which Web sites installed them. Individuals can also see what data has been stored in the cookies and delete any cookies they don't want. [Free].

NOTE   *The ZD Net Software Library, the online service operated by Ziff-Davis, publisher of dozens of computer magazines such as* PC Week *and* PC Computing, *is also one of the richest sources of PC freeware around.*

Another great source for locating shareware is Shareware. Com on CNet, an online news site and producer of computer television shows (www.shareware.com). Shareware.Com is a comprehensive index of more than 200,000 freeware and shareware titles, complete with links to download.

## chapter nine

Hiring Help

One of the smartest moves a company can make is to plan for getting help at the onset of an extranet project. Too frequently, this stage of development only occurs when the company runs into a snag. By then, time and resources have been wasted trying to solve a problem that would be easily conquered by someone more experienced.

Much better to plan for Murphy's Law and have Superman waiting on the sidelines—or better yet working side-by-side with the company.

Murphy's Law of Custom IT Development

If it can go wrong, it will.

If it's intuitive, get training.

If it's visual, grab the manual.

If it uses Wizards, put technical support on speed dial.

If the technical support person answers on the first ring, ask to speak to an engineer immediately.

If end users love the prototype, the production unit crashes.

If it works on your node, it won't work on your boss's.

If it works on your boss's node, management will decide to reengineer.

Superman basically comes in two forms: commercial resources that can be hired to perform tasks, then train and cost cash but save time; or resources that allow a company to teach itself and cost little cash, but eat time. As we saw in Chapter 7, often the soft cost of time can be far more expensive than the hard cost of hiring a consultant. The trick here is to chose the right consultant. Choose poorly, and the project ends up being expensive on both counts.

Most companies will find themselves in need of both types of help during the course of this project. In this chapter, we will guide you through the process of hiring commercial help, such as consultants, and offer resources where you can obtain training.

What Areas You Need to Know

Generally speaking, we recommend that companies become trained in several areas of extranet systems, even if they plan to hire consultants to create the project.

Security

Companies should understand what types of security they are using: SSL? VPNs? certificates? access control mechanisms? a combination of technologies? and so on. They should also be trained on how to properly configure this security. Moreover, the extranet team should also make sure that the security features of other network devices are configured properly throughout the entire IP network, particularly backbone devices such as routers.

This is not always as intuitive as it may seem. For example, recently, executives at a large international marketing firm hired a team of security professionals to audit the company's Internet security. The company had implemented some fairly complex security measures for their IP network, such as encrypted e-mail, and felt confident that they were "safe." But, as the Internet was becoming an increasingly important tool for conducting mission-critical business, these executives wanted the extra confidence an independent audit would provide.

What the security professionals found shocked them. The company had installed dozens of this same brand of IP router throughout the company to handle IP traffic from their intranet, extranet, and Internet. The IP router had security access control features, but the person who configured the routers had not understood how to properly set these switches. The result was that anyone from the Internet could log into these routers and gain administrative-level security clearance to these routers—the company's backbone. A hacker could have reconfigured those routers to do all sorts of mischief, from sniffing all IP traffic as it traveled across the network to corrupting the network and data on the network beyond repair. Had the company hired a consultant to configure even a single system, while training an internal network administrator on the process (or even contacted the vendor for instructions), such a gaping security hole would never have occurred.

While it isn't always practical to turn someone in the IT department into a computer security guru, the company should at least hire the expertise, then shadow the hired security gun and learn what choices were made with the company's systems.

Web Content Management

Even if the company hires a consultant to design and create an interactive Web page, the company would be wise to learn how to make minor changes on the site itself. It should be able to update static pages, for instance. Or it should have the abilities to update and/or alter the data in a backend database. In fact, it should be able to perform all of the routine tasks of maintaining the Web site so that it can keep this site as fresh as possible. That is, after all, the great benefit of going online. To assign this task to a consultant in many ways defeats the purpose of installing the system. If the company must schedule and pay for a consultant every time routine changes in the Web's data are required, the company is a lot less likely to perform these tasks as often as they should be done. This would be like hiring out to perform network backups or new software installations.

Consequently, most consultants do not prefer to be called on to perform minor, low-cost maintenance tasks, as it restricts them from scheduling larger, more profitable development projects. The result is that customers who require a lot of minor, low-paying attention, tend to get dropped to the bottom of the consultant's queue. Such a situation may seem infuriating to the customer that depends so heavily on the consultant. However, from the consultant's point of view, prioritizing menial, low-paying tasks after larger, more profitable jobs is mandatory if the consultant's business is to remain solvent. (And a consultant that goes out of business is bad news for both the consultant and the clients that depend on its services.)

On the other hand, several areas exist where most companies would benefit from outside expertise. These include security, Web/database integration, Java applets, and business-to-business electronic commerce. Companies may also need to hire expertise in remote access/management, e-mail integration, network design, and capacity planning. These areas require rather intense knowledge that is not easily obtained through a training course alone. There is a need for hands-on experience in a wide variety of areas before someone is truly proficient. Consequently, hiring consultants for these tasks can save the company money because (1) the company is paying less for worker hours because the hired gun works more efficiently than internal people who must climb a learning curve to achieve the same outcome, and (2) the project gets to production sooner so returns on investment can start to accrue sooner as well.

How to Find a Good Consultant

Finding a good computer consultant is like finding a good auto mechanic or a good doctor. There are a lot of them out there, some good, some not. Picking the perfect apple from the bushel is daunting, confusing, and risky.

Taxonomy of Consultants

Still, some sure-fire methods for finding the perfect extranet consultant exist, and we are here to guide you through them. A variety of taxonomies can be used to categorize consultants. For our purposes, we are going to separate them by their biases, by which we mean their preferences or inclinations. Biases are not necessarily bad; in fact they are part of the human condition. No one goes through life without generating an opinion, and then making decisions based on that opinion. It is more important to match biases between consultant and client than to search for a consultant that doesn't have any.

Representatives of Vendors

One of the most successful ways of finding a well-matched consultant is by choosing which tools the company wants to use and asking the vendor to provide a list of its trained and certified value-added resellers (VARs). VARs are companies that resell the vendor's products, but, in theory, must also be experts at using the tool and must be able to apply that knowledge to specific implementations. These implementations may be aimed at a vertical market, such as the banking or insurance industries. Or they may be applied to a horizontal market in a geographic location, such as computer security, database integration, and/or electronic commerce in greater Cincinnati.

For companies, this is a promising method for finding a consultant because it matches biases well. The consultant's bias is to use this particular product above any other, because the sale of that product generates profit and taps into that VAR's specialized skills. The company has a bias toward the product as well, as the conclusion to its product research.

Typically, the vendor requires that its VARs partake in training and commit to selling a specific amount of product. It may have a hierarchy of VAR certificates, where it has heavily trained partners that have a large business with the product, moderately trained partners that do a moderate amount of business, and sparingly trained partners that have a small business with the tool. Novell Corporation is the premier example of this kind of reseller partner hierarchy, with its Platinum and Gold resellers, for instance, but it also sells products at the local retailer.

We say, tongue in cheek, that such is the "typical" method of qualifying resellers. However, in recent years, some companies have created hierarchy systems based on a VAR's commitment to resell products alone, not on the training that the VAR undertakes. This causes a big, scary problem for end users looking to hire consultants. They are told that a VAR is a "premium" partner, the highest level achievable, but what they don't realize is that the only requirement to become a premium partner is to agree to sell a zillion units and pay a steep fee.

These VARs may then turn around and get their training on your nickel, learning how to use the tool during your implementation. Such a practice is, of course, attractive to some VARs, whose training costs are typically among their biggest overhead expenditures. If training courses can be avoided and they can still become a qualified reseller of a product, they can earn income and train at the same time—while working with clients. Good for them, bad for you.

On the other hand, for vendors that take their reseller accreditation programs seriously, vendor referrals become a great source for finding consultants. Resellers in these types of programs have already made a strategic decision to develop an extranet business. They have trained with this product, and, most likely, implemented other previous extranet projects which drew them into the business. They are tapped into what is and isn't possible with the current state of the technology.

So, despite a few bad apples, we believe vendors are rich sources for consultant referrals, as long as the company understands the vendor's qualification practices before relying on this information. A quick chat with a company's manager of VAR programs should suffice. (This might be called the *channel manager,* as "channel" is the term used to designate the reseller industry.) The following questions might assist in this interview.

Which Tool Vendors Should You Question? Beyond the potential for cheesy qualification processes, a couple of other disadvantages exist in using vendors as consultant references. First of all, this means that the company must do some pretty serious product evaluations before turning to a consultant. We believe that such product evaluations are often the best way for a company to proceed. However, in some cases, one of the values a consultant can offer is assistance with selecting tools. By performing all of the product research yourself you may have eliminated one of the most valuable functions of the consultant.

Questions for Vendors Offering Referrals

1. Can you refer me to qualified VARs in my geographic area?

2. What do you look for in a VAR?

3. What must a reseller do in order to become a qualified reseller of your products?

4. Are there different levels of qualification? Please explain to me what those levels are, and tell me their designated names.

5. What differences in training for VARs exist between these levels? Can a VAR opt to get additional training on your tools in this market from you? What types of training are there? What are the indications that a VAR has completed it satisfactorily? (For instance, is a certificate issued?)

6. How many resellers do you have?

7. Do you primarily recruit resellers based on the vertical markets that they serve or on geography?

8. If I hire one of your qualified resellers, am I still entitled to any free support from you?

9. What types of support would I be entitled to?

Relying exclusively on vendor referrals can also pose an additional dilemma: What does a company do when it has selected a series of tools and can't find a VAR that's qualified on more than one of them?

The answer is to query only your most strategic vendors. For instance, let's say there is a Lotus Notes shop that wants to build an extranet that allows business partners to supply Web content onto a Domino Web server. Finding a consultant experienced with Notes would be far more important than finding one experienced with the brand of HTML editor the company wants to use.

Companies that engage in this method of finding consultants should evaluate tools in stages, rather than decide on every tool at the beginning of the project. The first set of tools evaluated should be strategic. With a consultant in place, other tools can be decided upon with that consultant's aid, again keeping in mind that this consultant may have a bias toward the products that it is qualified to resell. (And if such tools work, why not use them, bias or not?) Yet, the company should remain aware of the potential biases a consultant might have and assign one member of the development team to remain on the lookout for other, even greater products that might be available but are outside the scope of the consultant's qualified palette of products.

Vendors as Consultants

Vendors can be a source of referrals, but often they provide consulting services themselves. This is particularly true of the Internet security market. For instance, Secure Computing Corporation of Roseville, MN (www.sctc.com) is the creator of the Sidewinder Firewall and also the vendor of the BorderWare firewall (which it acquired). In addition, the company offers a full line of security consulting services, from policy making to auditing. Similarly, Network-1 Software & Technology, Inc. of New York (www. network-1.com) is a vendor of firewalls and a full-service network integrator and computer security consultant.

Vendors as integrators is hardly a new situation. In the old days when computers were a room full of transistors, the vendor and consultant were nearly always one and the same. Many vendors of the mainframe era still operate full consultant services. For instance, Digital Equipment Corporation has several entire business units dedicated to Internet/intranet/extranet systems integration (www.digital.com/info/internet). The same can be said about IBM.

However, this type of consultant must be approached with the same understanding of bias as the vendor representative and then some. Obviously, the company can offer integration services, but those services will heavily feature their products, maybe to the absolute exclusion of all others. In the case of VARs referred by the company, this is *not* usually the case. VARs tend to be authorized resellers of numerous brands. If something better comes along from another company it is in the VAR's best interest to possibly switch over or add that product to their palette.

So, if the company, through its own independent analysis, has determined that a particular vendor offers the right tool, it may make sense to consider that vendor's consulting services as well. The training issue will be nullified. No one will know the product better or be better able to customize it.

The drawback is, of course, that by hiring vendor consultants the company may be locking itself into a one-vendor solution. (This kind of spawned the open systems revolution that was the breeding ground for the Internet in the first place, remember?)

Consultants that Sell Their Own Tools

Another type of consultant creates and sells its own tools for use in its own implementations. We consider these consultants, rather than vendors, because these tools are either (1) not marketed on the open market as the company's primary source of revenue (although they may be sold upon request there), or (2) nearly always require the expertise or customization of the consultant and are not typically intended to be configured by end users.

One example of this type of consultant is Thawte Consulting, Inc., an international computer security consultant with a U.S. office in Raleigh, NC (www.thawte.com). Thawte offers a secure server, certificate management software, and other Internet security tools which it uses for its clients.

This type of consultant achieves success because it offers a means to be independent of dominant players in the industry, while still having functional, customized tools. This is a great solution for those who believe multi-billion-dollar software companies have an arrogant attitude toward their customers, or who don't want to wait for hours to talk to a technical support person, only to be given misinformation, or who don't want to buy into a product based on market hype, only to find that it's as buggy as a beta version.

Typically, such consultants don't rely exclusively on their own tools, but fill in the gaps with commercial products in areas where they don't have extreme expertise or don't feel the need to reinvent the wheel. For example, a consultant might have developed its own custom SSL Web server, but will use Allaire's Cold Fusion to perform the database integration.

Of course, the trade-off is that the tool had better perform. The consultant had better be reliable and stable and the relationship had better be long term. Otherwise, the company has spent its cash on a proprietary product that it can't upgrade, alter, or hire someone else to repair.

Independent Consultants

These are the rarest, but they do exist. These are consultants who are not authorized resellers of *any* products, on the supposition that this eliminates their biases toward particular products. It is true that if a consultant is being brought in specifically to assist a company to evaluate tools, an independent consultant is the best choice over other types of consultants described here. However, don't be lulled into a false sense of security. These companies will still have biases toward particular tools, based on the products they know best (provided those products perform well). For instance, if the consultant has 10,000 hours on Oracle databases, odds are it will argue in favor of Oracle over Informix or Sybase when evaluating tools. The consultant knows that projects can be developed more quickly and profitably on the platforms its technicians know best.

Of course, the greatest benefit of an independent consultant is that if the product (or the vendor) doesn't perform well, it's outta there. The consultant doesn't have a contractual obligation to continue to resell it, or a huge capital expenditure in training to recoup. So, while the company may lean toward favorite tools, it does so strictly because it honestly believes those tools perform best.

That said, we would like to point out that for the vast majority of VARs, the above statement holds true as well. VARs that prefer to become authorized are not necessarily locked into the partnership for better or worse and VARs are some of the toughest technical people a vendor must please. (VARs are the vendor's sales force, after all.) If a product performs less than adequately, VARs don't hold still for it. If the vendor doesn't improve the product, the VAR dumps it and becomes authorized with someone else's tool. Simply speaking, it doesn't make a lot of business sense to stick with tools that don't perform well.

Independent consultants are not in any way more innately ethical than authorized VARs. They also have to work harder to stay on top of the market in which they play. One of the benefits of becoming authorized is that the vendor will then make a huge effort at keeping its VARs updated about new features, pricing, upcoming products, the company's strategy, and so on. Independent consultants have to read about this stuff in the trades, just like any Joe Technician. So, in many instances, the difference between independence and authorized resellers boils down to the level of commitment to a favored product.

The key to recognizing a good independent consultant is to find one that has vast experience in a specific category. Ultimately, it has done a number of implementations of, say, electronic commerce, using a variety of tools to perform the task. The consultant should also have a desire to try new tools as they emerge and should be able to chat intelligently about version 1.0 and betas on all sorts of products in its domain. This is a sign that the consultant is using its independence as a business strategy, and not a mere marketing ploy.

The drawback is finding them. Newsgroups are a potentially good source. Knowledgeable consultants will often frequent the newsgroups in which they have expertise as a marketing tool (and simply to share their knowledge).

Online searches are also a good technique, albeit time consuming. One shortcut is to access Yahoo's recently added Internet Consulting category to its comprehensive database (www.yahoo. com/Business_and_Economy/Internet_Services/Internet_ Consulting). This category is searchable by region.

How to Screen for Competence

Once a company thinks it has a live prospective consultant dangling on the hook, it's time to verify that the consultant is competent. This means references, references, references. First, talk to the consultant's customers and find out what they liked, and what they didn't.

If a company likes what it hears while talking to customer references, it's time to question the company. An interview should center on two items. First, these interviews should uncover the company's project management skills and style. This will include

Questions for Consultant's References

1. How did you find out about this consultant?
2. Did you review other consultants before hiring this one?
3. What did you like best about this consultant?
4. How big was the project?
5. How long did it take?
6. How many people did the consultant commit to it?
7. How many people did you commit?
8. Who did the project management?
9. What was the consultant's project management responsibilities?
10. Did they perform them well?
11. Did they manage expectations well?
12. Did they deliver the project on time?
13. Did it perform as expected?
14. Have bugs cropped up since it's been in use?
15. How did the consultant handle the bugs?
16. Did you contract for updates or new releases?
17. How do you expect those to be handled?

(Continued)

items such as meeting deadlines, managing personnel (its own and any team members assigned to the project), and managing expectations. Second, the interview should cover what services it can expect to be included and excluded in the contract. This will include technical support, training, and upgrades to custom applications, for example. It might include other issues such as Web hosting.

18. Did they train you on what they were doing?
19. Was this training included in the contract or did it cost extra?
20. Was it worth the cost and the time spent?
21. Did the consultant get along well with your people?
22. Did you have a single point of contact with the consultant or did you have to manage the consultant's staff?
23. What is the best way to manage a relationship with this consultant?
24. How did they handle conflicts over technical practices or other technical issues when they arose?
25. What could the consultant have done better?
26. Have you hired them again? Would you?
27. Would you hire them for projects other than the type they performed, or only in the same area?
28. Have you ever recommended them to anyone else, other than when they use you as a reference?
29. Do you recommend them highly and without reservation?
30. If not, in what situations would you *not* recommend them?

When to Hire Help

The best time to bring in outside consultants is at the beginning of a project, rather than at the point at which the company's developers run into trouble. Consultants can do more than simply execute what the company orders. They can help the company discover what it really wants and offer ideas on what is reasonable to do, which, in this fast-developing area, is often *greater* than what the company thinks is possible. For instance, the advertising company that decides it wants to implement a secure e-mail sys-

Questions for Consultants

1. What is your project management philosophy?
2. How many people do you anticipate assigning to this project?
3. Who is my contact person?
4. What type of commitment do you expect from us in terms of people, time, prototyping, predevelopment assessments, and so on?
5. How can I be sure that this project will be completed on time?
6. How can I be sure that this project will perform as well as expected?
7. How can I be sure that this project will remain confidential?
8. What do you do if your technical people disagree with my technical people on the team?
9. Does your typical scope of work include training? how much?
10. How much will it cost us to include upgrades in the contract?
11. What are areas that may require additional fees?
12. What are areas that you, as standard practice, include in your contracts?
13. What do you do when an area is beyond your level of expertise? Do you hire subcontractors?
14. If subcontractors are used, whose responsibility is it to manage and pay them?

tem so that it can route photos to customers for approval may really be better serviced by a photo database accessible with a Web front end.

Similarly, the time to develop reference resources is when the perimeter of the project is being formed, not when the developer runs into a wall. For example, if a company plans on implementing a secure server which uses SSL, its developers would be wise to subscribe to some of the newsgroups where people knowledgeable about SSL hang out. These include: netscape.security, netscape.devs-server-technical, comp.security.misc, and comp .security.unix. (Internet security newsgroups hosted by Netscape are accessible via http://help.netscape.com/nuggies/ security.html.) Good sources for other pertinent newsgroups are vendors, search engines that search newsgroups, such as Alta Vista, and the trade press.

By reading newsgroup traffic, the company can see the types of issues others struggle with. Extranet developers can then prepare to combat some of these obvious problems in advance, such as by going to a training course or hiring a consultant with specific set of skills.

A Few Consultants

The following is a short list of some of the many consultants skilled in extranet applications today. We offer them to you as a starting point for your search for the perfect consultant, but also to demonstrate the diversity from which consultants are entering this market. This list is by no means comprehensive, as new extranet consultants are born every day (by the hundreds!). We have also included a few resources to help you locate more in your region or particular industry. Again, we extend a disclaimer: this list does not constitute an endorsement. We highly recommend that companies fully research and evaluate the capabilities of these consultants, and any others up for consideration, before engaging them. All information included here was supplied by the consultant.

Business-to-Business Electronic Commerce

American Tech, Inc., Holmdel, NJ, 908-946-8844 (www .powriter.com/). Makers of PurchasingNet, an intranet or internet extension to any purchasing or accounting system; also will build custom extranet sites based on the company's products.

Bluestone, Inc., Mount Laurel, NJ, 609-727-4600 (www
.bluestone.com). Electronic commerce distribution and logis-
tics, distance learning over the World Wide Web, intranet
database applications, agents, collaborative work environment, general business functionality, applications over the
Web (human resources, accounting, etc.).

Intranet/Extranet System Integrators/Consultants/VARs

Alta Systems, Bolton, MA, 508-779-2738 (www.altasys.com).
Provides a wide range of computer services for small and
mid-sized businesses including interactive Web sites, remote
access to intranets, database integration, and extranets.

Amicus Networks, Austin, TX, 512-418-8828 (www.amicus
.com). Specializes in creating extranets and offers 7×24 computing centers Web hosts. Offers content and custom development.

BATS, Inc., Sunnyvale, CA, 800-811-BATS (www.bats.com).
Specializes in network design and reengineering, internet/
intranet services, server installation and configuration, Internet security, e-mail system upgrades/standardization, cross-
platform Internet access Web and FTP servers.

Black Diamond Consulting, Inc., Portsmouth, NH, 603-430-
7777 (www.bdiamond.com). Specializes in intranet access to
legacy systems, planning, application and user-interface
development, object-oriented analysis, database design, and
ActiveX developer. (Black Diamond is co-creator of the Surround Video SKD, listed in Chapter 8.)

Charter Systems Inc., West Newton, MA, 617-243-4000
(www.charter.com), New York (www.cnp-inc.com). Charter
specializes in network consulting, firewall security, comput-
erized simulation, LAN/WAN integration, and network
capacity planning.

Creative Networks, Inc., Palo Alto, CA, 415-326-9926
(www.cnilive.com). Specializes in collaborative computing
over the Internet, also Web services, client/server messaging,
information integration and access.

Digiratti Technologies, Inc., Petaluma, CA, 707-773-1015 (www.digiratti.com). Specializes in Web content management and a concept called WebEnterprises, or large mission-critical intranets that could span across extranets.

Digital Equipment Corp., Maynard, MA, 1-800-Digital (www .digital.com/info/internet). Broad background in network, systems integration, intranets, extranets, and computer security.

Intuitive Systems, Redwood City, CA, 415-361-8400 (www .intuitive.com). Internet developers responsible for the Internet Mall, one of the largest electronic commerce stores on the Internet.

Inventa Corp., Santa Clara, CA, 408-987-0220 (www.inventa .com/). An international systems integration firm that specializes in intranets and extranets and can guarantee deployment of certain projects in 10 weeks or less.

Penumbra Software, Inc., Norcross, GA, 770-352-0100 (www .penumbrasoftware.com). In addition to making the commercial Java development tool, Mojo, Penumbra also offers Web site development services, specializing in interactive Java-based Web sites.

Thomson Technology Consulting Group, Rockville, MD, 301-548-4000 (www.tomtech.com). With several offices nationwide and global, TTCG designs and implements Internet, intranet, and extranet applications (which they call the Virtual Community), multimedia, and collaborative groupware applications. TTCG's approach is to tailor off-the-shelf software packages to client's needs and processes. They have developed reusable "package-friendly" best-practice process models for doing so. They also perform custom development, when shrinkwrapped products won't suffice.

TriNet Services, Inc., 150 Fayetteville Street Mall, Suite 1340, Raleigh, NC 27601. Specializes in interactive Web sites using Java and Internet security.

USWeb Corp., Santa Clara, CA, 888-USWEB-411, ext. 402. (www.usweb.com/intranet). A nationwide consultant that specializes in high-end, interactive Web sites for the intranet/ Internet and extranet.

Computer Security Specialists

Secure Computing Corp., Roseville, MN, 612-628-2700 or 800-692-5625 (www.sctc.com). In addition to being a vendor of security products, such as the Sidewinder firewall and Border-Ware firewall, Secure Computing also offers a full line of security consulting services, from policy making to auditing.

Network-1 Software & Technology, Inc., New York, NY, 212-293-3068 (www.network-1.com). In addition to offering the FireWall/Plus for Windows NT, the company also offers a full suite of network integration, performance, and security services.

Thawte Computing, Inc., Raleigh, NC, 919-510 5544 (www.thawte.com). Thawte has extensive expertise in SSL Web development and has created its own secure Web server and certificate server, among other tools.

MicroCosm Computer Resources, Sunnyvale, CA, 408-774-0309 (www.mcr.com). An Internet security specialist that offers network and Internet security design, implementation, and auditing, including penetration testing.

Pacifica Technologies, San Diego, CA, 619-280-4223 (www.pacificatech.com). Designs, implements, and audits network and Internet computer security systems. Specializes in auditing including penetration testing.

Sources for Finding More Extranet Consultants

The Internet Developers Association is a professional trade group composed of more than 1,000 members (www.association.org).

InfoWorld's Web site (www.infoworld.com) offers a Reader's Service called "SourceIT" in which VARs of certain vendors can be searched by area of expertise. The number of vendors included is far from comprehensive yet, but it can be a great tool if your vendor is supported. This site also includes an IT trade show calendar, helpful for those who want to find help the old fashioned way—through face-to-face contact with vendors at trade shows.

Yahoo recently added an Internet Consulting category to its comprehensive database (www.yahoo.com/Business_and_Economy/Internet_Services/Internet_Consulting). This category is searchable by region.

Other Resources for Extranet Developers

Seminars and conferences:

International Quality & Productivity Center produces Web and intranet seminars (800-303-9160 or www.iqpc.com).

Network World Technical Seminars offers ongoing intranet and Internet security seminars (800-643-4668 or www.nwfusion.com).

Developer Camps Java training seminars (Hotline: 800-433-4224).

Numerous workshops conducted by various computer security professionals are put on all year long, every year, in cities throughout the United States by the Computer Security Institute (CSI), based in San Francisco (http://www.gocsi.com/wkshop.htm).

Security auditing seminars are conducted by Pacifica Technologies (www.pacificatech.com).

Online Resources

Security

Security research is endless. Here are a few good sources for keeping up with what the acedemics say:

http://seclab.cs.ucdavis.edu/

GeoSystems Global's Virus Alert site, devoted to tracking and combating computer viruses (www.antivirus.com).

Antivirus encyclopedia (http://www.antivirus.com/), maintained by Trend Micro Devices, Inc., a vendor of antivirus products.

The National Security Institute (http://nsi.org/) has a Web site that includes a wealth of information about computer security including a consultant and vendor directory.

RSA offers one of the most comprehensive Security FAQs on the Internet today (www.rsa.com).

A list of security resources and newsgroups is maintained by Intuitive Systems (http://www.intuitive.com/security/).

Other Helpful Spots

Web Design (www.desktopPublishing.com). Links to Web design tutorials and reference materials.

The Intranet Journal (http://www.brill.com/intranet/). All sorts of topics of interest to intranet developers.

Java information from Sun Microsystems (http://www.sun .com/java/list.html). A Web page that offers information on Sun's Java products, training, and related services.

One of the best sites about cookies on the Web is maintained by "Andy" at www.illuminatus.com/cookie.fcgi.

Nets, Inc., provides a primary service called Industry.Net, which matches buyers with customers in the business-to-business manufacturing space. It is a Web technology that in many ways rivals EDI. The Web site (www.industry.net) provides information to nonmembers.

Trade Compass, Inc. (www.tradecompass.com). A site for the import/export industry, but one that demonstrates many of the technologies being implemented in extranets, from EDI interfaces to a buyer/seller matching service.

Summary

No matter what the extranet application, one thing's for certain: At some point a company will need help with development. The most likely areas in the development curve where people get stuck are (1) the security implementation (which may not be evident until catastrophe strikes), (2) database integration, and (3) interactive applications such as those written in Java. Help can come in two forms: consultants and self-help resources such as newsgroups and books.

Hiring a consultant may be more pain than it's worth unless extreme care is taken to choose the right one. This involves understanding the biases by which consultants naturally operate and factoring those biases into decision-making time. Finding good consultants remains a challenge and can feel like looking for a needle in a Web stack. Once a list is compiled, good 'ole legwork, in the form of interviewing customers and consultants, is the best insurance that the consultant found will be worthwhile. Questions should cover not only technical expertise, but—even more important—project management skills.

Consultants are moving into the extranet space from all sides. Even a short list of some of the players reveals significant differences among consultants' backgrounds, abilities, and target businesses. Finding a good one is tough, but worth it.

## chapter ten

Competing Technologies and the Future of the Extranet

The extranet has many names. We've heard it called the inter-prise, the virtual IP network, the virtual workgroup, and the Webenterprise, to name a few. Regardless of the nomenclature, the concept is the same—open up the intranet in a secured manner and it becomes a shared resource for business partners to accom-plish common goals (such as collaboration) or intersecting goals (such as invoicing/payments).

We believe that an extranet offers companies the easiest, most cost-effective way to automate tasks between business partners. We hold this conviction because Internet protocols are standard-ized while at the same time use low-cost hardware and software. Low-cost hardware such as PCs (rather than mainframes or mini-computers) makes the technology accessible to a wider array of users, big and small. This creates a huge market in which many vendors and consultants can play and thrive. At the same time, standardization allows more vendors and consultants to compete head-to-head, generating a wide and deep knowledge base. The entire situation brings costs down and quality up, and allows the market to stabilize and mature quickly, yet in a controlled manner, under the supervision of standards bodies, not vendors. If all great minds are bent on the same task, the task is accomplished sooner and evolves in a better way than if every great mind creates a pro-prietary solution.

But we recognize that an extranet isn't the only way that partners can or will communicate. In fact, many an extranet application is actually a means to replace a "communication system" between company and partner rather than create a new one. In this chapter, we outline some of the technologies that the extranet replaces. We then close with a peek into the crystal ball and do our best to foretell the future of the extranet.

What Technologies Does the Extranet Compete With?

EDI

The quintessential example of the extranet phenomenon replacing other technologies concerns Electronic Data Interchange (EDI). EDI is the process by which two mainframes can exchange purchasing and payment information. The catch is that it remains a mainframe technology. Smaller players could play by renting time on host mainframes in business to offer EDI services to those without the means to perform the data transfers themselves, called value-added networks (VANs). VANs can be an expensive option for those players (which reduces the benefit of EDI—pitched as a means of reducing the costs associated with the accounts payable/receivable process).

In truth, the companies that use EDI as an integral part of their business strategy are *not* ditching it during this millennium. But they are searching for ways to integrate Web-based front ends to the system (or integrate electronic commerce systems wholly into their EDI frameworks). This opens up entirely new strata of partners that can now take part in automated accounts receivable/payable processes. Anyone that can afford a PC-based network, modem, and secure Web browsers (which are available for nothing) can take part in a current EDI implementation. The IETF is working on a standard for this situation right now. The solution basically parallels electronic commerce systems, that is, using encryption to pass EDI documents over the Internet. The group has yet to agree on a format for these documents, such as whether to use Secure MIME (S/MIME) or Pretty Good Privacy encryption, but will probably support several. The working group specification is available at URL ftp://ds.internic.net/internet-drafts/draft-ietf-ediint-req-01.txt.

Still, with secure Web-based business-to-business electronic commerce, who needs EDI? PC-based applications can now perform all of the same tasks over secured extranets and don't have the interoperability problems that have plagued these mainframe-based systems. This includes high-volume transaction-based applications for which EDI works so well. Companies that have not yet created an EDI system would be much better served by implementing a business-to-business electronic commerce server, rather than traditional, mainframe-based EDI technologies.

Even the major EDI players have recognized this. Companies such as Premenos Corporation (www.premenos.com) and Harbinger Corporation (www.harbinger.com), EDI systems vendors, have repositioned themselves as "electronic commerce" vendors, and have revamped their wares with Internet-enabled offerings.

An excellent FAQ about EDI and the Internet is available at ftp://ds.internic.net/rfc/rfc1865.txt. Premenos also offers an extensive resource guide on EDI- and Internet-based electronic commerce.

Facsimile

Another technology the Web is replacing is use of the fax machine. True, no one is tossing out their fax machines just yet. But, those of us who have already integrated the Internet into our daily work routines have discovered that the fax sits idle more than it ever has before. Sometimes, days go by without its familiar ring.

Why fax a document that would have to be reinput when we can now e-mail a MIME attachment, preserving document formatting? E-mail is nearly ubiquitous, and the cost of a local phone call to the ISP versus the cost of the long-distance phone call directly to the other fax machine can add up to some significant savings.

Better yet, why e-mail a document when it is posted on the Web already? This removes the need for dependency on another person to provide basic information. The information is already waiting there at 2 P.M. or 2 A.M., whenever it is needed.

Also, faxing can be integrated into a Web site, should there be a need. For instance, information can be made available even to those without access to a PC/modem/telephone line (such as a business traveler at the airport). One example is InfoPress from Castelle, Inc., of Santa Clara, CA (www.castelle.com).

Telephone Support/Live Conversation

E-mail, workflow, and video applications allow the Web to be the point of connection between two partners. This allows work to be accomplished in an asynchronous fashion, meaning that two parties can engage in a communications volley, but at different times. Mary e-mails John, who responds and copies Larry, and so on. With video, applications such as training, reviewing meetings, and even performing marketing presentations can be done asynchronously.

In addition, live two-way communication is also possible over the Web, considerably lowering the costs of performing synchronous communications. An Internet voice transmission can take place from York to New York for pennies on the dollar of what it costs to place that call using telephone carriers. Videoconferences can take place using lower-cost PC equipment, rather than the high-end equipment of standalone videoconferencing units or the travel costs associated with meetings.

The Data Warehouse

The concept of the data warehouse is already being replaced by the intranet. Data warehouse backends are still being created. But they are being accessed via browser front ends, searched by SQL-aware search engines, and formatted by CGI into HTML. With the intranet acting as a data warehouse, rather than a custom-made database and front end, the project becomes ripe for extranet use. Partners can contribute data directly to the data warehouse, maybe as content suppliers of information that the partner sells to the company, such as international trade statistics. Or a partner's retail stores can upload sales information on products to their distributors, allowing distributors to gauge which products to stock and in what quantities.

On the flip side, partners may be able to perform limited queries to a company's database in order to better serve or be served by a company. For instance, grocery stores may be able to query an orange juice manufacturer's crop statistics, to better plan for price fluctuations in the market. Or an advertising agency can query sales response databases in order to determine which television shows have given their clients the most response from ads.

In fact, the list of advantages of the extranet over previous methods of accomplishing communication with partners is virtually endless.

The Future of the Extranet

The question remains: with this market changing so rapidly, what will happen to my current investment in an extranet application? For the answer, let's use our crystal ball to look into the future of the Internet.

The Boundaries of the Network Will Blur

We are standing on the brink of a major change, both in network design/architecture and in philosophy. With the widespread adoption of extranets, the line between corporate networks will blur. Where does the partner's network begin and the company's network leave off? Where is the company's Information Systems *perimeter* when internal firewalls allow some partners access from the outside to some network segments, but restrict internal access to those same segments? In essence, networks will become task and workgroup oriented, rather than company oriented. This will, we believe, improve both the functionality of the network as a business tool and its performance.

IS Tools Will Shift

A shift in IS tools to manage this new shared network will be required. Partners may be given read-only rights to extranet servers, so that they can assist in the detection of network problems, for example. Traditional management tools will be stretched to accommodate this type of management scheme. A lot of work is being done on extending traditional network management tools into Internet-dedicated devices. Several pending standards deal with extending the Management Information Base (MIB) protocols to control Internet network devices, from ATM networks to objects.

Security

Security will become more inherent in the Internet itself. This will allow it to instill confidence, rather than fear, in users (somewhat like what telephone service does today). We think nothing of connecting a WAN via frame-relay or ISDN lines today. With the next version of the IP protocol (IP version 6, which includes security), we will have the same confidence in using the Internet for WAN-like networks, extranets, and intranets. When IP version 6 becomes the norm, the Internet, for the first time, will be inherently secure. Additional methods of standardized security will be available for refining its basic IP security and customizing it to match the needs of the application.

Agents

Agents will automate many of the networking tasks that are generally performed manually today. The first generation of these tools is coming online now. For instance, conducting research of Internet-published information will no longer be a matter of hopping on several public search engines and then surfing each list of responses. New "agents," or tools, will perform those tasks, present the findings and then learning from surfer's reactions which responses worked and which didn't. Increasing use of such agents will help indirectly increase their efficiency. Agents will also be used to perform backend, middlewarelike tasks, such as compiling standard reports from multiple Web sites that use live, backend databases.

Web Sites Will Start to Follow Uniform Style Guidelines

Web content providers will begin to adopt more uniform customs for publishing on the Web, much like nonfiction books have adopted the custom of the table of contents in the front of the book and the index in the back. These customs will allow sites to be more easily screened by agents to obtain valuable nuggets of information. Some of these customs are already beginning to appear in rough form. The site map, for instance, is being used by an increasing number of sites. Site maps are a hierarchical "tree" chart of the site, allowing users to navigate with vision rather than surfing blind. The Java-based pop-up menu is another early convention. More than text pop-ups that explain icons, these can be pop-ups of links to other pages. See Chapter 4 for general information on uniform content design.

The Browser Will Become the Universal User Interface

The browser will become the point at which computer users interact with their machines and network resources, rather than the operating system. A person will be able to sit down at a Unix box, a Mac, or a PC, and work, period. The browser will interpret whether the device is connected locally, through the physical network or through an IP network.

Video

Video will increase in use as the performance hit to use it lessens (partly due to increased bandwidth and partly due to improvements in digital video technology). Numerous RFCs are working on ways of increasing the performance of video over IP networks while decreasing the demand it makes on the network.

The Internet Backbone Will Become More Efficient

Internet access has become a basic business utility, like telephone service and electricity, with the mass adoption of intranets and extranets. However, this immediately gives rise to worries about the Internet's imminent "collapse." Will brown-outs and outages become so frequent as to make the Postal Service the fastest choice for delivering messages? No, thanks to a number of initiatives aimed at increasing the potential loads the backbone can manage. The Internet is already fundamentally reliable. However, its performance will improve as ISPs use new technologies, such as combining routing with switching. Even though usage of the Internet will climb, reliability and performance will improve.

Businesses will be able to mimic these improvements with their IP networks and extranets by applying new routing and more efficient routing protocols, such as the Inter-Domain Routing Protocol. This allows them to benefit from more efficient networking architecture, which can support more high-bandwidth activities and more business partners.

Forethought Breeds Good Planning

With an understanding of the trends of the Internet, a business can plan for its current deployment of an extranet while covering its future assets. For instance, we do not recommend spending a lot of time on developing a data warehouse that doesn't support HTTP/HTML or can't port to a Web platform today. Any warehouse developed today should simply use Web browsers as the front end because, shortly, the operating system as we know it today will look and feel very much like a browser. In fact, Microsoft has even announced that by version 5 of Internet Explorer, the browser will be so tightly integrated into the operating system that users won't even have to launch it to use it. It has IE version 5 slated for release in late 1997. Netscape is testing similar products today as well. This means that building a custom front end in, say, Visual Basic, and then training employees for its use will ultimately lead the company down a dead end with the project. It will forever become an albatross that requires special development and training for new employees. Conversely, one that uses HTML and browsers will become so intuitive for end users that training will be virtually nil.

Such lines of thought should be applied to every area of network, intranet, and extranet development. Ask yourself: where will this technology be in a year? two years? Where will the company's network be? Where will the partner's network be?

The World in Our Hands

Contrary to what the major vendors are telling us, the answer to all those questions lies in standards, not in vendor-driven strategies. A *desktop-centric* strategy may be important to Microsoft, but that shouldn't drive the commercial world's adoption of new technologies. Likewise, a *network-centric* strategy greatly benefits Sun Microsystems, but it may not be the right choice for end users. Until the mass adoption of the Internet, end users were forced to swallow vendor-driven strategies. Upgrading to Windows 95 is a prime example. Microsoft developed Windows 95, told us we needed it, made sure that all new Windows software would support only that product, and there we were, faced with having to upgrade or be left behind.

In contrast, the Internet is driven by standards bodies which consist of volunteers. The goal of these standards is to outline technologies that are useful to end users. It is true that many of the people on IETF working groups are from vendors who have a stake in seeing that their technologies get adopted as the basis of standards. But these working groups are *not* the vendors themselves and are therefore not inherently striving to enrich the pockets of a specific company. Their first duty is to the users of the Internet.

To learn about these standards, we need only read the abstract file of the Internic's Request for Comments (RFCs). Even better, IS managers can steer the process by reading RFCs that land within their areas of knowledge and submitting comments. No longer are we simply members of a user group that a vendor can choose to listen to—or ignore—based on its own bottom line. The world of information systems has turned a big, wide corner with the mass adoption of the Internet. We've gotten the democracy in information systems that we've always wanted. It is now our responsibility to be part of the system.

Summary

The extranet has many aliases, all of which refer to the same concept—creating a network that blurs the boundaries of ownership between company and partner. This allows the Web to compete with older technologies very favorably. The extranet has replaced much of the work that was once done via archaic EDI systems, over facsimile machines, even through the telephone. It expands the capabilities of data warehouses as well.

Several trends have become evident that point to what the future of Web-based applications will be. These include increases in security, automation, and backbone performance, among others. Trends are difficult to spot, because vendors are still trying to drive the boat and tell us what will happen, based on their own financial strategies. Now that we've steered ourselves into a true open-systems, standard-based environment it is our responsibility to protect it by staying involved in the standards development process. IS managers should read the Internic drafts available through Internic (www.internic.net) and comment on them. In this way, we will preserve our open future, and also remain tuned into where the Internet will take us next, and how it will get us there.

index